Quality of Life in Asia

Volume 6

This series, the first of its kind, will examine both the objective and subjective dimensions of life quality in Asia, especially East Asia. It will unravel and compare the contours, dynamics and patterns of building nations, offering innovative works that discuss basic and applied research, emphasizing inter- and multi-disciplinary approaches to the various domains of life quality. Thus, the series will appeal to a variety of fields in humanities, social sciences and other professional disciplines. Asia is the largest, most populous continent on Earth, and it is home to the world's most dynamic region, East Asia. In the past three decades, East Asia has been the most successful region in the world in expanding its economies and integrating them into the global economy, offering lessons on how poor countries, even with limited natural resources, can achieve rapid economic development. Yet while scholars and policymakers have focused on why East Asia has prospered, little has been written on how its economic expansion has affected the quality of life of its citizens. The series will publish several volumes a year, either single or multiple-authored monographs or collections of essays.

More information about this series at http://www.springer.com/series/8416

Daniel T.L. Shek • Po Chung
Editors

Promoting Service Leadership Qualities in University Students

The Case of Hong Kong

 Springer

Editors
Daniel T.L. Shek
Department of Applied Social Sciences
The Hong Kong Polytechnic University
Hunghom, Hong Kong, China

Po Chung
Hong Kong Institute of Service Leadership
  & Management Limited
Wanchai, Hong Kong, China

ISSN 2211-0550   ISSN 2211-0569   (electronic)
Quality of Life in Asia
ISBN 978-981-287-514-3   ISBN 978-981-287-515-0 (eBook)
DOI 10.1007/978-981-287-515-0

Library of Congress Control Number: 2015942824

Springer Singapore Heidelberg New York Dordrecht London

Printed on acid-free paper

Springer Science+Business Media Singapore Pte Ltd. is part of Springer Science+Business Media (www.springer.com)

Welcoming Speech by President of The Hong Kong Polytechnic University

This chapter outlines the welcoming speech delivered by Professor Timothy Tong, President of the Hong Kong Polytechnic University, at the "International Conference on Service Leadership Education for University Students: Experience in Hong Kong".

The Honourable John Tsang, Dr. Victor Fung, Dr. Po Chung, distinguished guests, ladies and gentlemen:

Welcome to the International Conference on "Service Leadership Education for University Students: Experience in Hong Kong". I would like to express my deepest gratitude to the Honourable John Tsang, Financial Secretary of the Hong Kong Special Administrative Region, for joining us today.

Economies around the world are increasingly dominated by service industries. Hong Kong is no exception with over 90 % of its GDP generated from the services sector. As our future relies on excellence in services, it is important to support development in this area. As educators, it is our responsibility and aspiration to equip our graduates with the competencies and virtues that will enable them to maintain their competitiveness in the service economy and contribute to the betterment of society with high-quality services.

Against this background, the Fung Service Leadership Initiative was launched in 2012 with the collaborative efforts of the Victor and William Fung Foundation, the Hong Kong Institute of Service Leadership & Management Limited and the eight University Grants Committee-funded institutions in Hong Kong.

Since inception of the Initiative, the eight institutions have successfully incorporated the Service Leadership framework in their curriculum or have included a wide variety of co-curricular activities such as service-learning, student leadership and civic engagement programmes. Research on Service Leadership is also growing. At the Hong Kong Polytechnic University, for example, several credit-bearing Service Leadership subjects and noncredit-bearing Service Leadership training workshops have been conducted with positive evaluation results.

In view of the impressive work that has been done across the institutions, this conference marks a milestone in the development of Service Leadership education in Hong Kong. By bringing together educators, academics and members of the business sector, the conference gives us an invaluable opportunity to better understand the issues surrounding the future of Service Leadership education.

University students from participating institutions have benefited tremendously from the Initiative. Apart from acquiring knowledge on service leadership, the students also demonstrate a more caring disposition after taking the courses. As such, let me commend you all on the remarkable progress you have made to foster Service Leadership education in Hong Kong.

In addition, I wish to thank the Victor and William Fung Foundation for not only providing generous financial support for this Initiative but also for their vision and passion for nurturing young service leaders in Hong Kong. I would also like to thank Dr. Po Chung for instigating the Fung Service Leadership Initiative.

Lastly, let me take this opportunity to thank all distinguished speakers, organizers and the Organizing Committee for their effort and support. I believe this conference will be an important step to advance Service Leadership education in Hong Kong and beyond. I wish all of you fruitful and rewarding exchanges in this conference. Thank you very much.

Congratulatory Message by the Chairman
of the University Grants Committee
# of Hong Kong Special Administrative Region

This chapter outlines the congratulatory message delivered by Mr. Edward Cheng, Chairman of the University Grants Committee of the Hong Kong Special Administrative Region, at the "International Conference on Service Leadership Education for University Students: Experience in Hong Kong".

The Honourable John Tsang, President Tong, Victor, Po, distinguished guests, ladies and gentlemen:

I take great pleasure in congratulating the remarkable achievements of the Fung Service Leadership Initiative and also the organisation of the International Conference on "Service Leadership Education for University Students: Experience in Hong Kong".

I have been a strong supporter of the Initiative from an earlier stage as it is truly a pioneering move in the local, Chinese and global contexts. I wish to extend my warmest greetings to the internationally renowned scholars and all participants joining the Conference. I am sorry that I cannot attend the Conference in person, but I would still hope to show my support through this video message.

As the Chairman of the University Grants Committee (UGC), I am pleased to see the successful collaborative efforts of the eight UGC-funded institutions on the Fung Service Leadership Initiative. I understand that the major objective of the Initiative is to benefit a prosperous and vibrant Hong Kong through nurturing the younger generation to meet the demands of the growing service economy and promoting service values.

It is an objective that is shared by the UGC. To the same end, I have focused the work of the UGC on two initiatives that also aim to better prepare students for the exciting future lying ahead, especially against the background of the new 4-year academic programme and the rise of Asia in particular China. As I briefly outline them here, you will see how the aims and values of the Li & Fung Service Leadership Initiative sit well with them.

The first is "Internationalisation and Engagement with Mainland China". Being a small and externally oriented economy, Hong Kong has been particularly sensitive, and responsive, to the effects of globalisation. We have been an active participant in the international community and must continue to do so. Our funded institutions must provide a platform for students to prepare for their future by exposing them to a multicultural learning and social environment, so that they will be willing and able and be competitive enough to work effectively in Asia and elsewhere, in Australasia, Europe, America or Africa.

In this connection, the UGC has put together a significant tripartite funding scheme to support four new initiatives on internationalisation. They are sponsorship of student-initiated projects or initiatives that encourage multicultural integration, setting up of a Hong Kong Pavilion in international education conferences, establishing a sector-wide search engine to provide easier access to information for prospective students and sponsoring students from families with financial difficulty to travel abroad to go on exchanges. We are also very happy to note that the Policy Address subsequently announced that the Government would support approximately 10,000 students every year to participate in exchange programmes outside Hong Kong. This echoes with our initiative in ensuring that no student will be denied the opportunities to fully experience diversified post-secondary student life because of lack of means.

The other work area that is also very close to my heart is "Teaching and Learning". The arrival of younger students with the new academic structure should become an incentive for institutions to go deeper with the Initiative to modify teaching approaches in the years to come. The goals are simple – to meet the learning needs of the new generation of students and to enhance their learning experiences. To further this end, another tripartite funding injection will be made available to provide motivation for institutions on this front in the 2012–2015 triennium.

I cannot emphasise enough how important the quality of teaching and learning is, as one of the core missions of all UGC-funded institutions. Globalisation has led to a sharper trend of competition as well as collaboration in the higher education sector among institutions and across different jurisdictions. The revolution of digital information technology has also brought about greater democratisation of access to information that has demanded a paradigm shift in our learning and teaching approaches. The need to put the focus back on teaching and learning has become a loud and clear message.

As I said a few moments ago, I believe that we all share the same values, and such a focus brings me back to supporting Service Leadership education. Your initiative has shown clear success in nurturing leadership of students, and Hong Kong awaits to see more of them serving and leading. I am confident that the Fung Service Leadership Initiative will continue to thrive in the rest of the project period and generate positive impact in the higher education sector within and beyond Hong Kong.

It is my sincere wish that you will enjoy the Conference as well as Hong Kong. Thank you very much!

Opening Address by Financial Secretary of the Government of Hong Kong Special Administrative Region

This chapter outlines the opening address delivered by Mr. John Tsang, Financial Secretary of the Government of the Hong Kong Special Administrative Region, at the "International Conference on Service Leadership Education for University Students: Experience in Hong Kong".

President (Tim) Tong, Victor, Po, distinguished guests, ladies and gentlemen: Good morning.

It is a great pleasure for me to join you for the opening of this International Conference on "Service Leadership Education for University Students: Experience in Hong Kong".

The theme of this conference is closely related to the prospects for Hong Kong's economic development and aligns with the Government's effort to enhance our city's overall competitiveness.

Economies globally have experienced great transformation in recent decades with service industries becoming more prominent in the overall picture. Hong Kong is a good example. Our economy is highly oriented around the provision of services delivered domestically and exported to other places. More than 90 % of our GDP is derived from services.

Hong Kong's advantage lies in its strong reputation for excellent service provision. This reputation has been built up over many decades, during which time Hong Kong has developed its spirit of service. This is based on the high quality, efficiency, trust and transparency of the services that Hong Kong provides.

In response to increasing external competition and new challenges, we are placing more focus on ways to strengthen Hong Kong's spirit of service to maintain our competitiveness and to enhance Hong Kong's status as a leading service economy.

The answer lies in developing our human capital, which is our city's greatest natural resource. We must nurture service leaders who respond effectively to the needs of this service era. Our prosperity depends on the quality of the next generation of service leaders.

It is important to foster young leaders who are not just capable of providing, but also willing to provide, high-quality service to others. I support the Service Leadership Model proposed by the Hong Kong Institute of Service Leadership and Management. The SLAM model considers leadership as a service aimed at ethically satisfying the needs of self, others and systems.

It is a common aspiration for people to strive for leadership positions and to acquire relevant knowledge and skills to achieve their personal goals. The SLAM model takes service leadership to the next level by underscoring the importance of personal qualities such as strong moral character and caring disposition.

The Fung Service Leadership Initiative is a valuable platform for nurturing self-leadership, continuous self-improvement, interpersonal trust and respect which are important attributes for successful service leaders.

The Fung Group has more than 100 years of history and expertise as a business leader in Hong Kong and knows what it takes to succeed. Through the Fung Service Leadership Initiative, our next generation of entrepreneurs will become better service leaders who are capable of adding value to their companies and to the overall economy.

In collaboration with the Hong Kong Institute of Service Leadership & Management and based on the ideas of Dr. Po Chung, the related projects have been progressing smoothly. I wish to thank the Victor and William Fung Foundation, the Hong Kong Institute of Service Leadership & Management and the participating tertiary institutions for their combined effort in fostering a new generation of service leaders.

Ladies and gentlemen, I firmly believe that nurturing university students to become service leaders is of great importance to the social and economic development of Hong Kong. I hope that service leadership education and research becomes a mainstay in our higher education sector and in other academic and commercial organisations.

No doubt, Hong Kong's experience will also provide unique insights into service leadership education for other economies and regions. I wish to thank the expert speakers and distinguished international guests for sharing your work and insights with us.

I wish you all a successful conference and our visitors an enjoyable stay here in Hong Kong.

Thank you very much.

Acknowledgement of the chapter is given to the Government of the Hong Kong Special Administrative Region.

Author's Note

The speech should not be used in such a way that the original intent of the work is distorted.

Development of the Service Economy in Hong Kong: Challenges and Opportunities

This chapter outlines the keynote speech delivered by Dr. Victor Fung, Chairman of the Fung Group, at the "International Conference on Service Leadership Education for University Students: Experience in Hong Kong".

Good morning, Prof. Timothy Tong, Prof. Dayle Smith, Prof. Shek, my good friend Po, professors, ladies and gentlemen:

It has been an honour and excitement for me to stand up and address you on a topic very close to my heart. First of all, let me thank our Financial Secretary, Mr. John Tsang, for giving us an opening address in person, despite his busy schedule. Second I also thank Mr. Edward Cheng for his congratulatory message.

So why did we initiate this Service Leadership Initiative?

I think, the future of Hong Kong's competitiveness lies in services and the development of services.

All of you know that 94 % of Hong Kong's GDP comes from services.

Beyond Hong Kong's own borders, I think one has to look to China. If you look at the Chinese 12th Five-Year Plan, there is a huge emphasis on services. Forty-three per cent of the Chinese economy is in services. That must be raised over time. We all know that any developed economy would have over 60 % of its GDP from services. So China has a long way to go. And even in the 12th Five-Year Plan that we see today, the plan is only to move services from 43 to 47 % in 5 years.

There's a huge role that Hong Kong can play if we get our own service sector right. And in terms of our positioning, vis-a-vis the Mainland, to be able to assist the Mainland to achieve a development of the service sector faster than it would otherwise, I think, would be a huge contribution.

To put it in another perspective, we go back 30 years to 1978, when Deng Xiaoping opened up the Chinese economy and Hong Kong started to develop in a new direction. What we saw at that time was a new growth model for China – in fact for the world. As you all well know, Hong Kong was in a very unusual position in having a manufacturing base here. And manufacturing was very important to Hong Kong.

What happened was the evolution of a model, which rationalized the manufacturing process on both sides of the border. It was a new growth model based on manufacturing. That model now gave birth to the global supply chain and the whole growth of China and indeed the whole world.

Looking back, we now see it was of course the beginning of the emphasis on the service sector. And what we really are thinking – what we should be thinking about – is how to look for that new growth model between Hong Kong and the Mainland, this time in services. We have been extremely successful in evolving from a manufacturing-based economy to an almost pure service-based economy. To my knowledge, no other region has done that transformation so completely and so quickly. Further the transformation was not dictated by a grand plan.

So what is that new growth model that would actually combine the advantages of both sides – to develop a new growth model, which without exaggeration could be driving China for the next 10, 20, or 30 years – and indeed the world. That's why I think the service sector is so important and why service is the absolute core of our competitiveness, both in terms of our own welfare, our own job creation inside Hong Kong, and in terms of our positioning to be able to actually help the entire country and the entire region and indeed the world – and maintain our leadership position.

That's why I'm so interested and excited to see that the Service Leadership Initiative is now into its second year and that it involves all of the eight institutions of higher learning in Hong Kong to develop a whole new curriculum and teaching in Service Leadership. Because unless we do that, we will not be a service leader.

So the whole basis of what we're trying to do here is to provide a little bit of seed capital as a catalyst for that effort.

What I really want to say is I have no wish to constrain at all what each of the institutions wants to do in terms of services. We want to provide you with some help, with a common platform and infrastructure, which we hope you will adopt and find useful.

But I also want a 100 flowers to bloom within the service sector. Find your own way. Find your own niche, in terms of which industries you want to emphasize, which aspects of service and so on.

But there are some common threads. That's where Po Chung, Tom Osgood and SLAM come in. And, that is, we think it depends a lot on the individual and what's inside an individual as opposed to what's the manufacturing process, which is much more of a command and control.

You know Po Chung who is my golfing partner is sort of brainwashing me every Sunday, saying that you know when my DHL couriers go out and they're running around the offices collecting parcels, I have absolutely no way to look over each person's shoulder to see whether he's being good to the secretary or pouring coffee over the secretary's desk. I may lose the customer and destroy DHL's reputation right there.

So, how do I actually motivate and indeed may I say the word "control" a system like this. It's very different from watching my 200 workers inside my factory walls, and I say "Do this; do that".

So it must depend a lot more on the individual – and that's really what the emphasis is. And that individual, you then, have to empower and trust that when he or she is in front of the customers. If that contact is repeated a million times every day, you really have no control over. That is the essence of Service Leadership and excellence in services.

So how do I get this whole ethics into our community and into our teaching? I think the best way is through being a catalyst, for each of the institutions of higher learning in Hong Kong to do their own thing. I like to emphasize, in the service sector, as long as you're contributing to the whole, I am very happy.

So this is really what it's all about. And you know, my goal is how to promote the teaching of excellence in services in Hong Kong. That's my goal. That's where I'm going. I don't care if you're an expert in teaching people how to be running hotel services or banking – you know it doesn't matter – as long as it is about serving others and yourself. I think we own everything in services. Maybe at some point, we'll have to then say: What are some of the common threads? What are some of the commonalities? Your researches will provide the insight into the new paradigm of Service Leadership.

And this, I'm very impressed by the work that's done now.

Basically, there's a lot of emphasis on the person: inside the mind of the person, the morals, and it's very Confucian actually. It's from within – out. And it's definitely not a control system.

So I just want you to know that this is where I'm coming from. It's from a very pragmatic basis. This is very important for Hong Kong. This is important for Hong Kong's future competitiveness.

K. M. Wong tells me that this may be a first in terms of this kind of cooperation in Hong Kong – where you're all doing your own thing and yet you're all moving in the same direction for Hong Kong.

I trust you appreciate what you are doing will have profound implication for Hong Kong, Mainland China and the world.

Thank you.

Where There Is No Vision, the People Will Perish

This chapter outlines the keynote speech delivered by Dr. Po Chung, Chairman of Hong Kong Institute of Service Leadership & Management Limited, at the "International Conference on Service Leadership Education for University Students: Experience in Hong Kong."

Good morning, ladies and gentlemen. I am pleased to speak to you today. We have gathered here to share our insights on a topic I've been working on for more than four decades. For the first 30 years, I was in the service leadership trenches – helping to design and grow DHL into one of the largest service companies in the world.

Although my experience rests on my years at DHL, today I will talk about three things that indirectly related to the courier business. First, I'll explain why it is that when there's no vision, the people will perish. Then, I will tell you what the vision is and explain the two invisible pillars of successful service. And finally, I'll give you a tip to remember, should you ever need to outrun a grizzly bear.

"Where there is no vision, the people perish." If you've never heard this before, it's from the book of Proverbs, in the Christian bible. It doesn't matter what your culture or religion happens to be because it's the wisdom of the message that's important.

The fact is that Hong Kong needs a new vision, the right path as we compete against China. We need a vision to move forward or else we will slowly but surely get overwhelmed. I'm only using Hong Kong as an example as you will recognize that all major metropolitan hubs are facing the same problem, whether it is Tokyo, Seoul, Taipei, Shanghai, Bangkok, Kuala Lumpur, or Singapore in addition to the entire collection of developed countries.

Let's look at Hong Kong's history. For a long time, business was booming because we were one of the world's major manufacturing hubs. Then, as China opened up and started importing our expertise into China and developing its own expertise in manufacturing, Hong Kong lost its competitiveness. We adapted from manufacturing to service. We gradually stopped running production lines at home, and our people went across the border to provide teaching and technical service to the new manufacturing giants that sprouted across China. So what we have today is the "China Story" – and it's a loud echo of the old Hong Kong Story. In other words, China now follows the vision we used to have in Hong Kong.

So what is our new vision? Because without it, we will perish.

For Hong Kong, it's differentiate or die. Our new vision is to be the best service hub in the region.

Hong Kong's manufacturing economy is dead or gasping. But in its place we find something better. Our new higher-value-added economy is even stronger than our old one. We now have a healthy Service Economy.

It's crystal clear. Hong Kong's new economy is service-driven. We see it every day and you can see as soon as you step out of this room. About 93 % of the city's GDP is from our service industries. More than 90 % of our workforce is working in service. If there ever was a transition that Hong Kong needed to make – from manufacturing to service – it already happened. We don't need to look farther because we're already here.

We must appreciate and understand this fact and do our best to support our strengths. This support must come from many directions. It has to come from the Government, come from academic institutions, come from the business community, and in fact, from every one of us.

So that's the vision. Strengthening our service leadership is how we can differentiate and thrive. I will now move to part two and tell you the two invisible pillars of a superior service operation.

Our invisible pillars are our values DNA. On the one hand is our regional and global respectability and trustworthiness, and on the other hand is our ability to think critically and independently. The first set is on being, and the second is on doing.

We benefit from our traditional Chinese values and thrive when an organization needs bottom-up and top-down management. We are also comfortable with trusting to our frontline service people to improvise on the spot and make decisions.

These, after all, are the ingredients of a healthy service network and explain why we have earned the trust and respect from our neighbors and trading partners from around the world.

This is a good moment to bring up two points I learned from running DHL:

First, we can't run a head office, regional, or country service office without having a clear moral compass. In other words, we couldn't run a global service network if everyone in our network didn't trust and respect one another. Trust and respect for one another means that people aren't wasting energy fighting one another, and they aren't holding grudges or getting into bad office politics. To succeed, everyone must be united in doing what the organization is really meant to do, which is to provide the best service at every service moment.

So setting the moral tone is what leaders do, so it's crucial that leaders get it right.

The next thing from my DHL years is that you can be the best at making goods and products, but to be competitive you must have a superior service mentality. This must run from the supply chain to the point of sales.

In other words, even if you make great things, people won't buy them without superior service behind you.

What we do at DHL is we wrap superior service around each package we pick up and deliver.

In the transportation and logistics industry, we are known as the "last miler": couriers are defined by how they handle the last mile between the city operation hub and their customers' door.

However, DHL was the first "last miler" who brought the service even closer: we brought our service promise to the last 3 ft, the last yard. We went from looking at the last mile to the last yard. When you're only 3 ft away from your customer, the quality of your service promise better be good.

Mainland organizations simply don't work this way. The Mainland management systems don't appreciate why trustworthiness and having service people who can think critically and independently are so important when working with customers – each one with unique demands and requirements.

We are now in the Service Age, and Hong Kong's history, values, and culture give us an edge in providing superior professional and management services. These ingredients are how we will stay ahead in the race. If the Mainland has a production-line, cookie-cutter mentality, we use more of a customized, service mentality. To borrow from Anita Rodrick, the late founder of The Body Shop, this is what lets us go where our competitors aren't, can't, or won't go.

Because of our values DNA and thinking ability, we are the home base of the world's best global bank, the best international airline, the best courier network, the best supply chain company, and one of the best professional services communities of lawyers, auditors, and arbitrators. We house the regional head office base of top-tier advertising agencies, trading companies, HR and PR companies, as well as the headquarter of several top-tier hotels.

Hong Kong needs to recognize why we are so competitive. We must understand and articulate the uniqueness of what we have and connect the dots. We must stop doubting and moaning the loss of our vision from the last century, and we must train our young how to keep developing our service expertise.

The new vision for Hong Kong is to serve as Mainland's closest ally, especially when it is to purchase foreign companies. We must help the Mainland avoid repeating the same failure that Japan did in the 1970s and 1980s, when the nation bought thousands of service companies around the world but ended up selling them soon after. Their failure was that they didn't realize the importance of having the right culture and skills needed to run those kinds of service networks. In Hong Kong, we live in both worlds. We straddle both cultures. We know what it is to succeed through superior service.

I outlined the vision we can follow if we want to remain competitive against such a powerful force coming from the Mainland. I then told you about the ox versus the horse mentalities, showing the ingredients that Hong Kong has for delivering superior service in global organizations. I will now wrap up by telling you a story about what you should do when you need to outrun a grizzly bear.

Once upon a time two friends went camping. One morning, as they got out of their tent, they suddenly saw a grizzly bear running down the hill toward them. One guy shouted, "Run! There's a bear is coming for us!"

The second friend immediately sat down and started putting on his running shoes.

The first guy screamed, "What are you doing? You can't outrun a bear!"

And the second guy yelled back, "I don't need to outrun the bear, I only need to outrun you!"

I love that story. The reason I like it so much is because it's a great tool to explain how to strategize your competiveness. I'm not suggesting we need to focus on being the best in the world at being trustworthy, having a strong character, and improvising. They are important in their own right. Instead, we need to focus on beating our competitor using the best path available to us. For us, we can't compete on manufacturing, but we can stay ahead when it comes to service leadership.

As I said when we began: where there is no vision, the people will perish. We now have the vision, and it's simply about staying on track and committing to what we've been doing as global service leaders.

We must explain all of these so parents, students, teachers, and the broader community understand what we need to succeed and that our ability to deliver superior service through trustworthiness and improvisation is something very hard to copy. Even after several generations, the competition may never catch up!

Thank you for your attention, and thank you for putting your time and effort into this conference. I want to give special thanks to my dear friend, Victor Fung, and the Victor and William Fung Foundation. I wish you all great success on our shared goal of building a bright, bold, and sustainable future built on service excellence.

Preface

The shift from manufacturing to service economy has taken place in many places. With specific reference to Hong Kong, the services sector contributes to over 92.9 % of the gross domestic product in 2013. The growth of the service economy poses new demands on the workforce. Leaders in the manufacturing economy are commonly autocratic and directive, and workers are expected to be followers in the assembly lines following the instructions of the leaders. However, in a service economy, leaders are expected to be flexible, creative, and possess a wide range of competencies and knowledge. Yet, a few traditional leadership theories are developed with reference to the needs and characteristics of the service economy. Against this background, the Service Leadership and Management (SLAM) Model was proposed by the Hong Kong Institute of Service Leadership and Management Limited (HKI-SLAM) based on the seminal work of Po Chung. According to the SLAM model, besides possessing relevant task competencies, effective service leaders also have character strengths and a caring disposition.

In order to maintain Hong Kong's competitiveness in the global market and to develop leaders with a human face, there is a need to strengthen our service leadership. This should begin with nurturing service leaders in tertiary education. However, there are a few credit-bearing and non-credit-bearing leadership courses in university settings that aim at promoting students' service leadership attributes. As such, the Fung Service Leadership Initiative was launched as a collaboration between HKI-SLAM and the Victor and William Fung Foundation in 2012, where HK$40 million was pledged by the Foundation to support projects of service leadership education in eight tertiary institutions funded by the University Grants Committee in Hong Kong. The Initiative was intended to address the needs to nurture service leaders for today's economy.

It is clear that employers nowadays do not hire employees solely based on their "hard skills" (e.g., discipline-specific knowledge or task-based skills). Actually, employers also pay special attention to the "soft skills" (e.g., leadership and interpersonal skills) and character (e.g., integrity and trustworthiness) of their employees. One of the unique features of the service leadership model is its holistic nature. While most existing leadership education and training programs predominantly focus on the functional or expertise dimension of leaders, the service leadership model advocates the development of well-rounded service leaders who are equipped with both intrapersonal and interpersonal competencies across the Doing, Thinking, Being, and Growing domains. It is argued that the ingredients to success depend on the nurturance of the above domains. Therefore, one of the greatest missions as educators is to encourage students to thrive, enhance their overall development and well-being holistically, prepare them to become responsible, and contribute citizens to society. In the first chapter "Service Leadership Qualities in University Students through the Lens of Student Well-being," the authors argue that service leadership qualities are in line with attributes of well-being proposed in various student well-being models. In other words, effective service leadership qualities in the SLAM model are resonant with models on student well-being. Besides, empirical evidence to support the relationship between service leadership attributes and student well-being is provided, which suggests that the nurturance of service leadership qualities is promotion of student well-being.

Since the inception of the Fung Service Leadership Initiative, institutions have designed a wide range of credit-bearing courses, non-credit-bearing programs, and co-curricular and extra-curricular activities to promote service leadership. In addition, research has also been conducted in this area. To provide a forum to share our experience on service leadership education, the "International Conference on Service Leadership Education for University Students: Experience in Hong Kong" was held on May 14–15, 2014, at The Hong Kong Polytechnic University in Hong Kong. The Conference was an overall success which attracted scholars, teachers, students, and stakeholders both locally and internationally.

To document the conference, it is our great pleasure to edit this book which includes addresses, keynote speeches, and papers presented at the Conference. In Chaps. 2, 3, and 4, the welcoming speech delivered by Professor Timothy Tong, President of the Hong Kong Polytechnic University, a congratulatory message by Mr. Edward Cheng, Chairman of the University Grants Committee of Hong Kong Special Administrative Region, and an opening address by Mr. John Tsang, Financial Secretary of the Government of Hong Kong Special Administrative Region are included. In Chap. 5, the keynote address titled "Development of the Service Economy in Hong Kong: Challenges and Opportunities" by Dr. Victor Fung, Chairman of the Fung Group, is presented. In Chap. 6, the keynote address on "Where There Is No Vision, the People Will Perish" by Dr. Po Chung, Chairman of the Hong Kong Institute of Service Leadership and Management Limited, is presented.

Following the speeches are chapters outlining the implementation of the service leadership initiative at respective institutions (Chaps. 7, 8, 9, 10, 11, 12, 13, and 14). For instance, the role of service leadership in general education and the importance of service leadership for higher education are presented. Various conceptual models and frameworks for student leadership development and social entrepreneurship are put forth based on the SLAM model. The overview of service leadership courses, programs, and related activities at different institutions is also outlined. In

Chaps. 15, 16, 17, 18, and 19, papers pertaining to the application of service leadership are presented. In terms of research, findings from evaluation studies using different evaluation strategies are presented to demonstrate the effectiveness of service leadership education at various institutions. Regarding pedagogy, there are chapters presenting the development and use of video-assisted case sets and the establishment of a service leadership community to facilitate the nurturing of service leaders in and outside of the classroom.

As service leaders, we engage in constant reflection and seek for continuous improvement. As such, in the concluding chapter titled "Service Leadership Education for University Students: Seven Unfinished Tasks," the authors identified areas that researchers and practitioners should further work on to strengthen the theoretical conceptualization and enhance the practical applications of service leadership.

It is evident we have walked a long way since the inception of the Fung Service Leadership Initiative and much has been achieved in terms of both teaching and research across the eight institutions in Hong Kong within a short period of time. Although the SLAM model was developed in Hong Kong, it is a contemporary leadership model that is applicable globally. Primarily, the rise of the service economy is a universal trend, which results in a new set of leadership skills needed to meet the changing demands. Second, promoting healthy adolescent development and well-being is the priority of all educators. As such, experience and insights presented in this book are useful as tertiary institutions may model after the courses, activities, and pedagogical approaches proposed to promote service leadership attributes and well-being of students and to conduct further research in the area. We would like to take this opportunity to express our gratitude to the Victor and William Fung Foundation for their generous support to the Fung Service Leadership Initiative, which brings great benefits to our next generation of service leaders. We would also like to thank the work of Hildie Leung and Jocelyn Lin, two Managing Editors of this book for their wonderful support.

Hong Kong, China   Daniel T.L. Shek
Hong Kong, China   Po Chung

Contents

Contributors

Ben Y.B. Chan is the associate director of the Center for Engineering Education Innovation and assistant professor of Engineering Education in the Department of Civil Engineering at the Hong Kong University of Science and Technology. Chan has published more than 40 journals and conference papers in civil engineering and engineering education. He is the undergraduate program coordinator for all the first-year students in the School of Engineering. He is also a member of the Engineering Undergraduate Studies Committee and the coordinator for school-sponsored courses within the school.

Carman Ka Man Chan is a senior project officer at the Office of Service-Learning at Lingnan University. She has been developing and coordinating various service-learning and civic engagement projects for several years. Currently, she actively engages in the program development of service leadership and student development through service-learning at Lingnan. Her research interests are leadership, civic engagement, and social entrepreneurship. She coauthored "A Leadership Training Manual for Service-Learning Stars" of Lingnan and has published in the *Journal of Management Education.*

Kin-man Chan received his PhD from Yale University and is currently associate professor of sociology at the Chinese University of Hong Kong where he has served as director of Centre for Civil Society Studies, director of the Universities Service Centre, and associate director of Center for Entrepreneurship. He was visiting professor of sociology and chair of the board of directors, Institute for Civil Society in Sun Yat-sen (Zhongshan) University and chaired the Beijing Normal University One Foundation Philanthropy Research Institute. He has been on the editorial boards of the *Journal of Civil Society*, *China Non-Profit Review*, and *Third Sector Review* and has served China Projects Committee, Oxfam Hong Kong, Hong Kong Democratic Development Network, the Hong Kong Civil Education Foundation, and Hong Kong Social Enterprise Incubation Centre. He is the author of numerous books and articles on democracy, Hong Kong political development, and civil society and is a cofounder and leader of Occupy Central with Love and Peace.

Maureen Yin Lee Chan is senior research fellow of management at Lingnan University. She received her PhD from Lancaster University. Her research interests are student learning and development, leadership, and organizational learning, and her teaching interests are in human resource management, organizational behavior, and management. Before joining Lingnan, she worked professionally in training and human resource development. Currently, she is engaged in research on service leadership and the development of the Service Leadership Education curriculum. She has published in the *Journal of Management Education.*

Yanto Chandra is assistant professor in the Department of Public Policy and the Department of Management at the City University of Hong Kong. Chandra's research focuses on social entrepreneurship, entrepreneurship, and research methods to study entrepreneurial actors. Chandra won the Outstanding Paper Award at the Literati Network Awards for Excellence 2010. He serves on the editorial board of the *Journal of International Marketing* and the *Journal of Data Mining and Digital Humanities.* His work has been published in, among others, *Asia Pacific Journal of Management, Journal of International Marketing,* and *Journal of World Business.*

Raysen W.L. Cheung is currently assistant professor in the Department of Applied Social Sciences of the City University of Hong Kong. He obtained his PhD in vocational psychology from Loughborough University and is an editorial board member of the *Journal of Vocational Behavior.* He teaches and researches in areas of life-career development and well-being at work. Previously, he had served the City University of Hong Kong as a counselor for over 13 years in student counseling, psychological education, and career guidance. Currently, he promotes student development through leadership initiatives of Project Flame and delivering a Gateway Education course.

Hang Chow is a senior research associate in Project Flame: Social Innovation and Entrepreneurship at CityU. He obtained his BSocSc in Policy Studies and Administration from the City University of Hong Kong and MA in China Development Studies from the University of Hong Kong. Currently, he has special responsibilities to promote social innovation and entrepreneurship both inside and outside campus and organize student activities for Service Leadership Education.

Jessie Mei-ling Chow is the Assistant Director (Experiential Learning) of the Faculty of Social Sciences at the University of Hong Kong. Before joining HKU, she worked as an educational psychologist at mainstream schools, schools for maladaptive children, NGO and private edutainment centers. Ms Chow has also conducted numerous workshops and trainings for both pre-service and in-service teachers, gifted adolescents and parents with gifted children at different organizations and tertiary institutions. Her specialization focuses on giftedness and twice exceptionality.

Susanna Chui is pursuing her doctoral degree in leadership at the Durham University Business School. Her research interests include leadership in the third sector, social impact measurement, and corporate social responsibility. Her deep interest in applying action and experiential learning in leadership and management education resulted in proven course development including the "Leadership in Sustainability" and "Business Communications" courses, all of which have received good student evaluation. Susanna has completed her master of research degree in leadership with the University of Exeter. Her first master's degree in mass communications research was obtained from the University of Leicester, and she holds a bachelor of arts degree in English from the University of York (UK).

Po Chung is a cofounder of DHL Asia Pacific and chairman emeritus of DHL Express (Hong Kong) Ltd. He is passionate about the nature and value of service in world societies and global centers of commerce. His professional life has been dedicated in large part to understanding how to provide superb service, how to educate others as service leaders, and how to design and operate service-sector organizations. As chairman of Hong Kong Institute of Service Leadership & Management Limited, Dr. Chung is a champion of the effort to develop service-oriented courses and programs in Hong Kong's major universities. Dr. Chung is also author of the *Character Leadership* book series which includes *The First Ten Yards* and *Service Reborn*. Two new titles in the series, *The 12 Dimensions of a Service Leader* and *25 Principles of Service Leadership*, will be published in 2015.

Paula Hodgson is a doctoral graduate of the University of South Australia investigating organizational change for technology integration in universities in Hong Kong. She has been working in higher education since 1997 and is enthusiastic about innovative practices in university teaching, learning, and assessment. Although majority of her research focuses on assessment and evaluation, her recent research is focused on flipped classroom and mass open online courses (MOOCs) after her successive completion in three MOOCs. Peer-reviewed journal papers and conference papers of her work can be accessed at https://www.researchgate.net/profile/Paula_Hodgson2?ev=prf_highl.

A. Reza Hoshmand is the director of general education at Hong Kong Baptist University. Prior to coming to Hong Kong as a Fulbright Scholar in 2008, Professor Hoshmand was the associate dean for Graduate Studies and chair/professor of Business and Management Division at Daniel Webster College in Nashua, New Hampshire. He has taught at Harvard, Tufts, the University of Hawaii, and the California State Polytechnic University in Pomona. He has published seven books in statistical analyses and research methods and business and economic forecasting. His work has also been published in numerous journals.

Leo K.W. Hui is a teaching associate at the Center for Engineering Education Innovation in the Hong Kong University of Science and Technology. He received his PhD degree in chemical and biological engineering from the University of British Columbia in Canada. His research interests are engineering education, student learning, and leadership.

Shui-fong Lam is an associate professor in the Department of Psychology at the University of Hong Kong. She obtained her doctoral degree (school psychology) from the University of Minnesota. Since 1994, Dr. Lam has been teaching in the Department of Psychology at the University of Hong Kong and responsible for providing professional training to school psychologists. Her research interests lie in achievement motivation, parenting, instructional strategies, and positive psychology. She is also concerned with the improvement of psychoeducational services in school system.

Moon Y.M. Law is a teaching fellow of the Hong Kong Polytechnic University and the project manager of the Project P.A.T.H.S. She was a social worker and field-work supervisor for master's degree students of counseling. Apart from providing training for teachers and social workers in Hong Kong and mainland China, she has taught different courses for university students, including counseling, leadership, and service-learning. Her research interests include positive youth development, leadership, and Internet addiction, and her work appears in journals such as *International Journal of Adolescent Medicine and Health* and *International Journal on Disability and Human Development*.

Hildie Leung (Managing Editor) is a research assistant professor in the Department of Applied Social Sciences at the Hong Kong Polytechnic University. She obtained her PhD degree in psychology at the Chinese University of Hong Kong. Her research centers on positive youth development and its application to the promotion of healthy adolescent development and the prevention of problem behaviors among children and adolescents. Her work appears in journals such as *Social Indicators Research*, *International Journal on Disability and Human Development*, and *Journal of Behavioral and Decision Making*. She has also coauthored book chapters in the area of positive youth development and positive psychology.

Joan Y.H. Leung is an associate professor in the Department of Public Policy at the City University of Hong Kong. She obtained her bachelor's degree, two master's degrees, and PhD from the University of Hong Kong. She teaches and researches on public sector management, integrity management, and education policy in Hong Kong. She was a winner of the CityU Teaching Excellence Award (2003–2004). Recently, she extends her interest to develop general education courses on service leadership, social innovation, and entrepreneurship. She is also the associate director (professional/academic development) of Project Flame: Social Innovation and Entrepreneurship at CityU.

Loretta M.K. Leung is associate head of Wofoo Whole Person Development Centre and section head of Leadership and Service-Learning of the Hong Kong Institute of Education (HKIEd). She is responsible for planning, developing, and implementing a variety of workshops and programs to promote students' whole person development. Ms. Leung is an experienced trainer with substantial professional qualifications such as Certified Master of Neuro-Linguistic Programming (NLP) practitioner, Certified Facilitator of the Student Leadership Challenge, and Certified MBTI practitioner and Master of Education in Counseling. She conducted student leadership development training programs to university students for over 17 years. She also worked collaboratively with the academic staff in teaching cocurricular service-learning courses in the past four years.

Li Lin (managing editor) is an instructor in the Department of Applied Social Sciences at the Hong Kong Polytechnic University. She currently teaches leadership course for university students. Her research interests largely involve development of adolescence and emerging adulthood, particularly parent-child relationship, positive youth development, adolescent risk behavior, and sociocultural influence. Her publications cover many adolescent issues, such as positive youth development and adolescent materialism, adolescent risk behavior, as well as program evaluation.

Carol Hok Ka Ma is assistant director at the Office of Service-Learning and adjunct assistant professor at the Department of Sociology and Social Policy at Lingnan. She is director for the International Center for Service-Learning in Teacher Education and for the International Association for Research on Service-Learning and Community Engagement. She coedited *Service-Learning in Asia: Curriculum Models and Practices* and coauthored a paper for UNESCAP. She has published in the *International Journal of Community Research and Engagement*, *Asian Journal of Gerontology and Geriatrics*, *Journal of Management Education*, and *Journal of New Horizons in Education*. She is coediting "Rethinking Social Responsibility for Higher Education in Asia," with UNESCO chairperson, Dr. Rajesh Tandon.

Cecilia M.S. Ma is an assistant professor in the Department of Applied Social Sciences at the Hong Kong Polytechnic University. She received her PhD from the University of South Carolina. Her research interests include psychometrics, structural equation modeling, and program evaluation. She has published peer-reviewed papers in journals such as *Research on Social Work Practice*, *Social Indicators Research*, and *International Journal on Disability and Human Development*. She has also coauthored book chapters and articles in the area of Chinese adolescents' psychological development. Her current research projects focus on positive youth development programs and the development of a university leadership program.

Neil C. Mickleborough is the former director of the Center for Engineering Education Innovation and professor of civil engineering at the Hong Kong University of Science and Technology. His engineering education research interests are associated with problem-based learning in engineering and in civil engineering related to tall building design and prestressed concrete. He is the coauthor of the book entitled *Design of Prestressed Concrete* published by Taylor and Francis.

Daniel T.L. Shek is associate vice president (Undergraduate Programme) and chair professor of the Applied Social Sciences at the Hong Kong Polytechnic University, advisory professor of East China Normal University, and honorary professor of Kiang Wu Nursing College of Macau. He is chief editor of the *Journal of Youth Studies* and *Applied Research in Quality of Life* and editorial board member of several international refereed journals, including *Journal of Adolescent Health, Social Indicators Research, International Journal of Behavioral Development*, and *International Journal of Adolescent Medicine and Health*. He is chairman of the Family Council of the Government of Hong Kong Special Administrative Region.

Andrew M.H. Siu is an associate professor in rehabilitation science of the Hong Kong Polytechnic University and is an occupational therapist who specializes in rehabilitation counseling and psychiatric rehabilitation. He teaches courses in emotional health, rehabilitation psychology, counseling, psychiatric rehabilitation, vocational rehabilitation, and psychometrics. He has published over 60 journal papers in the areas of positive youth development, psychiatric and work rehabilitation, and in the development of psychosocial and rehabilitation outcome measures.

Robin Stanley Snell is professor of management at Lingnan University, Hong Kong, where he also served as director of the Business Programmes. He received his PhD from Lancaster University. His research interests are business ethics, organizational learning, and qualitative organizational research. He was editor of *Management Learning* and wrote the book *Developing Skills for Ethical Management*. He has published in many journals, including *Asia Pacific Journal of Human Resources, Asia Pacific Journal of Management, Business & Society, Business Ethics Quarterly, British Journal of Management, Human Relations, Human Resource Management Journal, International Journal of Human Resource Management, International Business Review, Journal of Business Ethics, Journal of International Management, Journal of Management Education, Journal of Management Studies, Management Learning*, and *Organization Studies*.

Rachel C.F. Sun got her BSocSc and PhD at the University of Hong Kong, Hong Kong. She is assistant professor of the Faculty of Education at the University of Hong Kong. She is a principal investigator of school misbehavior research studies and coprincipal investigator of positive youth development programs and a service leadership program in Hong Kong. Her research areas include academic achievement motivation, school satisfaction, life satisfaction, positive youth development, problem behavior, school misbehavior, adolescent suicidal ideation, and psychological health. She is a member of the editorial boards of *Research on Social Work Practice* and *Frontiers in Child Health and Human Development.*

Hugh Thomas received his PhD from New York University and is currently associate professor of finance at the Chinese University of Hong Kong where he has served as the director of the Center for Entrepreneurship. He has a bachelor of arts from the University of Alberta, postgraduate diplomas from Beijing Language and Culture University and Nanjing University, and an MBA from CUHK. He has published numerous articles and cases in banking and finance. He participated in founding the National Center for Industrial Science and Technology Management at Dalian in 1980 and subsequently worked in banking and consulting in Hong Kong for seven years. Prior to joining CUHK, he was tenured at McMaster University in Canada.

Alice Wong is the executive officer of the General Education Office of Hong Kong Baptist University. Working for the project of "Service Leadership Across the General Education Curriculum and Whole Person Education," Alice is mainly responsible for the management of the project as well as the coordination with different faculty and offices in running different courses and organizing various activities, which aim at developing in students the capacity to deliver services with competence, character, and care. Alice is also actively involved in the Action Research Team to share the good practices of Service Leadership Education initiatives with other higher institutions in Hong Kong.

Linda Wong is visiting professor in the Department of Public Policy. She is founder and director of Project Flame, the City University of Hong Kong's platform to promote social innovation and social entrepreneurship for faculty and students. Started in 2012, Project Flame now comprises over 30 members from 18 academic and administrative units in the City University. She has been a social worker and social planner before joining the academia. Her teaching and research interests include social welfare, the third sector, social entrepreneurship, comparative social policy, and China studies. She has published widely in monographs, book chapters, and top journals.

Lu Yu is an assistant professor of the Department of Applied Social Sciences at the Hong Kong Polytechnic University. She was trained in clinical medicine, psychiatry, education, and positive psychology. Her research interests include positive youth development, mental health and addiction, leadership, cross-cultural studies, gender development, and instrument development and validation. Her work appeared in *Personality and Individual Differences, Archives of Sexual Behaviors, Journal of Autism and Developmental Disorders, BMC Public Health, International Journal on Disability and Human Development, Journal of Pediatric and*

Adolescent Gynecology, Journal of Sex Research, Sex Roles, The Scientific World Journal, Asian Journal of Counseling, and *International Journal of Child Health and Human Development.*

Catherine Zhou is a teaching associate at the Center for Engineering Education Innovation within the Hong Kong University of Science and Technology (HKUST). She received her PhD degree in computer science and engineering from the Chinese University of Hong Kong. She has been working in teaching and learning since July 2010. Her research interests include professional skills development and the postgraduate research experience. Dr. Zhou is also a co-opted member of the HKUST Task Force on Research Postgraduate Education.

Service Leadership Qualities in University Students Through the Lens of Student Well-Being

Daniel T.L. Shek and Hildie Leung

Abstract With the emergence of the knowledge-based and service economies, the demand for service leadership is obvious. However, there are few models specifically designed for service leadership. Besides, most of the leadership models developed for university students are elitist leadership models, assuming only elites can be effective leaders. To promote service leadership in the higher education sector in Hong Kong, the Hong Kong Institute of Service Leadership and Management (HKI-SLAM) proposed the service leadership model. In this chapter, the basic qualities of effective service leaders are highlighted with reference to the attributes of student well-being commonly proposed in different student well-being models. Besides presenting evidence on the linkage between service leadership attributes and well-being, the chapter also examines the concordance of service leadership attributes and student well-being attributes described in different models. It is argued that through nurturing service leadership qualities in university students, their well-being is also enhanced.

Introduction

During the industrial age, employees were merely expected to acquire discipline-specific knowledge and task competencies (i.e., the "hard" skills). However, these qualities are no longer sufficient in the contemporary world where service economies are growing. Obviously, on top of professional knowledge, graduates are expected to possess "soft" skills (e.g., intrapersonal and interpersonal competencies) because human interaction is basic in service economies (Shek et al. in press-a). However, with specific reference to university students, validated leadership programs

The preparation for this work and the Service Leadership Initiative are financially supported by the Victor and William Fung Foundation.

D.T.L. Shek, Ph.D., S.B.S., J.P (✉) • H. Leung, Ph.D.
Department of Applied Social Sciences, The Hong Kong Polytechnic University, HJ407, Hunghom, Hong Kong, China
e-mail: daniel.shek@polyu.edu.hk; hleung@polyu.edu.hk

© Springer Science+Business Media Singapore 2015
D.T.L. Shek, P. Chung (eds.), *Promoting Service Leadership Qualities in University Students*, Quality of Life in Asia 6, DOI 10.1007/978-981-287-515-0_1

are lacking and most of them are elitist orientated, with the emphasis that only elite people possess leadership skills. Against this background, the Hong Kong Institute of Service Leadership and Management (HKI-SLAM) argued for the development and implementation of service leadership education which attempts to nurture university students to become effective service leaders.

At the same time, although contemporary student development approach focuses on whole person development and aims at promoting students' overall wellness (Hermon and Davis 2004), research has showed that university students increasingly show mental health problems (Kitzrow 2003). Compared with US adolescents, Hong Kong adolescents reported relatively low levels of self-assessed health status and life satisfaction (Kwan 2010). Similarly, in a study comparing mainstream adolescent Hong Kong students, Chinese immigrant students, and South Asian students, Yuen (2014) found that Hong Kong students were least satisfied with their lives and reported the lowest levels of spiritual health across all personal, communal, environmental, and transcendental domains. These findings raise serious concerns and questions as to how educators can provide a university environment and curricula that would nurture our graduates to become contributing members to the society as service leaders while maintaining a healthy well-being. Of course, one possible solution is to promote student well-being through promoting their service leadership qualities.

In this chapter, the linkage between service leadership and student well-being is described. In particular, we will present the literature to support why developing service leadership attributes among university students would enhance their well-being, including subjective well-being, life satisfaction, and happiness.

Leadership and Wellness

Existing research on leadership and wellness mainly focuses on investigating how effective leadership may impact on *employees'* or *followers'* well-being or job satisfaction. For instance, Bono and Ilies (2006) reported that charismatic leaders enable their followers to experience positive affective well-being. Arnold et al. (2007) found that transformational leadership exerted positive influence on the psychological well-being (i.e., affective well-being and mental health) of workers. Moreover, servant leaders exerted positive influence on subordinates' eudaemonic well-being by creating healthy work environments (Chen et al. 2013). It is established in the literature that certain leadership styles (e.g., post-heroic or engaging leadership styles) may positively impact on followers' well-being at work (Alimo-Metcalfe et al. 2008), yet relatively few studies have been systematically conducted to investigate the influence of leadership on the well-being of leaders. Besides, there are few studies examining the linkage between leadership training as well as cultivation of well-being in the process of training. The dearth of research in this area, especially in the higher educational context, points to the need to further understand how leadership qualities may benefit leaders and students' well-being.

Theoretically, some scholars have suggested certain leadership styles are associated with leaders' well-being. First, regarding ethical leadership, Wright and Quick (2011) contended that since ethical leaders often possess virtuous characters (e.g., being fair, responsible, forgiving), it is reasoned that these qualities may help enhance leaders' own well-being and health. Indeed, happier individuals perceive themselves to be more ethical and intelligent (Myers and Diener 1996). Second, research suggested possible linkages between spiritual leadership and well-being. Spiritual leaders possess character strengths including spirituality, forgiveness, humility, gratitude, hope, and kindness. Research also demonstrated that individuals who had more forgiveness, gratefulness, and optimistic experience displayed higher levels of life satisfaction (Szcześniak and Soares 2011). Spirituality was also positively associated with individuals' psychological well-being. Spiritual individuals were also more likely to be extraverted, high in openness, and emotionally stable (Unterrainer et al. 2010).

Third, regarding self-leadership, Dolbier et al. (2001) conducted two studies with university students and corporate employees investigating the relationship between self-leadership and well-being. Results revealed that for university students, self-leadership was related to better psychological functioning as well as better health status. For the corporate sample, self-leadership was related to greater perceived wellness and lower levels of work stress. It was reasoned that self-leaders know what is healthy and unhealthy and regulates oneself to opt for health-promoting coping styles to maintain their well-being.

Fourth, Ilies et al. (2005) proposed authentic leadership to be related to eudaemonic well-being. Particularly, they argued that leaders who demonstrate authentic behavior are likely to experience flow and intrinsic motivation at the workplace, have higher self-esteem, and are more expressive when leading. However, there is no existing literature that directly discusses the impact of service leadership on students' well-being. In short, the limited literature suggests that there is a positive relationship between leadership qualities and indicators of well-being.

Service Leadership and Student Well-Being

According to the HKI-SLAM, service leadership "...is about satisfying needs by consistently providing quality personal service to everyone one comes into contact with, including one's self, others, groups, communities, systems, and environments" (Chung 2010). The service leadership model asserts that we are all leaders who provide service to people around us. In order to provide high-quality service, leaders must be able to positively manage their own personal brand. Chung (2015a) identified 12 dimensions of one's personal brand that characterize successful leaders in the service age. The 12 dimensions are categorized into four domains, including doing, thinking, being, and growing. Many of the proposed dimensions are closely related to individuals' well-being such as "health" in the physical domain, "happiness" under the emotional domain, and "habitat" under the spiritual domain. It is argued that one's health "must be stable in order for us to succeed... why we need to review and enhance this dimension is to maintain an optimal level of stamina and energy" (Chung 2015a, p. 6).

A key characteristic of the service leadership model that differentiates it from existing leadership theories (e.g., servant leadership) is its focus on satisfying the needs of both the follower and that of the leader. Leaders' individual needs are also taken into consideration because "a leader is unable to optimize his or her ability to lead others well unless he or she is healthy in mind, body, and spirit" (Shek et al. in press-b). Given the importance of health and well-being to service leaders, the present paper outlines research demonstrating how the development of leadership competencies (i.e., intrapersonal and interpersonal), moral character, caring disposition, self-reflection, and self-leadership and continuous improvement, as advocated by the service leadership model (Chung 2012), are intimately linked to student well-being.

At the same time, we argue that there is an intimate link between leadership qualities in university students and student well-being because many desired leadership qualities are in fact attributes of student well-being. Scholars have proposed numerous conceptual models delineating domains that are intrinsic to student well-being. For instance, Masters (2004) outlined five aspects of student well-being including spiritual, emotional, mental, physical, and social. He argued that "the development of student well-being depends on growth in these areas, as well as on their increasing integration into a balanced whole" (p. 2). Similarly, Fraillon's (2004) review identified five substantive dimensions (i.e., physical, economic, psychological, cognitive, social) that were consistently found to be central to student well-being. Kia-Keating et al. (2011) also proposed developmental domains including social, emotional, behavioral, moral, physiological, cognitive, educational, and structural aspects which will have positive impact on adolescents' healthy development. According to Allardt (1989), well-being refers to "a state in which it is possible for a human being to satisfy his/her basic needs" (p. 82) including "having," "loving," and "being." "Having" refers to material conditions; "loving" represents the needs to relate to others; and "being" is about personal growth and integration into the community. The aforementioned holistic approaches to student development and well-being are clearly in line with what is advocated by the service leadership model.

Effective Service Leadership Qualities

In the service leadership model proposed by the Hong Kong Institute of Service Leadership and Management, several attributes of effective service leadership are proposed. These include leadership competence (intrapersonal and interpersonal competencies), moral character, caring disposition, self-leadership and continuous self-improvement, and self-reflection. In this section, these qualities are highlighted and their relationship to mental health and student well-being.

Intrapersonal Competencies

Service leadership is "about promoting inspiring competitive advantage by the use of smartness, EQ, SQ, and inspiration rather than by only smartness and hard power" (HKI-SLAM 2013). Hence, service leaders should be equipped with leadership competencies on both an intrapersonal (e.g., the ability to solve problems, manage, and be aware of one's and others' emotions, to overcome adversity, to transcend materialistic pursuits; Shek and Lin in press) and interpersonal level (e.g., communication and conflict management skills). In this discussion, service leadership attributes in terms of cognitive competence, emotional competence, resilience, and spirituality are focused upon.

Regarding cognitive competence, Gillham and colleagues (2011) found intellectual strengths, as operationalized as interest and passion for learning, to significantly predict adolescents' life satisfaction. Chang et al. (2003) reported that actual academic test scores predicted life satisfaction among children and reasoned that cognitive competence and academic development may be means to achieving life satisfaction. Similarly, students' perceived academic scores were also positively correlated to their self-satisfaction and friend, family, and school domains of life satisfaction as well (Leung et al. 2004). Deniz (2006) found that when faced with stress, students who used a vigilance decision-making style by clarifying objectives, seeking alternatives, and social support were more satisfied with their lives. Individuals who have an effective decision-making style report higher levels of life satisfaction (Bacanli 2000). In the workplace, Judge et al. (2010) found that general mental ability had an indirect effect on subjective well-being. In particular, individuals who were more intelligent reported higher levels of occupational prestige, economic well-being, and physical health, which were associated with subjective well-being. Indeed, problem-solving skills training in the workplace has shown to increase employees' positive emotions, higher job satisfaction, and life satisfaction (Ayres and Malouff 2007). Based on the literature, it can be reasoned that promotion of problem-solving skills in leadership programs helps to enhance student well-being.

Emotional intelligence is also a common focus in leadership training, and it is intimately linked to student well-being. Ciarrochi and Scott (2006) found that low levels of emotional competence predicted higher levels of depression, anxiety, and stress among university students. Individuals who had higher emotional intelligence reported higher levels of past satisfaction with life, concurrent life satisfaction, and future expectation of life satisfaction (Austin et al. 2005). Emotional intelligence was positively associated with psychological well-being components including self-acceptance, life satisfaction, and self-esteem (Carmeli et al. 2009). Emotionally intelligent individuals also had higher levels of stress tolerance and are generally more hopeful (Bar-On 2012). Individuals' capacity to experience positive emotions and alleviate negative emotions optimizes ones' health, subjective well-being, and psychological resilience (Fredrickson 2000). Particularly, it is believed that happy individuals are more satisfied with their life not only because they are able to feel better, but rather, their ability to develop resources such as resilience for living well (Cohn et al. 2009). Nelis and colleagues (2011) also reported the impact of an emotional competence intervention which enhanced participants' happiness, life satisfaction, as well as employability longitudinally.

Besides, resilience forms an integral part of leadership training as well as student well-being. Indeed, when confronted with challenges and adversities, resilient individuals are more likely to adapt flexibly to the situation, cope effectively with the associated stress, and ultimately become successful, healthy, and happy in the future (Ong et al. 2006). As such, it has been argued that "as a protective factor for quality of life, resilience can also help people enhance their life satisfaction" (Liu et al. 2012, p. 834). In a recent study of resilience among university students in the USA, Australia, and Hong Kong, results showed that less resilient students reported higher levels of psychological distress (Pidgeon et al. 2014).

Finally, to provide high-quality service, service leaders should possess spirituality which enables service recipients to see that he/she is committed to concerns that are greater than oneself (Chung 2015a). Spiritual development is a powerful resource for positive human development (Benson et al. 2003). In a recent international study of over 6,000 adolescents, Scales et al. (2014) found that youths with higher spiritual development had better physical and psychosocial well-being as compared with counterparts who scored lower on the Youth Spiritual Development Index Scale.

Being able to find positive meaning is crucial to one's well-being. Finding positive meaning in both ordinary daily life, such as feeling connected to others and optimism (Folkman 1997), and experiences of adversities has been shown to predict long-term psychological well-being and health (Affleck and Tennen 1996). Furthermore, individuals' level of transcendence (e.g., appreciation of beauty, gratitude, hope, humor, religiousness) is positively associated with life satisfaction (Peterson et al. 2007). There are also research findings showing the positive influences of spirituality on one's physical and mental health (George et al. 2000).

Interpersonal Competencies

Good interpersonal skills are intrinsic to an effective service leader. Theoretically, interpersonal skills are effective leadership skills, and they are also regarded as essential attributes of student well-being. Interpersonal skills including cooperation, communication, and social etiquette are needed to satisfy the needs of service recipients and to gain trust from, inspire, and mentor followers (Shek et al. in press-c); it is also part of one's wellness. Segrin and Taylor (2007) found social skills (i.e., social and emotional expressivity, sensitivity, and control) to be positively associated with different indicators of psychological well-being, including life satisfaction, environmental mastery, self-efficacy, hope, happiness, and quality of life. In a longitudinal study, Segrin (2000) found that adolescents with poorer social skills in high school reported more depressive symptoms and worsening of loneliness once they entered college. Individuals better equipped with social and communication skills (e.g., ability to decode others' facial expression) showed more satisfying and supportive interpersonal relationships and hence healthier psychological well-being (Carton et al. 1999).

Having positive relationships with others plays an important role in quality of life. Individuals value communicating, understanding, helping, and being helped by others. Being in relationships with love, trust, and support constitutes to one's quality of life (Flanagan 1978). Particularly, in Confucian societies where harmony is greatly emphasized, interpersonal relationships contribute far more than one's knowledge or wealth attainment in shaping a happy life (Shin and Inoguchi 2009). In terms of college student development, Lounsbury et al. (2005) emphasized the "importance of developing mature interpersonal relationships, particularly friendships, social bonds, and connections with other students" (p. 719) and argued that higher education should create environments that will enable students to develop their potentials and form positive interpersonal relationships.

Moral Character

According to the service leadership model, moral character is an indispensable part of service leaders. Similarly, morality is seen as an important attribute in student well-being. As pointed out by the HKI-SLAM (2013), "positive judgments about leadership quality and effectiveness and service satisfaction are influenced significantly by whether or not a leader or service provider violates moral intuitions or social norms." A service leader should have a well-developed personal code of ethics, as characterized by moral qualities including integrity, respect, humility, and fairness (Chung 2015b). Krieger (2004) underscored the importance of professionalism and upholding values of integrity, wisdom, and compassion. He argued that professionalism and satisfaction are inseparable; very often unprofessional behaviors lead to depression as a result from a loss of integrity. Engaging in immoral behaviors such as lying is associated with the experience of psychological anxiety and physical stress (Zuckerman and Driver 1985). On the contrary, individuals who engage in prosocial behaviors experience greater happiness and higher levels of life satisfaction and self-esteem (e.g., Ellison 1991; Wheeler et al. 1998).

Moral virtues, including courage (bravery, honesty) and justice (fairness) were found to be positively associated with life satisfaction (Peterson et al. 2007). Sun and Shek (2010) also found that moral competence was positively related to life satisfaction of adolescents. Similarly, Alavi (2007) studied university students and identified both moral attitude and behavior to be positively associated with happiness. The author argued that "when we do a good deed, we are helping everybody, including ourselves" (p. 497) and further suggested that in order to increase students' happiness, educational systems should aim to improve their moral attitudes and behaviors as well. According to Park and Peterson (2006), "moral competence and good character in youth are the foundation of life-long optimal human development and the well-being of society" (p. 903).

A distinctive feature of the service leadership model is the inclusion of Eastern philosophies in its theorization. Chung (2012) asserted that "students in the Western nations know very little about Eastern spiritual traditions ... (while) Asian students have little background in Western theologies and ethical philosophies" (p. 58). Therefore, according to the SLAM model, while service leaders should possess character strengths as advocated in the literature from the West such as bravery, honesty, kindness, hope, and gratitude (Peterson and Park 2011), service leaders should also strive to develop Chinese cultural values and ideals including self-cultivation, recognition, and avoidance of vices (Chung 2012; Shek and Yu in press). The development of character strengths is beneficial to one's well-being. Peterson and colleagues (2007) found character strengths including love, hope, curiosity, gratitude, and perseverance to be closely linked with life satisfaction. Students who participated in a character strengths-based program, where they were asked to identify and reflect on their character strengths, experienced significant increases in life satisfaction postexercise, as contrasted with the control group (Proctor et al. 2011).

Caring Disposition

In addition to leadership competencies and moral competencies, service leaders must also possess a caring disposition by demonstrating sincerity, consideration, and empathy to service recipients while listening and attuning to their needs (Chung 2015b). According to Shek and Li (in press), awareness of service recipients' needs, love, and nurturing a caring disposition are essential elements of effective service leadership. Caring service leaders are able to influence and form positive relationships with followers and clients. Indeed, the presence of positive interpersonal relationships as characterized by warmth and trust is crucial to ones' psychological well-being. Individuals' "ability to love is viewed as a central component of mental health" (Ryff 1989, p. 1071). Character strength of humanity (e.g., kindness, love) and temperance (e.g., forgiveness, modesty) were associated with life satisfaction (Peterson et al. 2007). Those who are able to experience strong feelings of empathy and affection for others and capable of developing deeper friendships and greater love are more likely to attain positive psychological functioning (Ryff 1989).

Trait agreeableness, defined as being helpful, caring, and sympathetic, contributes to the fostering and creation of friendships and intimate bonds, which is ultimately associated with higher marital satisfaction (McCrae and Costa 1991) as well as life satisfaction (Heller et al. 2004). In a study of college students, Lounsbury and colleagues (2005) found that students who were more agreeable reported higher levels of general life satisfaction as well as collegiate life satisfaction (e.g., how satisfied they were with their learning, grade point average (GPA), academic major). Valois et al. (2009) argued that empathic relationships served as a developmental asset for youths, as students who reported absence of this quality reported lower levels of life satisfaction. According to Bevis (1981), nurturing a caring disposition enables one to develop capabilities for patience, kindness, compassion, and love and gains a sense of satisfaction and achieves actualization, where caring is a life force that "helps to prevent disease, promote health, heal or help the vulnerable, educate the population, and raise human relationships to satisfying experiences" (p. 49).

Self-Leadership and Continuous Self-Improvement

In the service leadership model, it is asserted that leading oneself is a fundamental condition of leading others. "Service includes self-development efforts aimed at ethically improving one's competencies, abilities, and willingness to help satisfy the needs of others" (Chung 2010; Shek et al. in press-b). Chung (2015b) asserted that if one can lead him/herself in positive, productive, and healthy ways, it is the best indication that he/she can also lead others. Thus, a service leader should first be able to lead oneself. Self-leadership is "a process through which people influence themselves to achieve the self-direction and self-motivation necessary to behave and perform in desirable ways" (Houghton and Neck 2002, p. 672). It is concerned with how individuals lead oneself to attain personal standards and natural rewards that carry intrinsic motivational value (Manz 1986). Self-leadership plays an important role in individual happiness (D'Intino et al. 2007). In a study of college students, Kasser and Ryan (1993) found that students who were intrinsically oriented (i.e., focusing on goals such as affiliation, community feeling, and physical fitness) reported less depression and anxiety and greater self-actualization and feelings of vitality. On the other hand, those who focused on extrinsic goals (e.g., financial success, popularity, attractiveness) reported lower levels of well-being and happiness. Indeed, service leadership education encourages students to be intrinsically motivated in their service provision. The emphasis on self-leadership is consistent with the notions of self-regulation and self-efficacy which are intrinsic to the existing conceptions of student well-being (Witmer et al. 1998; Hermon and Hazler 1999).

Another unique feature of the service leadership model is its emphasis on continuous self-improvement (Chung 2010; Shek et al. in press-b). This emphasis is in line with the contemporary view of well-being. Ryff (1989) argued that personal growth is an important dimension of well-being. "Optimal psychological functioning requires not only that one achieve the prior characteristics, but also that one continue to develop one's potential, to grow and expand as a person" (p. 1071). Service leadership is about "constantly striving to provide the highest quality service one affords to everyone one comes into contact with and whose lives are affected by one's actions or leadership" (Chung 2010; Shek et al. in press-b). Chung (2012) underscored the importance of self-fulfillment/actualization (Maslow 1998) and goal attainment in service provision. In a systematic review of literature on goals and happiness, Emmons (2003) concluded that goals are related to individuals' long-term levels of happiness and life satisfaction. Individuals who adopt an approach goal orientation (i.e., striving to achieve positive and desirable goals) report higher levels of subjective well-being, as opposed to those with an avoidance goal orientation (i.e., striving to avoid negative and aversive goals).

Self-Reflection

Service leaders must engage in constant reflection on one's character and service provision in order to seek for continuous improvement both professionally and personally (Chung 2012). Boehm and Lyubomirsky (2009) reported that self-reflection is an adaptive strategy that happy people use to enhance and maintain their happiness. Hunt (2001) asserted that engaging in reflection will contribute to collective well-being and encouraged students to approach spirituality through reflective practice in order to gain a sense of connectedness. In fact, student reflection is often a part of service learning courses. Research showed that students who engaged in reflection exercises reported reduced anxiety and depression and improved academic attainments (Bringle and Hatcher 1999). In analyzing students' reflections, Pennebaker (1990) found that students who were able to explore and extract personal meaning from experiences showed subsequent health improvements. The focus on reflection in the service leadership model echoes the student well-being models that reflection is part of well-being (Soutter et al. 2014).

Conclusion

In this chapter, the relationships between effective leadership qualities and attributes of student well-being are focused upon. In particular, how student well-being is viewed using the lens of service leadership is explored. Essentially, the qualities of effective service leaders in the service leadership model are consistent with those attributes of student well-being intrinsic to some of the models of student well-being. Being able to serve with leadership, moral competencies, and a caring disposition generates positive sentiments and is beneficial to one's well-being, as astutely put by the two scholars,

> Service leadership is about "understanding services more deeply so that (one) can find more joy in giving and receiving them." (Chung 2012, p. 58)

> I slept and I dreamed that life is all joy. I woke and I saw that life is all service. I served and I saw that service is joy. (Khalil Gibran, 1883–1931)

At the same time, the leadership qualities emphasized in the service leadership model are resonant with those attributes in the student well-being model. As such, nurturing university students to be effective service leaders simultaneously promote their well-being.

Acknowledgments The service leadership research project at The Hong Kong Polytechnic University is financially supported by the Victor and William Fung Foundation.

Appendix 1 Qualities of Effective Service Leadership and Attributes of Student Well-Being Based on Different Models on Student Well-Being

Attributes of student well-being	Service leadership attributes							
	Cognitive competence	Emotional intelligence	Spirituality	Interpersonal skills	Moral character	Caring disposition	Self-leadership and continuous self-improvement	Self-reflection
Student well-being model (Allardt 1989; Soutter et al. 2014)								
Having							✓	✓
Being			✓		✓		✓	✓
Relating				✓		✓		
Feeling		✓						
Thinking	✓							✓
Wheel of wellness (Witmer et al. 1998)								
Spirituality			✓					✓
Self-direction		✓					✓	✓
Work and leisure	✓							
Friendship				✓	✓			
Love				✓	✓	✓		
Domains of healthy adolescent development (e.g., Kia-Keating et al. 2011; Fraillon 2004)								
Social				✓		✓		
Emotional		✓						
Behavioral (e.g., prosocial activities)				✓	✓	✓		
Moral character					✓			
Physiological (e.g., self-regulation skills)							✓	✓
Cognitive (e.g., spiritual beliefs and hopes)	✓		✓				✓	✓
Educational	✓						✓	✓
Structural (e.g., safety)							✓	✓

References

Affleck, G., & Tennen, H. (1996). Construing benefits from adversity: Adaptational significance and dispositional underpinnings. *Journal of Personality, 64*(4), 899–922.

Alavi, H. R. (2007). Correlatives of happiness in the university students of Iran (a religious approach). *Journal of Religion and Health, 46*(4), 480–499.

Alimo-Metcalfe, B., Alban-Metcalfe, J., Bradley, M., Mariathasan, J., & Samele, C. (2008). The impact of engaging leadership on performance, attitudes to work and wellbeing at work: A longitudinal study. *Journal of Health Organization and Management, 22*(6), 586–598.

Allardt, E. (1989). *An updated indicator system: Having, loving, being. Working papers 1989: 48.* Helsinki: Department of Sociology, University of Helsinki.

Arnold, K. A., Turner, N., Barling, J., Kelloway, E. K., & McKee, M. C. (2007). Transformational leadership and psychological well-being: The mediating role of meaningful work. *Journal of Occupational Health Psychology, 12*(3), 193–203.

Austin, E. J., Saklofske, D. H., & Egan, V. (2005). Personality, well-being and health correlates of trait emotional intelligence. *Personality and Individual Differences, 38*(3), 547–558.

Ayres, J., & Malouff, J. M. (2007). Problem-solving training to help workers increase positive affect, job satisfaction, and life satisfaction. *European Journal of Work and Organizational Psychology, 16*(3), 279–294.

Bacanli, F. (2000). Development of indecisiveness scale. *Turkish Psychological Counseling and Guidance Journal, 2*(14), 7–16.

Bar-On, R. (2012). The impact of emotional intelligence on health and wellbeing. In A. Di Fabio (Ed.), *Emotional intelligence – New perspectives and applications* (pp. 78–92). Croatia: Intech.

Benson, P. L., Roehlkepartain, E. C., & Rude, S. P. (2003). Spiritual development in childhood and adolescence: Toward a field of inquiry. *Applied Developmental Science, 7*(3), 205–213.

Bevis, E. O. (1981). Caring: A life force. In M. Leineiger (Ed.), *Caring: An essential human need. Proceeding of the three national caring conferences* (pp. 49–59). Detroit: Wayne State University Press.

Boehm, J. K., & Lyubomirsky, S. (2009). The promise of sustainable happiness. In S. J. Lopez (Ed.), *Handbook of positive psychology* (pp. 667–677). Oxford: Oxford University Press.

Bono, J. E., & Ilies, R. (2006). Charisma, positive emotions and mood contagion. *The Leadership Quarterly, 17*(4), 317–334.

Bringle, R. G., & Hatcher, J. A. (1999). Reflection in service learning: Making meaning of experience. *Educational Horizons, 77,* 179–185.

Carmeli, A., Yitzhak-Halevy, M., & Weisberg, J. (2009). The relationship between emotional intelligence and psychological wellbeing. *Journal of Managerial Psychology, 24*(1), 66–78.

Carton, J. S., Kessler, E. A., & Pape, C. L. (1999). Nonverbal decoding skills and relationship well-being in adults. *Journal of Nonverbal Behavior, 23*(1), 91–100.

Chang, L., McBride-Chang, C., Stewart, S., & Au, E. (2003). Life satisfaction, self-concept, and family relations in Chinese adolescents and children. *International Journal of Behavioral Development, 27*(2), 182–189.

Chen, C. Y., Chen, C. H. V., & Li, C. I. (2013). The influence of leader's spiritual values of servant leadership on employee motivational autonomy and eudaemonic well-being. *Journal of Religion and Health, 52*(2), 418–438.

Chung, P. P. Y. (2010) *Distinguishing characteristics of service leadership and management education.* Hong Kong Institute of Service Leadership and Management. Available at: http://hki-slam.org/index.php?r=article&catid=2&aid=29

Chung, P. P. Y. (2012). *Service reborn: The knowledge, skills and attitudes of service companies.* Hong Kong: Lexingford Publishing.

Chung, P. P. Y. (2015a). *Your second skin: Managing the 12 dimensions of your personal brand for the service age.* Unpublished manuscript.

Chung, P. P. Y. (2015b). *The 25 principles of service leadership.* Unpublished manuscript.

Ciarrochi, J., & Scott, G. (2006). The link between emotional competence and well-being: A longitudinal study. *British Journal of Guidance & Counselling, 34*(2), 231–243.

Cohn, M. A., Fredrickson, B. L., Brown, S. L., Mikels, J. A., & Conway, A. M. (2009). Happiness unpacked: Positive emotions increase life satisfaction by building resilience. *Emotion, 9*(3), 361–368.

D'Intino, R. S., Goldsby, M. G., Houghton, J. D., & Neck, C. P. (2007). Self-leadership: A process for entrepreneurial success. *Journal of Leadership & Organizational Studies, 13*(4), 105–120.

Deniz, M. (2006). The relationships among coping with stress, life satisfaction, decision-making styles and decision self-esteem: An investigation with Turkish university students. *Social Behavior and Personality: An International Journal, 34*(9), 1161–1170.

Dolbier, C. L., Soderstrom, M., & Steinhardt, M. A. (2001). The relationships between self-leadership and enhanced psychological, health, and work outcomes. *The Journal of Psychology, 135*(5), 469–485.

Ellison, C. G. (1991). Religious involvement and subjective well-being. *Journal of Health and Social Behavior, 32*(1), 80–99.

Emmons, R. A. (2003). Personal goals, life meaning, and virtue: Will springs of a positive life. In L. M. Keyes & J. Haidt (Eds.), *Flourishing: A positive psychology and the life well-lived* (pp. 105–128). Washington, DC: American Psychological Association.

Flanagan, J. C. (1978). A research approach to improving our quality of life. *American Psychologist, 33*(2), 138–147.

Folkman, S. (1997). Positive psychological states and coping with severe stress. *Social Science & Medicine, 45*(8), 1207–1221.

Fraillon, J. (2004). Measuring student well-being in the context of Australian schooling: Discussion paper. *The Australian Council for Educational Research, 1–54.

Fredrickson, B. L. (2000). Cultivating positive emotions to optimize health and well-being. *Prevention & Treatment, 3*(1), 1–25.

George, L. K., Larson, D. B., Koenig, H. G., & McCullough, M. E. (2000). Spirituality and health: What we know, what we need to know. *Journal of Social and Clinical Psychology, 19*(1), 102–116.

Gillham, J., Adams-Deutsch, Z., Werner, J., Reivich, K., Coulter-Heindl, V., Linkins, M., ... Seligman, M. E. (2011). Character strengths predict subjective well-being during adolescence. *The Journal of Positive Psychology, 6*(1), 31–44.

Heller, D., Watson, D., & Ilies, R. (2004). The role of person versus situation in life satisfaction: A critical examination. *Psychological Bulletin, 130*(4), 574–600.

Hermon, D. A., & Davis, G. A. (2004). College student wellness: A comparison between traditional and nontraditional age students. *Journal of College Counseling, 7*(1), 32–39.

Hermon, D. A., & Hazler, R. J. (1999). Adherence to a wellness model and perceptions of psychological well-being. *Journal of Counseling & Development, 77*(3), 339–343.

Hong Kong Institute of Service Leadership and Management Limited. (2013). Essential Knowledge Strands (eKs) [Internet]. Hong Kong: Hong Kong Institute of Service Leadership and Management Limited. Available at: http://server.gopublic.com.hk:3993/slam/index.php?r=article&catid=3&aid=42

Houghton, J. D., & Neck, C. P. (2002). The revised self-leadership questionnaire: Testing a hierarchical factor structure for self-leadership. *Journal of Managerial Psychology, 17*(8), 672–691.

Hunt, C. (2001). A way of wellbeing? Approaching spirituality through reflective practice. *Adult Learning, 12*(3), 7–9.

Ilies, R., Morgeson, F. P., & Nahrgang, J. D. (2005). Authentic leadership and eudaemonic well-being: Understanding leader–follower outcomes. *The Leadership Quarterly, 16*(3), 373–394.

Judge, T. A., Klinger, R. L., & Simon, L. S. (2010). Time is on my side: Time, general mental ability, human capital, and extrinsic career success. *Journal of Applied Psychology, 95*(1), 92–107.

Kasser, T., & Ryan, R. M. (1993). A dark side of the American dream: Correlates of financial success as a central life aspiration. *Journal of Personality and Social Psychology, 65*(2), 410–422.

Kia-Keating, M., Dowdy, E., Morgan, M. L., & Noam, G. G. (2011). Protecting and promoting: An integrative conceptual model for healthy development of adolescents. *Journal of Adolescent Health, 48*(3), 220–228.

Kitzrow, M. A. (2003). The mental health needs of today's college students: Challenges and recommendations. *Journal of Student Affairs and Practice, 41*(1), 167–181.

Krieger, L. S. (2004). Inseparability of professionalism and personal satisfaction: Perspectives on values, integrity and happiness. *Clinical Law Review, 11*(2), 425–445.

Kwan, Y. K. (2010). Life satisfaction and self-assessed health among adolescents in Hong Kong. *Journal of Happiness Studies, 11*(3), 383–393.

Leung, C. Y. W., McBride-Chang, C., & Lai, B. P. (2004). Relations among maternal parenting style, academic competence, and life satisfaction in Chinese early adolescents. *Journal of Early Adolescence, 24*(2), 113–143.

Liu, Y., Wang, Z. H., & Li, Z. G. (2012). Affective mediators of the influence of neuroticism and resilience on life satisfaction. *Personality and Individual Differences, 52*(7), 833–838.

Lounsbury, J. W., Saudargas, R. A., Gibson, L. W., & Leong, F. T. (2005). An investigation of broad and narrow personality traits in relation to general and domain-specific life satisfaction of college students. *Research in Higher Education, 46*(6), 707–729.

Manz, C. C. (1986). Self-leadership: Toward an expanded theory of self-influence processes in organizations. *Academy of Management Review, 11*(3), 585–600.

Maslow, A. (1998). *Toward a psychology of being*. New York: Wiley.

Masters, G. N. (2004). Conceptualizing and researching student wellbeing. Paper presented at *Supporting student wellbeing: What does the research tell us about the social and emotional development of young people?* Radisson Playford Hotel, Adelaide, South Australia, October 24–26 (pp. 2–6). Melbourne: ACER.

McCrae, R. R., & Costa Jr, P. T. (1991). Adding liebe und arbeit: The full five-factor model and well-being. *Personality and Social Psychology Bulletin, 17*(2), 227–232.

Myers, D. G., & Diener, E. (1996). The pursuit of happiness. *Scientific American, 274*(5), 70–72.

Nelis, D., Kotsou, I., Quoidbach, J., Hansenne, M., Weytens, F., Dupuis, P., & Mikolajczak, M. (2011). Increasing emotional competence improves psychological and physical well-being, social relationships, and employability. *Emotion, 11*(2), 354–366.

Ong, A. D., Bergeman, C. S., Bisconti, T. L., & Wallace, K. A. (2006). Psychological resilience, positive emotions, and successful adaptation to stress in later life. *Journal of Personality and Social Psychology, 91*(4), 730–749.

Park, N., & Peterson, C. (2006). Moral competence and character strengths among adolescents: The development and validation of the values in action inventory of strengths for youth. *Journal of Adolescence, 29*(6), 891–909.

Pennebaker, J. W. (1990). *Opening up: The healing power of confiding in others*. New York: Morrow.

Peterson, C., & Park, N. (2011). Character strengths and virtues: Their role in well-being. In S. I. Donaldson, M. Csikszentmihaly & J. Nakamura (Eds.), *Applied positive psychology: Improving everyday life, health, schools, work, and society.* (pp. 49–62). New York: Psychology Press.

Peterson, C., Ruch, W., Beermann, U., Park, N., & Seligman, M. E. (2007). Strengths of character, orientations to happiness, and life satisfaction. *The Journal of Positive Psychology, 2*(3), 149–156.

Pidgeon, A. M., Rowe, N. F., Stapleton, P., Magyar, H. B., & Lo, B. C. (2014). Examining characteristics of resilience among university students: An international study. *Open Journal of Social Sciences, 2*(11), 14–22.

Proctor, C., Tsukayama, E., Wood, A. M., Maltby, J., Eades, J. F., & Linley, P. A. (2011). Strengths gym: The impact of a character strengths-based intervention on the life satisfaction and well-being of adolescents. *The Journal of Positive Psychology, 6*(5), 377–388.

Ryff, C. D. (1989). Happiness is everything, or is it? Explorations on the meaning of psychological well-being. *Journal of Personality and Social Psychology, 57*(6), 1069–1081.

Scales, P. C., Syvertsen, A. K., Benson, P. L., Roehlkepartain, E. C., & Sesma Jr, A. (2014). Relation of spiritual development to youth health and well-being: Evidence from a global study. In A. Ben-Arieh, F. Casas, I. Frones & J. E. Korbin (Eds.), *Handbook of child well-being* (pp. 1101–1135). Dordrecht: Springer.

Segrin, C. (2000). Social skills deficits associated with depression. *Clinical Psychology Review, 20* (3), 379–403.

Segrin, C., & Taylor, M. (2007). Positive interpersonal relationships mediate the association between social skills and psychological well-being. *Personality and Individual Differences, 43*(4), 637–646.

Shek, D. T. L., & Li, X. (in press). Nurturing students to be caring service leaders. *International Journal on Disability and Human Development.*

Shek, D. T. L., & Lin, L. (in press). Intrapersonal competences and service leadership. *International Journal on Disability and Human Development.*

Shek, D. T. L., & Yu, L. (in press). Character strengths and service leadership. *International Journal on Disability and Human Development.*

Shek, D. T. L., Chung, P. P. Y., & Leung, H. (in press-a). Manufacturing economy versus service economy: implications for service leadership. *International Journal on Disability and Human Development.*

Shek, D. T. L., Chung, P. P. Y., & Leung, H. (in press-b). How unique is the service leadership model? A comparison with contemporary leadership approaches. *International Journal on Disability and Human Development.*

Shek, D. T. L., Yu, L., & Siu, A. M. H. (in press-c). Interpersonal competence and service leadership. *International Journal on Disability and Human Development.*

Shin, D. C., & Inoguchi, T. (2009). Avowed happiness in Confucian Asia: Ascertaining its distribution, patterns, and sources. *Social Indicators Research, 92*(2), 405–427.

Soutter, A. K., O'Steen, B., & Gilmore, A. (2014). The student well-being model: A conceptual framework for the development of student well-being indicators. *International Journal of Adolescence and Youth, 19*(4), 496–520.

Sun, R. C. F., & Shek, D. T. L. (2010). Life satisfaction, positive youth development, and problem behaviour among Chinese adolescents in Hong Kong. *Social Indicators Research, 95*(3), 455–474.

Szcześniak, M., & Soares, E. (2011). Are proneness to forgive, optimism and gratitude associated with life satisfaction? *Polish Psychological Bulletin, 42*(1), 20–23.

Unterrainer, H. F., Ladenhauf, K. H., Moazedi, M. L., Wallner-Liebmann, S. J., & Fink, A. (2010). Dimensions of religious/spiritual well-being and their relation to personality and psychological well-being. *Personality and Individual Differences, 49*(3), 192–197.

Valois, R. F., Zullig, K. J., Huebner, E. S., & Drane, J. W. (2009). Youth developmental assets and perceived life satisfaction: Is there a relationship? *Applied Research in Quality of Life, 4*(4), 315–331.

Wheeler, J. A., Gorey, K. M., & Greenblatt, B. (1998). The beneficial effects of volunteering for older volunteers and the people they serve: A meta-analysis. *The International Journal of Aging and Human Development, 47*(1), 69–79.

Witmer, J. M., Sweeney, T. J., & Myers, J. E. (1998). *The wheel of wellness.* Greensboro: Authors.

Wright, T. A., & Quick, J. C. (2011). The role of character in ethical leadership research. *The Leadership Quarterly, 22*(5), 975–978.

Yuen, C. (2014). *HKIEd survey: Spiritual health critical to life satisfaction of local youth.* Available at: http://www.ied.edu.hk/web/news.php?id=20140610

Zuckerman, M., & Driver, R. E. (1985). Telling lies: Verbal and nonverbal correlates of deception. In A. W. Siegman & S. Feldstein (Eds.), *Multichannel integrations of nonverbal behavior* (pp. 129–147). New York: Lawrence Erlbaum Associates.

The Role of Service Leadership
in the University's GE Curriculum:
The HKBU Experience

A. Reza Hoshmand

Abstract The concept of service leadership is not only new to Hong Kong but also to other parts of the world. Most universities in North America and elsewhere have adopted service learning as a strategy for engaging students in community service and extracurricular activities in support of their academic course offerings. The philosophy of service leadership is to develop leadership capabilities in students for providing service of any type with care and competence. This chapter will elaborate on how the ideals of service leadership education that include character, virtues, and values could be incorporated into the General Education courses. The process of course development and elements of strategy in implementing service leadership will also be discussed. Student reflections from service leadership courses at Hong Kong Baptist University will be presented to highlight the impact of these courses on student learning.

Introduction

Among the many initiatives in the last few years that Hong Kong public tertiary institutions have launched is the Service Leadership Initiative. One of the objectives of this initiative was to engage the universities to introduce the concept of service leadership to students and in particular develop curricular and cocurricular activities that will broaden students' working knowledge, appreciation, and commitment to continuously develop their service competencies, character strength, and care (Chung 2011). To put this initiative in perspective, this chapter will elaborate on why leadership is important and how service leadership can help our graduates of tomorrow to be prepared for the many challenges that we face. It will also highlight how Hong Kong Baptist University (HKBU) has attempted to incorporate the ideals of service leadership in its General Education Program.

In a global community of the twenty-first century, it is imperative that our students get exposed to the concept of service leadership and how they can use

A.R. Hoshmand (✉)
General Education Office, Hong Kong Baptist University, Room AAB 805A, 15 Baptist University Road, Baptist University Road Campus, Kowloon, Hong Kong
e-mail: hoshmand@hkbu.edu.hk

© Springer Science+Business Media Singapore 2015   17
D.T.L. Shek, P. Chung (eds.), *Promoting Service Leadership Qualities in University Students*, Quality of Life in Asia 6, DOI 10.1007/978-981-287-515-0_2

leadership as a tool in solving the many problems we face. Turbulence, conflict, change, surprise, challenge, and potential possibilities are all words that describe today's world and that evoke myriad emotions ranging from fear and anxiety to excitement, enthusiasm, and hope. Clearly, the problems and challenges that we face today – global warming, religious and ethnic conflict, the maldistribution of wealth, the decline of citizen interest and engagement in the political process, the increasing ineffectiveness of government, and the shift from an industrial to a knowledge-based society and from a national to a global economy – call for adaptive, creative solutions that will require a new kind of leadership (Heifetz 1994; W. K. Kellogg Foundation 1999).

Higher education institutions play a major part in shaping the quality of leadership in our modern world. Our colleges and universities not only educate each new generation of leaders in government, business, science, law, medicine (whether it is Chinese or Western), and other advanced professions but are also responsible for setting the curriculum standards and how such education is to be delivered. What is important to remember is that in educating the new generation of leaders, the conventional models of leadership that are predicated on individual achievement, management, and position may not be able to provide what we wish to achieve in service leadership. The postindustrial theories of leadership that are associated with a concern for the common good, process orientations, and shared responsibility may be closer to the values espoused in service leadership (Northouse 2010). The concept of service leadership as envisioned by the Service Leadership and Management Institute in some ways parallels those important characteristics that are central to servant leadership. Servant leadership has been defined as a lifelong journey that includes discovery of one's self, a desire to serve others ethically, and a commitment to lead (Greenleaf 1977).

College and university faculty also exert important influences on the leadership process through their research and scholarship, which seeks both to clarify the meaning of leadership and to identify the most effective approaches to leadership and leadership education. In this connection, we have been fortunate to have received funding from the Victor and William Fung Foundation to introduce the concept of service leadership to higher education institutions in Hong Kong. But before we discuss specifically about the aims of service leadership, it is important to understand how leadership is perceived. Generally speaking, leadership is looked upon as a service that elected and appointed public officials perform. But critically important is the civic work performed by those individual citizens who are actively engaged in making a positive difference in the society. A leader, in other words, can be anyone – regardless of formal position – who serves as an effective social change agent. In this sense, every faculty and staff member, not to mention every student, is a potential leader.

A major problem with contemporary civic life in Hong Kong as well as in other parts of the world is that too few of our citizens are actively engaged in efforts to effect positive social change. Viewed in this context, an important "leadership development" challenge for higher education institutions in Hong Kong is to empower students, by helping them develop those special talents and attitudes that will enable them to become effective social change agents. To this end, as educators we have a responsibility to educate our students in these learnable leadership practices that include modeling behaviors to achieve goals, inspire a shared vision, challenge the process, enable others to act, and encourage the heart (Kouzes and Posner 2007). To achieve this is both an individual and an institutional challenge. Students will find it difficult to lead until they have experienced effective leadership as part of their education. They are not likely to commit to making changes in society unless the institutions in which they have been trained display a similar commitment. If the next generation of citizen leaders is to be engaged and committed to leading for the common good, then the institutions which nurture them must be engaged in the work of the society and the community, modeling effective leadership and problem-solving skills, demonstrating how to accomplish change for the common good. The recent theoretical models of college students leadership development programs such as servant leadership (Greenleaf 1996) and the practices in *The Leadership Challenge* (Kouzes and Posner 2007) can play an important role as a training tool within a program but should not be used as an undergirding theoretical foundation (Dugan and Komives 2011).

In the classroom, faculty continue to emphasize the acquisition of knowledge in the traditional disciplinary fields and the development of writing, quantitative, and critical thinking skills, giving relatively little attention to the development of those personal qualities that are most likely to be crucial to effective leadership: self-understanding, listening skills, empathy, honesty, integrity, and the ability to work collaboratively. Most of these qualities exemplify aspects of what Goleman (1995) would call "emotional intelligence." One seldom hears mention of these qualities or of "leadership" or "leadership skills" in faculty discussions of curricular reform, even though goals such as "producing future leaders" are often found in the catalogues and mission statements of colleges and universities. While there have been some very promising developments in the cocurricular area – for example, an increased emphasis on programs for student leadership development that can have lasting impacts on students, institutions, and communities (Thorns and Blasko 1998) – the General Education Programs in most institutions are still notably lacking in requirements or other content that focuses either directly or indirectly on leadership. And despite the mounting evidence that student engagement in community service substantially enhances the development of leadership skills (Astin and Sax 1998; Astin et al. 1999; Eyler and Giles 1999), service learning and the notion of service leadership remain an essentially marginal activity on most campuses. For this reason, we have taken the initiative to bring service leadership as a component of our General Education Program at HKBU. On a more practical level, our students are probably going to be influenced at least as much by what we academics do as by what we say in our classroom lectures and advising sessions. In other words, we are implicitly modeling certain leadership values in the way we conduct ourselves professionally: how we govern ourselves, how we deal with each other as professional colleagues, and how we run our institutions. If we want our students to acquire the qualities of effective leaders, then we have to model these same qualities, not only in our individual professional conduct but also in our curriculum, our pedagogy, our institutional policies, and our preferred modes of governance. Fortunately for us at HKBU, the ethos of whole person education is grounded on the notion that "whole person development" is a process through which the intellectual, physical, professional, psychological, social, and spiritual capacities of an individual can be holistically enhanced. We intend to use service leadership courses in the process of whole person development.

Practically all of the modern authorities on leadership, regardless of whether they focus on the corporate world or the nonprofit sector, now advocate a collaborative approach to leadership, as opposed to one based on power and authority (Bennis 1989; Heifetz 1994). In this context, it would be helpful for us to take a brief look at how leadership development programs in colleges have been formulated and how they foster leadership capabilities in the students.

Key Leadership Theories and College Student Leadership Development

It is in recent times that leadership development of college students has received more attention. Employers have demanded that institutions of higher learning need to address how students are engaged in class as well as outside of the classroom in activities that develop their leadership skills. There are numerous theories of leadership development that can be used to develop leadership skills in college students. However, we will only highlight a few that are closely aligned with our notion of leadership development in students.

It has been pointed out by Komives (2011) that the discussion about theories of college student leadership development began with the philosophy of servant leadership. The conceptual framework of servant leadership was laid down by Greenleaf (1977, 1996) who believed that people were better off for working together toward some shared outcome. His emphasis on a process orientation and value-based framing of positional leadership is the building block of the model. Some higher education institutions have used this in their service learning activities so as to develop the leadership skills in their students. Another theoretical model that has often been mentioned in the literature (Bass 1985; Bass and Avolio 1990) that has a positive effect on student leadership development is the transformational leadership model that was put forward by Burns (1978). In this model, leadership is seen as one that is concerned with followers' needs and the pursuit of shared goals. In this context, leaders genuinely care about their work and the people around them, and they want everyone to succeed in accomplishing goals that are facilitated through trust and excitement. Kouzes and Posner (2007) in their study asked people about the top things they look for, admire, and willingly follow in a leader, and they found that people prefer the following five characteristics in a leader: honesty, forward-looking, competent, inspiring, intelligent, and fair-minded. Hence, they identify five actions for successful leadership: modeling the way, inspiring a shared

Fig. 1 Social change
model of leadership
development (Adapted from
Higher Education Research
Institute 1996)

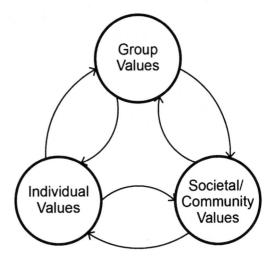

vision, challenging the process, enabling others to act, and encouraging the heart. These positive, collaborative views of leadership relate to leadership models developed specifically with college students in mind.

In 1993, a grant by the US Department of Education was given to a group of scholars to "enhance student learning and development of leadership competence" and "to facilitate positive social change." The outcome of this research was the 1996 social change model of leadership. This model approaches leadership as a dynamic, collaborative, and values-based process grounded in relationships and intending positive social change (Higher Education Research Institute 1996). Focused on college students, the model is a framework for personal development and for working with others to create positive change for society. The underlying assumptions of the model are that leadership is collaborative, is a process versus a position, and is value based. Other key themes are that all students are potential leaders, regardless of holding formal leadership positions, and that service is an important way any student can develop leadership skills. Figure 1 shows the interrelationship between the individual, group, and society and how the values of each interact with each other to develop the leadership capacities.

Subsequently, the conceptual framework of applied relational leadership was introduced (Komives et al. 1998). This model was applied to a variety of college students who were interested in developing as leaders. Leadership in this model is viewed as "a relational and ethical process of people together attempting to accomplish positive change." The virtue of this approach to leadership development lies in how a healthy, ethical, effective group can be developed and supported through the five elements of being inclusive, empowering, purposeful, ethical, and process oriented.

The leadership identity development theory, put forward by Komives et al. (2009), explores how college students develop the social identity of being collaborative, relational leaders who interdependently engage in leadership as a group process. In this model, student leadership development is viewed as an intersection between relational leadership and student development theory. To establish leadership identity, psychosocial and cognitive stages to development have to come together. There are six stages with transitions of increasing complexity that individuals experience, resulting in students reflecting on their roles of doing leadership in groups and expanding their views of leadership. Since its inception, the theory has been used in various studies on college student leadership. All of the above theories align well with our conception of service leadership and how the courses developed in this area at our institution will help students develop the desired leadership skills.

At many institutions, leadership is often taught in the management departments in business schools. While this exposes some group of students to the concepts of leadership, a majority of the students may not benefit from such exposure unless they are a student of business. For this reason, we have attempted to incorporate service leadership courses in our General Education Program. Since GE is a requirement for graduation, and that we have introduced service leadership in a variety of disciplines, the likelihood of exposure to leadership principles, and where students may show their leadership in practice, has increased. Given the breadth of the theoretical knowledge in leadership, it would not be possible to expose the students to all the elements of leadership. Hence, we have framed our courses in service leadership with the following conception of leadership.

What Is Leadership?

From our perspective, leadership is a process that is ultimately concerned with fostering change. In contrast to the notion of "management", which suggests preservation or maintenance, leadership implies a process where there is movement – from wherever we are now to some future place or condition that is different. Leadership also implies intentionality, in the sense that the implied change is not random – "change for change's sake" – but is rather directed toward some future end or condition which is desired or valued. Accordingly, leadership is a purposive process which is inherently value based. If we adopt the social change model of leadership development, then we see that leadership is concerned with change, and we view the "leader" basically as a change agent, i.e., "one who fosters change." Leaders, then, are not necessarily those who merely hold formal "leadership" positions; on the contrary, all people are potential leaders. Furthermore, since the concepts of "leadership" and "leader" imply that there are other people involved, therefore leadership is, by definition, a collective or group process. Educational institutions are also deemed as a collective environment where leadership can be developed and applied. In short, our conception of leadership comprises the following basic assumptions:

- Leadership is concerned with fostering change.
- Leadership is inherently value based.

- All people are potential leaders.
- Leadership is a group process.

Even though there are many opportunities for faculty, staff, and students to serve in formal leadership positions, our conception of leadership argues that every member of the academic community is a potential leader (i.e., change agent). The challenge for leadership development in higher education is thus to maximize the number of faculty, students, administrators, and staff who become committed and effective agents of positive social change. Leadership development programs and experiences for students can capitalize on the power of the student peer groups through classroom, hostel living, and various cocurricular activities. With these elements of leadership and how we have framed the concept of leadership for our students, the next section will provide a view on service leadership courses in general education at Hong Kong Baptist University.

Service Leadership Development at Hong Kong Baptist University

With that conceptualization of leadership, our university decided to develop service leadership courses in its General Education Program. Our vision of leadership development for our students is to develop thoughtful, skilled, and reflective practitioners equipped to effect positive social change. Our hope is that through exposure in curricular and cocurricular activities in these service leadership courses, our students will gain knowledge on how to develop themselves and become thoughtful, skilled, and reflective practitioners serving the needs of their profession and make positive contributions to society.

As has been noted elsewhere, too many leadership programs exist because of the interest of a single professional who builds a program that fails to become institutionalized (Komives 2011). We believe that with the development of service leadership courses throughout the academic programs in the university, the students will be able to take advantage of these courses in developing those valued characteristics of leadership and at the same time satisfy their General Education requirements in the distribution category of our GE offerings. Additionally, courses that have been developed and those that will be developed become part of the institutional offerings of our university. As was mentioned earlier, the notion of service leadership is new to the institutions of higher learning in Hong Kong. This meant that we had to introduce our faculty to the basic philosophy of service leadership and to engage them in the broad discussion of how courses in various disciplines could embed the concepts of service leadership.

To develop the courses in service leadership, a call for proposal was sent out in 2012 to the entire university community encouraging faculty colleagues to collaborate with one or two departments in developing interdisciplinary courses in service leadership. At the same time, workshops were presented to the university community on how to design, develop, and deliver the service leadership courses. Each proposal was vetted by external reviewers. Such vetting process allowed our colleagues to refine the course content and/or the pedagogy involved. With reference to the Hong Kong Institute of Service Leadership and Management (SLAM) Curriculum Framework, specific elements of service leadership such as learning how to provide services ethically and with care to those who receive the service were incorporated in each course. Learning and habituating leadership competencies including such elements as character strengths and caring disposition were emphasized. Additionally, the courses are to address the importance of positive social relationships and its impact on leadership effectiveness. All of the courses that have been developed so far are supported with cocurricular activities. We believe that such cocurricular activities immediately reinforce the theoretical notions of service leadership and enhance our student capabilities in meeting the challenges of today. Using the SLAM Curriculum Framework, the following intended learning outcomes are to be achieved:

1. Explain the leadership capabilities aimed at ethically satisfying the needs of self, others, groups, communities, systems, and environments.
2. Explain the key elements of effective leadership and how it can be improved to provide exceptional service.
3. Analyze different leadership models and how they impact quality of professional practices.
4. Identify ways to improve his/her leadership capabilities with character and care in providing excellent service.
5. Reflect and review ethical practices in their professional areas.
6. Develop service leadership plans/business plans in an entrepreneurial spirit with the intent to make potential social impact.

In the first year of the project, we developed three service leadership courses, namely, "Leadership in Sustainability," "Service Leadership in Action (Health Services)," and "Service Leadership and Emotional Intelligence." They are all interdisciplinary courses which are categorized into different areas of learning under the distribution requirements of our GE program.

To illustrate, the aims of the courses are highlighted below:

"Leadership in Sustainability": It aims to help develop responsible business graduates who can decipher the importance of leadership practiced by sustainability leaders in the corporate world. The aspects of good practice include environmental protection, good governance, quality and safe product and service offerings, motivational human resources management, and proactive stakeholder engagement. Students will be able to develop the right values for ethical and responsible management and be prepared to become change agents.

"Service Leadership in Action (Health Services)": Service leadership and management is about creating new personal service propositions and consistently providing high-quality caring service to everyone that comes into contact with.

The aim of this course is to introduce the concepts of service leadership and their actualization in health services, with particular emphasis on Chinese medicine. It is envisaged that through the sharing of experiences from stakeholders of the different sectors of health services in Hong Kong, it will provide a foundation for the students to deliver services in health care with competence, responsibilities, and care in the future.

"Service Leadership and Emotional Intelligence": It brings together two significant components of service leadership, namely, leadership and emotional intelligence (EI) through the joint expertise of the two units. It aims to familiarize students with leadership theories, leadership styles, and skills, to introduce the key concepts of EI, and to develop emotional abilities relating to self and social awareness and management.

With these aims in mind, we have extended our courses beyond the classroom and regularly arrange field visits, experiential activities, and outdoor games. In Leadership in Sustainability, perhaps the most favorably talked-about thing among students was the one-day leadership challenge. Students were challenged through a wide range of activities to learn about leadership first hand. They found that the challenge made their learning more memorable where they could internalize what was taught in lectures through personal experience. They saw how easily it was to overlook others' needs when they had placed achieving goal as the first priority; they started thinking about the importance of communication when they had to work in a team; they were also touched when their group mates did not "blame" them for their mistakes but comforted them.

Other experiential learning in this course included a game called Pollutant and Dialogue in the Dark. Both left the students with deep impression on how to develop empathy for those who are disadvantaged.

> What in the Dialogue in the Dark impressed me the most was not the training on leadership but self-reflection. Visually impaired tour guides lead us throughout the activity. This made me think about how I could also contribute to society by utilizing my own strengths. The activity is a worthwhile experience.

Students found the biweekly reflection essays required in this course helped strengthen their knowledge learned in the course. Among the reflections, we found comments by students who indicated that they sometimes found there was a conflict between what was taught and the reality. The course talked about corporate social responsibility and how to be an ethical business practitioner, but in reality not many leaders cared about social and environmental issues.

Other feedback from the students who took the service leadership courses was as follows:

> Leadership was about giving guidelines to others to follow was my previous understanding. However, the course made me realize that everyone can be a leader instead of just adhering to a strong individual. No one is perfect. We have both strengths and weaknesses. When a group shares a common goal, everyone in the group will strive for it.

As leaders, it is vital for us to put ourselves into others' shoes because sometimes leaders do not know the possible obstacles faced by team members. The experience in the course made me more considerate to others' need.

I think achieving goals is not the most important thing to a leader, but team building is. What makes our group different from the others is that we had a close and warm relationship. We were considerate to each other and did our best in our own roles.

In my opinion, a good leader should possess several important elements. First, a good leader should have good communication skills and getting along with other group members. Second, a good leader should have a sense of responsibility in performing job duties. Third, a good leader should be considerate. When a member fails to finish the task, the leader should try to understand the reasons behind it first instead of blaming the member.

In my perception, leaders in business sector are more money-oriented and aiming at maximizing profits. However, this course talked about corporate social responsibility and how to be an ethical business practitioner. In reality, not many leaders care about social and environmental problems.

In our case study, we found that an all-rounded leader should have knowledge of sustainability and needs to take environmental preservation, social and ethical responsibility into consideration besides operational costs.

In Service Leadership in Action (Health Services), students were exposed to Hong Kong's leading players in Chinese herbal medicine. Additionally, guest speakers came from a variety of companies including DHL, Nong's Company Ltd., and NGOs like Christian Action. This course also provided the students an opportunity to interact with the Knowledge Transfer Office at HKBU. This office is involved with intellectual property rights and its protection. Students appreciated learning more about how to setup businesses that involved providing services to the community.

Students' biggest gain in these two courses was that they had developed leadership and communication skills. They had a better understanding on the roles and responsibility of a leader and a team member. A leader to them was no longer someone with a high status but rather a facilitator. They understood that a leader, different from a manager, needs to be open to team members' ideas and opinions, because they might not always be right about everything. The students also realized that achieving the common goal was important but not nearly as much as being considerate to other people's feeling. They agreed that a leader should be assessed not only by achievements but also good communication. They had a better idea after the course what qualities an all-rounded leader should possess.

Students also learned that cooperation was essential to decision making and that people from different positions within the group had to work together to achieve the common goal. They agreed that by sharing their difficulties, they could have a better understanding toward each other. Students realized that everyone had a responsibility to build up a team, and everyone needed to be involved to carry out the tasks.

Besides leadership skills, students also shared that they had improved their writing and persuasion skills. One student said she became more assertive rather than keeping her ideas to herself.

When asked how service leadership courses had impacted their major studies, students said that they could take the mediation and leadership skills learned and serve as a better leader in group projects for other courses.

Conclusion

In an attempt to broadly educate our students to be of service to themselves, their community, and the world, we incorporated the service leadership courses in our General Education Program. The basic premise of these courses is to develop leadership capabilities in our students with the knowledge that no matter what industry they are engaged in, the service they provide must be delivered with care and competence.

Our experience in the last 2 years indicates the positive effect of these courses on our students. We will continue to develop additional courses in service leadership as we hope to allow as many faculties/schools/academy to take part in this initiative. Through this project, it is hoped that our faculty colleagues will become more effective facilitators in training students to be good service leaders. In addition, this project will demonstrate the importance of service leadership to improve student experiences as a learner and how their service leadership experiences contribute to their understanding of their discipline and its impact on society.

References

Astin, A. W., & Sax, L. J. (1998). How undergraduates are affected by service participation. *Journal of College Student Development, 39*(3), 251–263.

Astin, A. W., Sax, L. J., & Avalos, J. (1999). Long-term effects of volunteerism during the undergraduate years. *The Review of Higher Education, 22*(2), 187–202.

Bass, B. M. (1985). *Leadership and performance beyond expectations.* New York: Free Press.

Bass, B. M., & Avolio, B. J. (1990). The implications of transactional and transformational leadership for individual, team, and organizational development. *Research in Organizational Change and Development, 4,* 231–272.

Bennis, W. (1989). *On becoming a leader.* Reading: Addison-Wesley.

Burns, J. (1978). *Leadership.* New York: Harper & Row.

Chung, P. (2011). *Hong Kong Institution of Service Leadership & Management (SLAM) curriculum framework.* Unpublished manuscript.

Dugan, J. P., & Komives, S. R. (2011). Leadership theories. In S. R. Komives, J. P. Dugan, J. E. Owen, C. Slack, W. Wagner, & National Clearinghouse of Leadership Programs (Eds.), *The handbook for student leadership development* (2nd ed.) (pp. 35–58). New York: Wiley.

Eyler, J., & Giles Jr., D. E. (1999). *Where's the learning in service learning?* San Francisco: Jossey-Bass.

Greenleaf, R. (1977). *Servant leadership.* New York: Paulist Press.

Greenleaf, R. (1996). *On becoming a servant leader.* San Francisco: Jossey-Bass.

Goleman, D. (1995). *Emotional intelligence.* New York: Bantam.

Heifetz, R. (1994). *Leadership without easy answers*. Cambridge, MA: The Belknap Press of Harvard University Press.

Higher Education Research Institute. (1996). *A social change model of leadership development guidebook. Version III*. Los Angeles: Higher Education Research Institute.

Komives, S. R., Lucas, N., & McMahon, T. R. (1998). *Exploring leadership: For college students who want to make a difference*. San Francisco: Jossey-Bass.

Komives, S. R., Longerbeam, S. D., Mainella, F., Osteen, L., Owen, J. E., & Wagner, W. (2009). Leadership identity development: Challenges in applying a developmental model. *Journal of Leadership Education, 8*(1), 1–47.

Komives, S. R. (2011). Advancing leadership education. In S. R. Komives, J. P. Dugan, J. E. Owen, C. Slack, W. Wagner, & National Clearinghouse of Leadership Programs (Eds.), *The handbook for student leadership development* (2nd ed.) (pp. 1–32). New York: Wiley.

Kouzes, J. M., & Posner, B. Z. (2007). *The leadership challenge*. San Francisco: Jossey-Bass.

Northouse, P. G. (2010). *Leadership theory and practice* (5th ed.). Thousand Oaks: Sage.

Thorns, M., & Blasko, D. (1998). *Leadership evaluation report on the leadership institute and the W. K. Kellogg Foundation*. Battle Creek: W. K. Kellogg Foundation.

W. K. Kellogg Foundation. (1999). *Building leadership capacity for the 21st century: A report from global leadership scans*. Battle Creek: W. K. Kellogg Foundation.

Service Leadership in an Uncertain Era

Kin-man Chan and Hugh Thomas

Abstract The Service Leadership Initiative (SLI) at The Chinese University of Hong Kong involves an interdisciplinary general education three-credit 14-week course based on the premise that all students possess the potential to be service leaders. The course aims to promote service leadership through cultivating appropriate knowledge, skills, character, and care. It introduces students to theories of leadership from the disciplines of management, political science, psychology, and sociology with instructors from the appropriate faculties and departments teaching the classes. The first two classes introduce service from sociological and management perspectives based on classics of Heifetz (1994) for the former and Drucker (1968) for the latter with an overview of leadership theories provided by Northouse (2013) and Zigarelli (2013). As effective leadership requires sensitivity to oneself and to others, the course deepens students' understanding in the third and fourth classes by adopting a psychological perspective on leadership, based on the works of Siegel (2007). Each student reflects on these theories by submitting, in week 4, a short essay on how each has experienced being a leader and how that experience reflects theories of leadership.

The remainder of the course and its articles, cases, videos, and guest speakers highlight business, social enterprise, NGO, and political leaders to stimulate students' reflections on effective leadership. The course uses five video-assisted cases (each comprised of a 15–20-page written description plus a 15–30 min video) developed specifically for SLI. These cases include service leadership in the goods producer company, frontline leadership in banks, and leadership in NGOs and social enterprises. The leaders are individuals from the local community facing challenges in organizations to create value and maintain viability. Students are

K.-m. Chan, Ph.D. (✉)
Department of Sociology, The Chinese University of Hong Kong, Sino Building, The Chinese University of Hong Kong, Shatin, N.T. Room 431, Hong Kong, Hong Kong
e-mail: kmchan@cuhk.edu.hk

H. Thomas, Ph.D. (✉)
Department of Finance, Center for Entrepreneurship, The Chinese University of Hong Kong, Room 1201, Cheung Yu Tung Building, 12 Chak Cheung Street, Shatin, N.T., Hong Kong, Hong Kong
e-mail: hugh-thomas@cuhk.edu.hk

© Springer Science+Business Media Singapore 2015
D.T.L. Shek, P. Chung (eds.), *Promoting Service Leadership Qualities in University Students*, Quality of Life in Asia 6, DOI 10.1007/978-981-287-515-0_3

assigned case materials prior to classes and assess these cases interactively in class, participating in oral case discussions with the instructor calling on groups to express and defend their analyses. The videos show leaders reflecting on their authority, philosophies, objectives, traits, skills, situations, interactions, and effectiveness. Instructors adjust student group marks to reflect individual contribution to group performance by using student peer assessments. As Greater China in general and Hong Kong in particular are undergoing political changes, the course brings theoretical issuers of leadership to a contemporary focus, in a forum where leaders with different views on Hong Kong's political development debate their philosophies, strategies, and tactics.

Each student submits at the end of the course an essay on "A Good Leader That I Want To Follow." Upon completion of this course, students should be able to reflect on issues of leadership; understand how sensitivity to oneself and to others can enhance leadership; show an ability to summarize, classify, synthesize, and evaluate service leaders in business, nonprofit and political situations; and demonstrate knowledge of theories of leadership through using them to assess words and actions of recognized service leaders.

Introduction

By the Memorandum of Understanding between the Victor and William Fung Foundation and The Chinese University of Hong Kong (CUHK) of 16 March 2012 (the MOU), CUHK, through Kin-man Chan as principal investigator and Hugh Thomas as coprincipal investigator, undertook to "... structure an academically sound general education course on service leadership ... consistent with the HKI-SLAM Curriculum Framework's overarching education goals...." (the SLIGE course). We committed to "... produce locally sourced, globally applicable, current ... video-enhanced cases[1]..." to be used in the course (see Appendix I: Excerpts from Annex A of the MOU). To allow sufficient time for the CUHK approval for the SLIGE course and the production of the cases, we scheduled the first offering of the SLIGE course for the second term of the academic year 2013–2014. We also offered a SLI module for NGOs and social enterprises from Taiwan and the mainland. This paper discusses the structure and content of the SLIGE course and the SLI module.

---

[1] A description of the production and assessment of these video-enhanced cases is given in Chapter 17 "Developing Video Enhanced Pedagogical Cases in Service Leadership."

SLIGE Course Structure

Definition

The term "service leadership" may be defined in at least two different ways including (1) leadership ("... a process whereby an individual influences a group of individuals to achieve a common goal..."[2]) in organizations providing services (as opposed to goods) and (2) taking the initiative in providing personal service to benefit society. In the SLIGE course, we adopted the former, introducing students to classics in the leadership literature and examples of leadership from business, civil society sector, and politics. Yet we also maintained a philosophy of service in leadership consistent with the latter definition.

Form

We believe that learning by doing is preferable to traditional classroom learning. But the extreme difficulty of structuring a practicum in which novices enter service-providing organizations outside of the university and practice effective leadership within the time constraints of a 3-credit course led us to deliver SLIGE in traditional format: a 3-credit course delivered in 14, 3-h sessions using Cantonese and English. SLIGE was taught by five instructors from the Faculty of Social Science (Sociology, Psychology, and Government and Public Administration) and the Faculty of Business Administration (see Appendix II: Instructors).

CUHK university-level[3] GE courses need sponsorship by the Office of General Education and approval by the Senate, which we received in February and June 2013, respectively. In the process of obtaining approvals, we strengthened the SLIGE course's rigor, assessment mechanisms, and consistency.

SLIGE Course Content

The course had three parts: 4 weeks of theory, 8 weeks of examples and 2 weeks of synthesis.

---

[2] Northouse (2013), page 5.

[3] At CUHK, there is a distinction between university-level and college-level GE courses. The two required GE courses for all undergraduate students, *In Dialogue with Humanity* and *In Dialogue with Nature*, are offered by the CUHK Office of General Education. Almost all of the elective GE courses are offered by the offices of general education of CUHK's nine constituent colleges, which function as small student communities with hostels, canteens, sports and recreation facilities, and centers of counseling and moral education.

Theoretical Background

The theoretical background included the sociological/business and psychological perspectives in lectures 1–2 and 3–4, respectively. We introduced the differences between leadership with and leadership without authority (Heifetz 1994), the morality and process of leadership, and the technical and adaptive leadership as illustrated in Table 1, giving examples from social and political spheres as well as the theory of organizations (Drucker 1968) and ten modern theories of leadership from management theory (see Table 2 and Zigarelli 2013).

The psychological perspective drew on both Chinese Buddhism and mindfulness (Siegel 2007): the successful leader is self-aware and managed and socially aware and managed (Goleman 2011). The human mind can be appreciated in relation to

Table 1 Technical versus adaptive leadership

Situation	Problem definition	Solution and implementation	Primary locus of responsibility for work	Kind of work
Type I	Clear	Clear	Physician	Technical
Type II	Clear	Requires learning	Physician and patient	Technical and adaptive
Type III	Requires learning	Requires learning	Patient > physician	Adaptive

Table 2 Ten theories of leadership

Theory	Idea	Reference
Great man	Epics' and hero-centric histories' belief that nothing is nobler than following great men of destiny	Carlyle (1841)
Traits	Innate intelligence, self-confidence, determination, integrity, etc. define leaders	Stogdill (1948)
Skills	Technical, human, and conceptual skills that define leaders can be learned	Katz (1955)
Style	A leader's habitual style can be oriented on a concern for people (supporting) versus concern for results (directive) grid	Blake and Mouton (1964)
Situational	Leaders adopt styles to the abilities of subordinates on the supporting directive grid	Blanchard (1985)
Contingency	Effectiveness of leaders' habitual styles – people or results oriented – is contingent on the task structure	Feilder (1964)
Transactional	Contracts exchange of rewards for performance and management by exception	Bass (1990)
Transformational	Charisma, inspiration, intellectual stimulation, and individualized consideration increases leader effectiveness	Bass (1990)
Leader-manager exchange	Leader-follower dyads: in-groups negotiate relationships while out-groups receive supervision	Dansereay et al. (1975)
Service-leader	Hindu and Christian-based themes that leading begins with service and nurturing growth of followers	Greenleaf (1970)

Evolution of the mind

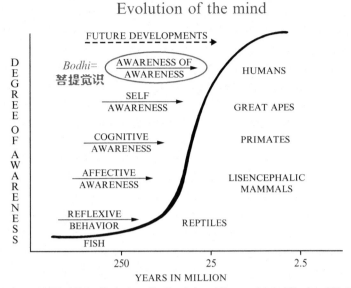

Parksopp, J.(1998). Affective Neuroscience: The Foundations of Human and Animal Emotions. NY: Oxford.

Fig. 1 Example of placing consciousness in perspective

the age of the Universe, Earth, life, and consciousness (see Fig. 1). The ABCs of our mental experience of the world are determined by this evolution from the **A**ffective appraisals to **B**iological reactions through **C**ognitive reactions (see Fig. 2). Mastering the affective appraisal – centered in the ancient amygdala of the brain, through training to achieve a state analogous to Bodhi (see Fig. 1) – helps one to achieve self-management. Empathy together with self-management is a solid mental basis for social management and leadership. We introduced stretching and breathing exercises to help this process.

Leaders in Different Spheres

The next eight sessions comprised sector-specific treatments of leaders in business, nonprofits, politics, and cross sector. We employed three guest speakers, four cases, and a forum. Po Chung discussed "Minding 12 Dimensions of a Service Warrior's Personal Brand." Michael Lai Kam-cheung, recently retired CEO of St. James' Settlement, spoke on nonprofits, and Ada Ho lectured on "The Balancing Act of Leadership and Management" and her social enterprise, *Love Plus Hope*. We used five of our SLI video-assisted cases, *China Merchants Bank*, *Constellation*, *Cisco*, *Diamond Cab*, and *WebOrganic*, to illustrate individual leaders from the chairman of the board through frontline sales staff in banking, information technology, and transport in for-profits and social enterprises.

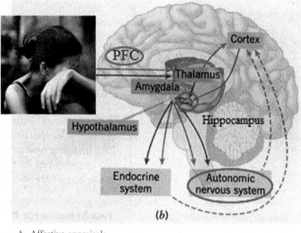

Amygdala: performs affective appraisals of stimuli in our environment. A stimulus can be appraised as positive, negative, or neutral.

Affective appraisal evokes bodily reactions.

Both affective and bodily signals travel back to prefrontal cortex (CEO of the brain)

PFC integrates all signals and makes cognitive interpretations and decisions.

A   Affective appraisals
B   Biological reactions
C   Cognitive reactions

Fig. 2 The ABCs of perception and action

Political events in Hong Kong offered the SLIGE course a living case in political service leadership without authority. The government will propose to the Legislative Council a law acceptable to the Chinese government, through whose National People's Congress the appropriate amendments to Hong Kong's Basic Law ultimately must be passed, setting out the 2017 election process for the Chief Executive of Hong Kong. Concerned that the national (and local) governments were insufficiently committed to specifying an election process that meets international standards, Chan Kin-man, the principal investigator of CUHK SLI, cofounded, with Professor Benny Tai Yiu-ting and Reverend Chu Yiu-ming, *Occupy Central with Love and Peace*, a civil society organization committed to pressure the government. Robert Chow Yung, a famous journalist, commentator, entrepreneur, and author, concerned that Occupy Central's plan of contingent civil disobedience might harm Hong Kong, founded *Silent Majority* in order to oppose *Occupy Central*. To bring into focus the political leadership styles, tactics, commitments, and ideas of the two political movement leaders, while avoiding a bias in the discussion, we held in the SLIGE class of March 11 a forum on *How to Achieve Democratic Election of the Chief Executive*. The forum was open to all members of the university community, and members of the local press and television stations also attended. The first hour of the forum was given to each side's presentation. The second hour was 10 min for each of the six student groups to discuss with the panelists, and the final half an hour was open to members of the public to ask questions. Figure 3 shows a picture of the forum with the discussants and moderator.

Fig. 3 Presentation of certificate of appreciation to Robert Chow at the forum

Table 3 Leaders

Leader	Role	Week	Mode
Mahatma Gandhi	Political/Indian independence	1	Lecture
Adolf Hitler	Political/German Third Reich	1	Lecture
Martin Luther King	Political/US civil rights	1	Lecture
Margaret Sanger	Social/planned parenthood	1	Lecture
Ma Weihua	China Merchants Bank chairman	2	Lecture
Chung Po	DHL International cofounder	6	Guest
Aglaia Kong	Business/Cisco China	7	Case
Sally Wong	Business/Bao An Bank (fictitious) sales rep	7	Case
Rodrigo Baggio	Social ent., Brazil/Center for Digital Inclusion founder	8	Video
Michael Lai Kam-cheung	St. James' Settlement CEO	9	Guest
Robert Chow Yung	Political/silent majority	11	Forum
Chan Kin-man	Political/Occupy Central	11	Forum
Andrea and Barry Coleman	Social ent. in Gambia/Riders for Health founders	13	Video
G. Venkataswamy	Social ent., India/Aravind Eye Care Hospital founder	13	Video
Ada Ho	L + H CEO and founder	14	Guest

Synthesis

We reviewed the 15 leaders we had introduced over the previous 14 weeks (see Table 3), through a summary of the major topics and concepts covered in the course. The final session, which occurred on the same day as students submitted their term papers, was devoted to a topical discussion around the major concepts, with students requested to discuss how each theme was relevant to the leader he or she wished to follow.

Assessment

We assessed students on three deliverables, one from each of the three parts of the course. At the end of the *Theoretical Background*, each student completed a written assignment describing an experience of being a leader and relating that to theory (20 %). During the *Leaders in Different Spheres* section, we assigned questions for students to discuss in groups prior to class and assessed student in-class contributions to discussion on a group-by-group basis (30 %). Attendance was taken at every class. Students sat in their groups and had name cards to facilitate discussion. To reduce the free rider problem in group work, students assessed peers through peer evaluations. On the last day of the *Synthesis* section, each student submitted a term paper describing a good leader and discussing how the leader demonstrates leadership consistent to the topics/concepts covered in the course (50 %). Appendix III gives the syllabus of the SLIGE course.

SLI Module in the NGO Internship Program

We developed an SLI module to promote service learning and offered it in the I-Care NGO Internship Program. Each year, more than 20 students are selected from a group of several hundred CUHK student applicants to serve in different NGOs and social enterprises in Mainland China and Taiwan for 8 weeks in the summer. Services have included designing a marketing plan for a "charity supermarket" in Inner Mongolia, serving ex-leprosy patients in Guangdong and assisting an anti-domestic violence campaign in Beijing. Table 4 gives the NGOs participating in 2013.

Before students are sent into the field, we require them to take a vigorous training program to teach the skills and attitudes necessary for delivering effectively their services. Following the program, we hold an elaborate debriefing session where students reflect on their experiences through discussion and publication of a booklet. During the training, students were instructed on service leadership, particularly emphasizing mindfulness, as introduced in the SLIGE course discussed above.

Table 4 NGOs in I-Care Internship Program in Greater China 2013

NGO partner	Location	NGO work
Shaanxi Gender Development Welfare Association	Mainland China	Rural development, child education
Handa Rehabilitation and Welfare Association	Mainland China	Rehabilitation service, community development
Aohan Women's Development Association	Mainland China	Micro-finance, community market women development
Lvgeng Center for Advancement of Rural–Urban Sustainability	Mainland China	Community economy, rural development, organic farming
Beijing Fanbao/Anti-Domestic Violence Network (ADVN)	Mainland China	Anti-domestic violence, policy advocacy
Media Monitor for Women Network	Mainland China	Media advocacy, gender equality
Peitou Culture Foundation	Taiwan	Community development, cultural conservation
Miaoli Community College	Taiwan	Community education, community development
NewHomeland Foundation	Taiwan	Community development, ecological conservation, education, social economy

Appendix IV gives the details of the CUHK I-Care SLI module in the Greater China NGO Internship Program.

Concluding Comments

The SLIGE and the SLI module, on their first offerings, have been successful. From our observations of the students, they have engaged at a level well above that of an average course at CUHK. From their assignments, class discussions, and reflections, they show understanding to some of the leadership theory and how they can apply it in Hong Kong's increasingly service-based for-profit economy, civil society sector, and politics. SLI's chief objective is to improve service leadership in Hong Kong through our students. We hope to further the attainment of this immeasurable learning outcome through continued offering of the SLIGE course and SLI modules.

Delivery of the SLIGE course and SLI modules forms one of the two major activities of SLI work at CUHK. We discuss second major activity, the production of pedagogical materials (the video-enhanced cases), in Chapter 17 of this volume. Through these two activities, we are committed to promote the concepts of service leadership to what we hope will become an increasingly receptive and growing community.

Appendices

Appendix I: Excerpts from Annex A of the MOU

Project Objectives

What does the project aim to achieve? What are the learning outcomes intended for participating students? In what ways are the intended learning outcomes related to system-level learning outcomes of Service Leadership Initiative?

We will produce locally sourced, globally applicable, and current pedagogical materials to be used in undergraduate and postgraduate-taught programs. The materials will be primarily video-enhanced cases ("Cases"), designed to focus instructor-led student discussion on service leadership. We will structure an academically sound general education course on service leadership (the "SLIGE course") consistent with the HKI-SLAM Curriculum Framework's overarching education goals to improve students' service leadership competencies, develop their characters, and nurture them in a caring disposition and social orientation. We will develop modules for undergraduate and postgraduate-taught program and diploma courses related to service leadership (the "Modules") which may use the Cases.

Services in Hong Kong account for over 90 % of our economy and over 100 % of our current account surplus. The career of every student who graduates from every university in Hong Kong is dominated by service; yet no coherent body of course materials exists to meet the pedagogical needs of service leadership. We propose to develop Modules and Cases with professors currently teaching aspects of service leadership. While the largest proportion of Modules and Cases will be management related, especially in the first year, service leadership is important to disciplines beyond schools of business. In subsequent years, we will approach professors in nonbusiness disciplines to augment their courses with Modules and Cases.

A Case may involve a service industry (e.g., accounting, banking, consulting, mobile, cultural, design, education, entertainment, healthcare, hospitality, Internet, insurance, law, logistics, real estate, retailing, software, social, trade) or a service function within the goods-producing enterprise. Each Case will highlight a decision that a leader must make, giving facts appropriate not only to the problem at hand but also to the background to that decision. The background will include information necessary for analysis of the ethical implications of the leader's decision and, for Cases used in Modules, information amenable to technical analysis of the discipline of the class using the Module.

Project Plan

How will the project be implemented and why? What are the key teaching and learning activities? How will student autonomy and peer learning be encouraged? What are the expected timeline and major milestones?

The plan includes three activities:

1. Case development
2. Course and Module design and delivery
3. Assessment

Course and Module Design and Delivery
We will promote service leadership philosophies consistent with HKI-SLAM's overarching education goals and among our students through two avenues: the SLIGE course and Modules.

The SLIGE Course. We believe that SLI at CUHK can achieve its greatest impact if it is integrated as a credit-bearing course in CUHK's general education (GE) program. At present, CUHK has no service leadership GE course. At CUHK, unlike other Hong Kong universities, GE courses are offered both through each of the nine constituent colleges of CUHK and through the university's GE program. Each of the constituent colleges can express its own mission through its own GE courses. The colleges enjoy considerable flexibility in introducing innovative GE courses, notwithstanding the requirement that those courses be approved at the CUHK level. This means that, in practice, introducing a GE course at the university-level is more rigorous, as it is held to the standard of engaging students "... on perennial issues of human concerns through reading of original texts of lasting significance. ..." We will work with university GE staff and academics to design texts, reading materials, projects, assessment systems, and examination methods to meet the university standards. The pedagogical materials are likely to include Cases developed above. We aim to apply for CUHK approval for the SLIGE course in late 2012 so that it can be on the books by September 2013. As part of that application, we, with the input of the sponsoring department (most likely the Department of Management), will draft appropriate student learning outcomes consistent with the SLAM-SLI objectives. This drafting process will be initiated within six months of funding the SLI award, and we expect that the structure of the SLIGE course, with approved learning objectives, will be finalized in early 2013.

Delivery of the SLIGE course will be financed, as with all credit-bearing courses, from the teaching budget of CUHK.

Assessment and Evaluation Plan

How will student learning be credibly assessed? How will the overall effectiveness of the project be evaluated? To what extent will assessment and evaluation data be used to adjust the project plan?

Assessment will be continuous within the implementation.

The process of development described in *Case Development* above is iterative so that the developing professor can affect how his or her pedagogical objectives are to be achieved in the Case as the Case is being developed.

The Cases will be used by the developing professor and SLI and their colleagues at other participating universities. We will poll the users of each Case to determine effectiveness and to make minor improvements to the Case for subsequent use. Feedback will also be used to improve the Cases under development.

We will encourage the SLI champions to use the Cases in their own universities. Following their use, we will solicit their comments for Case assessment and improvement.

Cases will be distributed through existing Case clearing houses (Harvard, Ivy, Babson, ECCH, NACRA, HKU, etc.). We will also try to secure publishing in book form in appropriate anthologies.

The numbers of users and/or sales can be used as a quantitative measure of success.

All students taking all for-credit courses at CUHK are polled in the course and teaching evaluation (CTE). The CTE is administered by the university, and its results are made available to the professors in each course. We will collect relevant parts of the CTE for Modules and for the SLIGE course and report those results to SLI.

Appendix II: Instructors in SLIGE Course

CHAN, Kin-man

Kin-man Chan received his Ph.D. from Yale University and is currently the Director of Centre for Civil Society Studies, Associate Director of Center for Entrepreneurship, and Associate Professor of Sociology at The Chinese University of Hong Kong. He serves in the editorial boards of Journal of Civil Society (USA), China Nonprofit Review (Beijing), and Third Sector Review (Taiwan). He is the coauthor of Stories and Theories of Democracy (with Choy Chi-keung), Contentious Views: Nine Debates that Changed Hong Kong (with Ng Shu Yui), One Country Two Systems (with Tsui Sing Yan), Trade Association and Social Capital (with Qiu Haixiong), and author of Towards Civil Society and Civil Society Perspective: Towards Good Governance.

CHOY, Ivan Chi-keung

Ivan Choy is a Senior Lecturer at the Department of Government and Public Administration of The Chinese University of Hong Kong. He received both his

Bachelor of Business Administration (where he was head of the Students Union) and his MPhil in Political Science from CUHK. He is a well-known television commentator and editorialist in Hong Kong politics. His research and teaching interests are in comparative politics, political leadership, and electoral and political parties' studies. Prior to joining CUHK, he was the Senior Lecturer at University of Macao and City University of Hong Kong.

LEUNG, Freedom

Freedom Y.K. Leung obtained both of his Bachelor's degree in Psychology and Doctorate degree in Clinical Psychology from Concordia University, Montreal, Canada. He joined The Chinese University of Hong Kong in 1993 and is currently an Associate Professor of the Department of Psychology. In 2004/2005, he won the Vice-Chancellor's Exemplary Teaching Award and the Faculty of Social Science Exemplary Teaching Award. Professor Leung's research interests include adult psychopathology, personality disorders, and mindfulness therapy. He is a member of the American Psychological Association and its Clinical Division and Hong Kong Psychological Society and its Clinical Division. Professor Leung had served in different capacities in Hong Kong Psychological Society including Honorary Treasurer, Vice-President, and President throughout 1994 to 1997. During 1998 to 2000, he was the Founding Editor of Journal of Psychology in Chinese Society.

THOMAS, Hugh

Hugh Thomas is an Associate Director of the Center for Entrepreneurship and an associate professor in the Department of Finance at The Chinese University of Hong Kong. He received his Bachelor of Arts in History from the University of Alberta, postgraduate diplomas in Chinese language from the Beijing Language and Culture University, history from Nanjing University, MBA from The Chinese University of Hong Kong, and Ph.D. in International Business and Finance from New York University. He participated in founding China's first business school, the National Center for Industrial Science and Technology Management at Dalian in 1980 and subsequently worked in banking and consulting in Hong Kong for 7 years. He is an award winning case writer. Prior to joining CUHK, he was an Associate Professor in the Finance Department of McMaster University in Canada.

YUEN, Terence

Terence Yuen is a researcher specializing in the fields of Civil Society and Public Policy. He is the Research Coordinator at the Centre for Civil Society Studies at The Chinese University of Hong Kong and oversees the center's research operations. An experienced Certified Public Accountant, he managed a leading charity in Hong Kong, disbursing over HKD200 million to over 100 charities per year prior to returning to academe to obtain a MPA and a Ph.D. in Politics and Public Administration, from the University of Hong Kong. He has served as a lecturer at the Community College of City University and is currently a member of the Hong Kong Social Entrepreneurship Forum, a founding member of Fullness Social Enterprise Society, and the Honorary Adviser to Fair Circle, a major fair trade organization in Hong Kong.

Appendix III: Syllabus for SLIGE Course

The Chinese University of Hong Kong
University General Education 2nd term, 2013–2014
UGED 1251: Service Leadership in an Uncertain Era
Fung King Hey Building – Swire Lecture Hall 2 – Tuesdays 1:30–4:15 pm

Coordinating Instructors
Prof. Chan Kin-man	3943–6610	kmchan@cuhk.edu.hk
Prof. Hugh Thomas	3943–7649	hugh-thomas@cuhk.edu.hk

Topical Instructors
Mr. Choy, Chi-keung Ivan	3943–7529	ivanchoy@cuhk.edu.hk
Prof. Freedom, Leung	3943–6575	fykleung@psy.cuhk.edu.hk
Dr. Yuen, Terence	3943–1423	tykyuen@cuhk.edu.hk

Teaching Assistants
Sharon Tam Ho Ying	3943–1691	sharon-tam@cuhk.edu.hk
Mandy Lam Kit Man	3943–7542	KitmanLam@baf.cuhk.edu.hk

Teaching Medium
Cantonese and English

Description

All students possess the potential to be service leaders. This course aims to promote a culture of service leadership through cultivating appropriate knowledge, skills, character, and care toward self, others, and society. The course will introduce students to theories of leadership from the disciplines of management, political science, psychology, and sociology. Because service is cocreated between the provider and the recipient and because leadership itself is a service, understanding effective service leadership requires sensitivity to oneself and to others. The course will include exercises to enhance this sensitivity. Using business, social enterprise, NGO, and political cases and through introducing students to leaders in different spheres, the course will stimulate students' reflections on how they can lead effectively in a world full of conflicts and uncertainties.

Objectives

Upon completion of this course, students should be able to:

- Reflect on the issues of leadership.
- Understand how sensitivity to oneself and to others can enhance leadership.
- Show an oral ability to summarize, classify, synthesize, and evaluate service leaders in business, nonprofit, and political situations.

– Demonstrate knowledge of theories of leadership through using them to assess words and actions of recognized service leaders.

Student Evaluation

Reflective Note due on Feb. 11   20 %
Group In-Class Oral Contribution   30 %
Individual Term Paper due on April 15   50 %

Schedule

Week	Date	Topic	Class readings and videos	Instructor
1	Jan 7	Theories of leadership I	Heifetz	Chan Kin-man
2	Jan 14	Theories of leadership II	Drucker; Northous, Zigarelli	Hugh Thomas
3	Jan 21	The mindful brain – sensitivity to oneself	Siegel	Freedom Leung
4	Jan 28	The mindful brain – sensitivity to others	–	Freedom Leung
5	Feb 4	Holiday – Chinese New Year		
6	Feb 11	Minding 12 dimensions of a service warrior's personal brand	Reflective note due; Chung; HKSLI Website	Hugh Thomas; Po Chung, Cofounder, DHL Intl; Founder, HKI-SLAM
7	Feb.18	Services in products and frontline service	Cisco China; Constellation;	Hugh Thomas
8	Feb 25	Nonprofits and social enterprises	Crutchfield & Grant; Diamond Cab	Terence Yuen
9	Mar 4	Leadership of nonprofits and social enterprises: two cases	St. James' Settlement Web: Intro	Terence Yuen; Michael Lai Kam-cheung, CEO, St. James' Settlement
10	Mar 11	Forum on political leadership in Hong Kong	–	Panel Chan Kin-man, Robert Chow Yung; moderator Hugh Thomas
11	Mar 18	Service leadership in politics	Alinsky; Rotberg	Choy Chi-keung Ivan
12	Mar 25	Cross-sector service leadership	Heifetz, Kania & Kramer; WebOrganic	Terence Yuen

(continued)

Week	Date	Topic	Class readings and videos	Instructor
13	Apr 1	Service leadership in social entrepreneurship	L Plus H Community Interest Co Web:Intro	Terence Yuen; Ada Ho, Founder of Love + Hope
14	Apr 8	A synthesis: service leadership in an uncertain era	–	Chan Kin-man; Hugh Thomas
15	Apr 15	Wrap up: your leaders	Individual term paper due	Chan Kin-man; Hugh Thomas

Required Readings

Week 1

1. Heifetz, R. (1994). Mobilizing adaptive work, *Leadership without easy answers*. Cambridge: Harvard University Press.
2. Heifetz, R. (1994). Creative deviance on the frontline, *Leadership without easy answers*. Cambridge: Harvard University Press.

Week 2

3. Drucker, P. (1968). Towards a theory of organizations. *The age of discontinuity* (pp. 188–211). Heinemann, London.
4. Northouse, Peter. (2013). *Leadership: Theory and practice*. Thousand Oaks: Sage. Chapter 1
5. Zigarelli, M. (n.d.). *Ten leadership theories in five minutes* [Video]. Available from https://www.youtube.com/watch?v=XKUPDUDOBVo

Weeks 3 and 4

6. Siegel, D. (2007). *The mindful brain: Reflection and Attunement in the cultivation of well-being*. New York: Norton.

Week 6

7. Chung, P. (2012).*Service reborn: The knowledge, skills and attitudes of service companies (Chapter 1, 10)*. New York: Lexingford. Available from HKSLI Website: SLI Introduction http://hki-slam.org/index.php?r=article&catid=3
8. HKSLI Website: SLI Introduction http://hki-slam.org/index.php?r=article&catid=3

Week 7

9. Lee, R., &Thomas, H. *Cisco and cloud-based education in China*. Hong Kong: SLI Case.

10. Thomas, H. *Constellation: The distribution of minibonds.* Hong Kong: SLI Case.

Week 8

11. Crutchfield, L., & Grant, H. (2008). *Forces for good: The six practices of high-impact nonprofits (Chapters 7 and 8).* San Francisco: Jossey-Bass.
12. Au, K., & Tsui, A. *Diamond cab: Investment of a venture philanthropy fund.* Hong Kong: SLI Case.

Week 9

13. St. James Settlement Web: Introduction. Available from http://www.sjs.org.hk/tc/index/main.php

Week 10 and 11

14. Alinsky, S. D. (1989). Of means and ends, *Rules for radicals.* New York: Vintage Books.
15. Rotberg, R. (2012). *Transformative political leadership* (Chapter 2). Chicago: University of Chicago Press.

Week 12

16. Heifetz, R. A., Kania, J. V., & Kramer, M. R. (2004). Leading boldly. *Stanford Social Innovation Review*, 2(3), 20–32. Available from http://www.ssireview.org/pdf/2004WI_feature_heifetz.pdf
17. Yu, J. Weborganic. *Creating a blue ocean for a social cause.* Hong Kong: SLI Case.

Week 13

18. L plus H Community Interest Company Web: Introduction. Available from http://www.lplush.com/index.php

Recommended Readings

Alinsky, S. D. (1989). *Rules for Radicals.* New York: Vintage Books.

Chung, P., & Ip, S. (2009). *The first ten yards: The five dynamics of entrepreneurship.* Singapore: Cengage.

Chung, P. (2012). *Service reborn: The knowledge, skills and attitudes of service companies.* New York: Lexingford.

Drucker, P. (1968). *The age of discontinuity.* London: Heinemann.

Goffman, E. (1959). *The presentation of self in everyday life* (Chapter 2 & 6). New York: Anchor Book.

Haifetz, R. A., Grashow, A., & Linsky, M. (2009). *The practice of adaptive leadership: Tools and tactics for changing your organization and the world.* Boston: Harvard Business Press.

Heifetz, R. (1994). *Leadership without easy answers.* Cambridge: Harvard University Press.

Northouse, P. (2013). *Leadership: Theory and practice.* Thousand Oaks: Sage.

Perry, J. (2010). *The Jossey-bass reader on nonprofit and public leadership.* San Francisco: Jossey-Bass.

Philips, D. T. (1998). *Martin Luther King, Jr. on leadershi.* New York: Warner Books.

Rotberg, R. I. (2012). *Transformative political leadership.* Chicago: University of Chicago Press.

Siegel, D. (2007). *The mindful brain: Reflection and attunement in the cultivation of well-being.* New York: Norton.

Sunstein, C. R. (2003). *Why societies need dissent.* Cambridge, MA: Harvard University Press.

Details of Student Evaluation

1. Individual Term Paper due on April 15 (50 %)

Each student is required to submit (in one hard copy and one soft copy through *VeriGuide*) an individual term paper of no more than 2,000 words in English on the subject "A Good Leader That I Want To Follow." The essay should describe a real leader in the field of government/politics, business, and/or civil society/NGO/social enterprise sector who has achieved sufficient fame to allow you to conduct secondary source research. Your essay should discuss how your leader demonstrates leadership consistent to the topics/concepts covered in the course. *Your leader may not be any of the leaders from the video-assisted cases or the guest speakers introduced in this class.*

2. Reflective Note due on February 11 (20 %)

Each student is required to submit (in one hard copy and one soft copy through *VeriGuide*) a reflective note of no more than 500 words in English on the subject "A Personal Experience of Leadership." The reflective note should describe how you have experienced being a leader and how this experience reflects theories of leadership as introduced in the first four classes in this course.

3. Group In-Class Oral Contribution (30 %)

The class will be divided into groups of four to five persons per group prior to the end of week 4. From week 5 through the end of the course, students will be assigned with case materials to analyze. During those classes, student will participate in oral case analysis with the instructor calling on groups to express and defend their analyses. The instructors will assess each group's oral analysis, and that assessment will result in a single group mark for each group. Instructors reserve the right to adjust marks to reflect individual contribution to group performance. Individual contributions will be determined by student peer assessment. During the final class, each student will be asked to complete the following peer assessment:

Group member	Contribution (x)			Comment
	None	Poor	Good	

Citations of Sources

Whatever work you submit must be your own. Claiming work written by others to be your own is plagiarism, a serious academic offense. Plagiarism will not be tolerated.

We encourage you to use any and all relevant sources, but whenever you quote directly, you must use quotation marks around your direct quote and insert a footnote and whenever you paraphrase another person's words, you must insert a footnote. In either case, your footnote must contain a full citation that will enable the reader to find the source, independently verify facts, determine the extent to which your ideas derive from the source, and follow your original reasoning.

The instructors hope that you will find this course informative, thought-provoking, and useful.

Appendix IV: Details of the SLI Module in the NGO Internship Program

Background

I-Care NGO Internship Program in Greater China is jointly organized by Centre for Civil Society Studies, Youth Civil Society, and the Office of Student Affairs of CUHK. This program offers students an opportunity to participate in an 8-week internship in NGOs between June and August. Students were assigned to work as interns in both cities and rural villages in Mainland China and Taiwan. The program offered internship opportunities to 21 and 28 undergraduate students in 2012 and 2013, respectively.

Program Objectives

1. To broaden the perspective and experience of participating students, so as to prepare them to better serve the community through extending classroom learning to hands-on workplace training in indigenous NGOs in Mainland China
2. To enhance students' understanding of contemporary sociopolitical and cultural developments in Mainland China, upon which students can make reflections on paralleled developments in Hong Kong
3. To cultivate students' long-term interest and commitment in serving communities, to understand the diversity of culture and values, and in the process to achieve sustainable personal growth

Program Design

Key design features of the program are as follows:

1. Duration: 8 weeks, falling between June and August.
2. Design: Placements at NGOs is matched with the preference and ability of the students.
3. Locations: Beijing, Guangzhou, Inner Mongolia, Xi'an, Taipei, Nantou, and Central Taiwan.
4. Targeted students: CUHK full-time undergraduate students from all disciplines.
5. Team formation: Students assigned to the same NGO will form a team of two to four. The multidisciplinary backgrounds of each team would provide new perspectives and learning opportunities to the participants.

Program Activities

Period	Program activity
Preplacement training	(a) Lectures on civil society and service leadership particularly mindfulness in service
	(b) Workshops on community study, interviewing, writing, and humanistic photographing
	(c) NGOs/social enterprise visiting
	(d) Film screening and discussion about civil society
Internship placement	(a) 8 weeks internship placement
	(b) Weekly reflection journals submitted by students
Post internship	(a) In-depth group debriefing and evaluation on internship experience
	(b) Public sharing session on students' reflections and experiences during internship
	(c) Overall reflection and reports submitted by students

Program Outcomes

1. Reflection on personal growth: Students reflected on their personal growth through the experience in the internship. It is shown that the 2 months allow students to understand their strengths and weaknesses and to learn to embrace problems encountered during internship.
2. Understanding of NGOs work: Students learned about NGO's mission, work, and development through participation in NGO's work. The program allows students to understand how NGOs apply creative and practical methods to solve different social problems as well as the constraints they face.
3. Understanding of sociopolitical developments in Greater China: Students learned the nature of social problems in the communities as well as the role of NGO/social enterprise in tackling these problems.
4. Continuous participation and study: Instructors helped students to reflect on their internship experience and how it would affect their career planning. Most students are still exploring various possibilities of their future career. Some students continuously develop their interest and ability in NGO work. A few students successfully seized job opportunities in the NGO sector.

References

Bass, B. M. (1990). From transactional to transformational leadership. *Organizational Dynamics, 18*, 19–31.

Blake, R. R., & Mouton, J. S. (1964). *The managerial grid*. Houston: Gulf.

Blanchard, K. H. (1985). *Leadership and the one minute manager: Increasing effectiveness through situational leadership*. New York: Morrow.

Carlyle, T. (1841). *On heroes, hero-worship and the heroic in history*. London: James Fraser; republished ElecBook, 2001

Dansereay, F., Graen, G., & Haga, W. (1975). A vertical dyad linkage approach to leadership in formal organizations. *Organizational Behavior and Human Performance, 13*, 46–78.

Drucker, P. (1968). *Towards a theory of organizations: The age of discontinuity*. New York: Harper and Row.

Feilder, F. (1964). A contingency model of leadership effectiveness. In L. Berkowitz (Ed.), *Advances in experimental and social psychology* (pp. 149–190). New York: Academic Press.

Goleman, D. (2011). *Leadership: The power of emotional intelligence*. Northampton: More Than Sound Publisher.

Greenleaf, R. K. (1970). *The Servant as leader*. The Robert K. Greenleaf Center for Servant-Leadership

Heifetz, R. (1994). *Leadership without easy answers* (pp. 188–211). London/Cambridge/Heinemann: Harvard University Press.

Katz, R. L. (1955). Skills of an effective administrator. *Harvard Business Review, 33*(1), 33–42.

Northouse, P. (2013). *Leadership: Theory and practice*. Thousand Oaks: Sage.

Siegel, D. (2007). *The mindful brain: Reflection and attunement in the cultivation of well-being*. New York: Norton.

Stogdill, R. M. (1948). Personal factors associated with leadership: A survey of the literature. *Journal of Psychology, 25*, 35–71.

Zigarelli, M. (2013). *Ten leadership theories in five minutes* [Video]. Retrieved from https://www.youtube.com/watch?v=XKUPDUDOBVo

Service Leadership Education Embedded in a Social Innovation and Entrepreneurship Framework

Linda Wong and Yanto Chandra

Abstract Despite the importance of services in Hong Kong's economy and the role of leadership in the services sector, little is known about how Hong Kong's universities played a role in nurturing future service leaders. Drawing on the notion that "everyone can be a leader" which rejects the trait-based perspective of leadership, we demonstrate how City University of Hong Kong (CityU) pioneered the development of service leadership education that is embedded in the social innovation and entrepreneurship framework. We elaborated CityU's approach to service leadership and showcased how we implemented the framework in two undergraduate courses that embrace the spirit of service learning and social entrepreneurship. We conclude that universities in Hong Kong need a "paradigm shift" in how they sharpen and unleash the creative potential of their target beneficiaries and should give a greater focus on discovery-enriched learning to better prepare young future leaders in the fast-changing world.

The Importance of Service Leadership

Service leadership is new to management and leadership theories. We owe it Po Chung, co-founder of DHL, to advocate the importance of service leadership in post-industrial economies where the services sector plays a determining role in creating income and employment. This is in contrast to the era of manufacturing dictated by the ethos of production, efficiency, and command chains. Chung is right to point out that our daily life subsists on service, which is defined as "any activity characterized by human interaction, including interaction by electronic means that satisfies a need" (Chung 2012, p. 3). To produce the best quality service, we must nurture the server. The rationale is that the server's qualities, traits, and abilities affect the service so much that the server essentially becomes the service (Chung 2012, p. 2). Given its importance we ignore the art and science

L. Wong (✉) • Y. Chandra
Department of Public Policy, City University of Hong Kong, Tat Chee Avenue, Kowloon, AC1-B7414, Hong Kong, Hong Kong
e-mail: linda.wong@cityu.edu.hk

© Springer Science+Business Media Singapore 2015
D.T.L. Shek, P. Chung (eds.), *Promoting Service Leadership Qualities in University Students*, Quality of Life in Asia 6, DOI 10.1007/978-981-287-515-0_4

of service to our professional and personal peril. Chung also reminds us that servers do not exist in a vacuum. Instead, they occupy a business or professional habitat. Fostering a healthy ecosystem will give good servers a germane habitat to render excellent service.

Chung's belief in service gives rise to a conceptual framework on how to foster service leadership. The guiding principles are his core beliefs in enhancing the knowledge, skills, attitude, and caring disposition of the server. This makes a lot of sense in Hong Kong. In 2014, Hong Kong does not have any primary or secondary industries to speak of. Our economy is defined by the tertiary sector, which accounts for 93 % of our GDP and employs 90 % of local manpower (Hong Kong Government 2013). To rise to the challenge, universities must strive to nurture service leadership among their students. Where City University of Hong Kong is concerned, two missions are paramount. One is the nurturing of well-rounded graduates to serve as competent professionals and future leaders of society. The second is the creation of applicable knowledge to support social and economic development and innovation.

City University is happy to be associated with the service leadership education initiative instigated by the Hong Kong Institute of Service Leadership and Management (HKI-SLAM) and the Victor and William Fung Foundation (VWFF). We firmly believe that service leadership education is vital for a number of reasons. First, service leadership education enriches student learning and grooms their leadership in delivering services in any work setting, be it in accounting, business, public administration, social work, engineering, technology, law, media, or other professions. More importantly, it enables students to broaden their perspectives to examine the interaction between business, government, and society so as to maximize their professional and civic responsibilities. In the process, students will strengthen their commitment to society, develop a desire to innovate, and grow an entrepreneurial mindset to tackle old and new problems to change society for the better. On a personal level, the accent on self-service, ethical practice, leadership development, and caring for others enhances character building and capacity for service leadership.

City University's Approach to Service Leadership

City University is one of the eight government-funded universities in Hong Kong. The university is firmly committed to innovative approaches to teaching and learning. In 2012, Hong Kong changed its university system from 3 years to four. This creates new space for our university's "discovery-enriched curriculum" approach with the aim to help students make an original discovery in knowledge and learning during their time of study. It is also a boon to our experiments with social innovation and service leadership.

From the very beginning, we have applied and adapted the original SLAM intellectual framework to our unique approach of blending service leadership to an integrated framework of social innovation, entrepreneurship, and student service leadership. The extramural grant gave us resources that we would not otherwise possess to build up a strong support team to carry out our programs. Starting as an informal group of faculty and administrators, the key movers came from the Departments of Public Policy, the Provost' Office, Asian and International Studies, Applied Social Studies, and Management. Membership then spread to other units – Marketing, Economics and Finance, Education Development and Gateway Education, Creative Media, Chinese, Translation, and Linguistics, Student Development Services, Electronic Engineering, Computer Science, and so on. Now our caucus has more than 30 members from 18 academic and administrative support units.

Initially, this bottom-up caucus was known as the Social Entrepreneurship Group. Since mid-2012, we took on the name of Project Flame. The imagery of flame derives from our assessment of the special feature of our age. We live in an era of discontent and uncertainty. Young people, university students included, struggle to find their place in society. However many feel frustrated by the perceived lack of opportunities, keen competition, and serious social inequality. Many feel powerless and lose their sense of self confidence. To energize our students, nothing is more important than keeping their passion and self-belief alive. Acquiring skills in innovation and problem solving through entrepreneurial approaches builds up their capacity for change making. As teachers with many years of experience in higher education, we are keenly aware of the characteristics of this new generation. They tend to be more inquisitive and demanding. They are adept in self-learning, given their prowess with media technology. Many embrace a broad outlook on life and citizenship. They ask for chances to do things rather than learn passively in the classroom. To most, getting a good professional education and a good job after college is still important. For many, it is not enough. A good many want to serve society and improve the environment. Some aspire to make a real difference by being creative in solution seeking. Fostering innovative and entrepreneurial mindset and skills will help our students to serve others and change society effectively.

Our approach encompasses programs that directly address core beliefs and concerns of service leadership as well as the vision and agenda of social innovation and entrepreneurship of Project Flame. In delivering service leadership education, we have carefully studied the service leadership framework, contextualized its contents and values against mainstream leadership theories, and came up with our own approach to treat service leadership as an area of learning and practice applicable to all practice settings. We believe our approach remains faithful to the service leadership framework and at the same time broadens its conceptual and application appeal.

Integration of Service Leadership and Social Entrepreneurship

At City University, our commitment to professional education is evidenced in our continuous search for innovative curriculum, pedagogy, outcome-based assessment, and whole-person development. In keeping with the demands of the knowledge and service-based economy, an infusion of social entrepreneurship and service leadership education extends and enriches student learning and leadership.

We integrate service leadership with social entrepreneurship because of the deep affinities between the two frameworks. We believe the synergy so created reinforces and strengthens each other.

Both paradigms embrace common values in the belief in the self, self-motivation, ethics, and care for others. This emphasis is intrinsically self-empowering as it increases the sense of individual autonomy and agency. Second, both share the assumption that leadership is possible whatever the setting – business, public service, or professional contexts. Third, central to both frameworks is the stress on an entrepreneurial approach in fulfilling one's needs and serving the needs of others, including customers, peers, society, and the ecosystem. Fourth, social innovation has a central place in both approaches. In social entrepreneurship, this is reflected in the inculcation of a mindset that is impatient with tried and failed solutions, courage in crossing organizational and disciplinary borders, initiatives to marshal new resources, and creation of new alliances to fight entrenched injustices. In SLAM, there is the belief in creating new personal service propositions and consistently providing high-quality personal service to everyone with whom one comes into contact.

The integrated approach enriches SLAM education and provides students with a wider space to explore the meaning of leadership, service solutions, and personal values. This approach marks an interesting foray alongside various approaches adopted by sister institutions in Hong Kong. The diversity of approaches underlay the rich potentials of service leadership education and the desirability to be creative in order to enlarge its impact.

A Holistic Model of Social Change and a Four-Pronged Approach

CityU's service leadership and social entrepreneurship approach embraces a holistic model of social innovation and social change underpinned by our belief that enduring and impactful change is a complex phenomenon. A multidimensional approach is necessary to create and deepen the desired outcomes. In an academic setting, for the impact to be sustainable, the change model has to be embedded in the multiple missions of a university. These missions include knowledge transmission, knowledge creation and evaluation, innovating new ideas, and service application. Each of these strands is interrelated and mutually reinforcing.

In knowledge transmission, the core task is the provision of meaningful curricular and co-curricular programs. In knowledge creation and evaluation, we pursue research to develop and assess knowledge and ideas. The integration of teaching and research will enrich education and our understanding of the world. In innovating new ideas, we seek to extend our grasp of change strategies and fine-tune them to produce the desired outcomes. In service application, we look for practice opportunities and learning through practice. The fruits of such learning will allow us to incubate creative approaches, invigorate our teaching, and construct more useful tools in research. We believe that all four missions must be embraced simultaneously. To leave out any one goal will produce incomplete results.

In our vision to combine social entrepreneurship and service leadership, we are committed to an energetic program of academic education and praxis. This will produce the desired graduates who possess the knowledge, skills, and aptitude to serve as future leaders in their fields and in society. At the same time, faculty and students can join hands to search for equitable and sustainable solutions to local and global problems. These goals are really daunting. They have to be pursued together if we are to achieve lasting effects.

Our missions are achieved through a four-pronged program which includes: professional and academic education, research and knowledge transfer, social innovation incubation, and student service leadership.

Knowledge Transmission Through the Program of Academic and Professional Education

In the area of academic and professional education, two new Gateway Education courses have been offered since 2012. In City University, Gateway Education courses are courses open to all undergraduates that broaden their horizons, perspectives, and skill sets across professional disciplines. The two GE courses are GE1218 Make a Difference: the Challenge to Social Entrepreneurship in a Globalized World and GE1220 Enhancing Your Service Leadership for the Twenty-First Century. These courses have enrolled over 650 students so far and have received excellent feedback. Three new GE courses, GE2245 Professions in Hong Kong: Critical Insights and Issues, GE2246 Changing Our Society: Turning Social Problems into Business Opportunities, and GE2247 Social Innovation and Entrepreneurial Venture Exploration, have been validated and are ready for offer. Yet another GE course, Designing Apps for Social Innovation, is on the drawing boards.

The GE courses have a number of core features. First, they are open to all students in the university. Second, they are multidisciplinary in nature, often team taught by teachers across departments and professions. Third, interactive and experiential learning is emphasized. Fourth, student reflective journals and group projects challenge students to probe into personal experiences and values and learn from one another. In a later section, we will provide further elaboration of our teaching approaches through the analysis of two courses.

An exciting milestone is the introduction of a new minor in social entrepreneurship. The aim of the program is to provide students with both the theoretical knowledge and practical skills to diagnose social problems and to generate intervention ideas for systemic change from multidisciplinary perspectives. The minor requires fifteen credit units of study comprising one core course and four electives. The disciplinary areas include public policy, social welfare, business management, marketing and finance. This program is the first in Hong Kong. The minor is expected to commence in Semester B, 2014/2015.

Service Application and Innovation Through the Program of Service Leadership

The student service leadership initiative received extramural funding from the Victor and William Fung Foundation and intellectual input from the Hong Kong Service Leadership and Management Institute. The various GE courses supply the academic content for service leadership and social entrepreneurship. A wide array of co-curricular activities reinforces student learning from practice and reflection. One program is student internships. Typically the students work in NGOs and social enterprises for 4–6 weeks. The destinations include Zhongshan and Shanghai. Another program is overseas study tours. Groups of students have visited Taipei, Shanghai, and Singapore to study the social enterprise landscape. A third program is local agency visits. This takes students to government departments, NGOs, social enterprises, and commercial companies to learn about different styles of leadership, service design, and innovative management practices. Yet another activity is guest sharing. Students learn from experienced practitioners and entrepreneurs to gain insights on leadership and social innovation. Lastly, we also organize service learning opportunities for students to help needful groups like single elders and children in deprived schools. These activities take students out of the classroom where they can connect with the community, agencies, and practitioners to maximize personal learning. Resources permitting, a learning commons, will be the next step to further to incubate student projects. This will provide the physical, human, and intellectual space for students to co-work on innovative ventures under the mentorship of faculty and experts.

Innovating New Ideas Through the Program of Social Innovation Incubation

Social innovation and entrepreneurship is new to most faculty and students. To introduce the notion and promise of social innovation to faculty and students is thus our priority. The intentions are to arouse interest through relevant activities and exposure via simulated practices. A kick-starter is the Social Entrepreneur in Residence program, a 3-day event featuring the founder of Dialogue in the Dark and a top local expert. The program targets university administrators, faculty, students, and community groups to explore the potentials of social entrepreneurship. Other programs include enrolling students to take part in competitions for charity, co-sponsoring the Social Enterprise Summit, and holding a Photo with a Message Competition and a mini-MaD workshop to develop proposals to eliminate food waste. A flagship program is Hand^2 Spot, our secondhand shop to promote innovation, entrepreneurship, and conservation where students receive training to run the business operation. An extravaganza was a green fashion show by students who paraded secondhand clothing down the catwalk to the amazement of the university community. A repeat performance was requested due to the success of the first attempt.

Knowledge Creation and Evaluation Through the Program of Research and Knowledge Transfer

In the area of research and knowledge transfer, a number of activities have been rolled out. A key project was the organization of two international symposiums on idea incubation and scaling up in 2013 and 2014. The symposia feature international and regional experts to share experiences and insights on the incubation of new ideas to the scaling up of social enterprises. Included in the event is pitching by start-ups and master coaching. The key achievement is our pioneering research on a Social Enterprise Endorsement System (SEE) for Hong Kong. An endorsement system seeks to promote proper understanding of social enterprises, raise public recognition, and enhance service effectiveness. The research is commissioned by the Hong Kong General Chamber of Social Enterprises with funding provided by a leading bank community foundation. Our research team was tasked to develop an endorsement tool on the basis of extensive research into international practice and consolidated views of the local social enterprise sector. The system design went through extensive consultations, experimental application, and feedback from pilot projects. The tool is meant to be inclusive. Criteria and benchmarks for social enterprises ranging from incubating, start-up, intermediate to advanced projects were designed. The first batch of twenty social enterprises which passed endorsement was announced in November 2014. The scheme will be extended to all local social enterprises on a voluntary basis. Eventually we hope to introduce the scheme to the Greater China region and Asia.

Our Curriculum Approach

Highlight of GE1220 Enhancing Your Service Leadership for the Twenty-First Century

GE1220 is the first of its kind service leadership course offered in the College of Liberal Arts and Social Sciences. The course adopts a discovery-enriched curriculum approach that aims to stimulate, develop, and refine students' interest and competence in designing innovative service ideas and present them a la Dragon's Den in front of a few judges. The course starts from a realization that the services sector generates 93 % of Hong Kong's economy (Hong Kong Government 2013) and that 9 out of 10 university graduates in Hong Kong are likely to join the services sector. Even China, the world's largest factory, has gradually moved toward providing value-added services for the global economy. In fact, a high proportion of services and knowledge-based sectors is a trait of advanced economies. Thus, a focus on creativity, design, and out-of-the-box thinking that combines with in-depth understanding of services management and marketing is critical. Our focus is to turn students into creators, not passive recipients of ideas and artifacts. We challenge our students to turn away from old thinking, break the norm, and offer alternative realities that meet users' needs.

Service leadership is a multidisciplinary area at the intersection of social science, psychology, technology, art/design, law, and ethical business, to name a few (Dacin et al. 2011; Moss et al. 2011). As an introductory course, GE1220 is opened to students from all disciplines, as was reflected by the actual enrolment in the past 2 years. The main theme of the course is to help students recognize that "every business is a service business" and that "everyone is a service leader" (Chung 2012; Grönfeldt and Strother 2006). The course is taught by two teachers with rich experience in management, business, and marketing.

The uniqueness of GE1220 is its fusion of perspectives and theories from services marketing, leadership, design, photo-elicitation methods, and sensitivity toward technological change to break the conventional wisdom and offer well-designed service experience (Zeithaml et al. 2013). One new foray is to have students integrate the use of 3-D printing facility to prototype products and work with CityU's Apps Lab. In fact, in each semester, more than half of the student group projects focus on designing ideas for apps that help businesses and the society.

Some of the unique points of GE1220 are highlighted below:

1. In-class game (e.g., building the tallest structure using used newspapers) as a way to break the ice and get students to reflect on team building, creativity, and respect for constraints.
2. Combining theories of leadership – as the conceptual cornerstone to manage leader–follower relationship – and services management as the fundamental building blocks to manage expectations, study the users, design services, plan for service failure and recovery, and reflect on ethical issues in services management.
3. Included photo-elicitation methods (a visual research technique using photos as stimuli to elicit information from users) and service design thinking as the methodological framework to build empathy, generate new ideas, prototype and test new ideas, and communicate them to the audience. This is the first time that such novel methods are used in a services-related course.
4. Guest speakers who are experts in the services business, such as the senior managers from Ocean Park, CEO of Photomax, the founder of DHL Hong Kong, CEO of Dialogue Experience, etc., have addressed the class. Company visits are organized for every class.
5. Group projects that give students opportunities to apply their theoretical knowledge of services and service leadership to design and propose new services, new meanings, and new experience to the audience.
6. Dragon's Den approach where two or more expert judges are present to challenge, ask questions, and refine students' new services design project. Our Dragon's Den approach has been very successful in helping students refine their ideas and make them real and novel.

The assessment methods involve individual and group work. Students are asked to reflect on their experience as a customer of a service and critique and link their experience with the theories/concepts (i.e., Service Diary), writing and presenting their new service design to the audience, and a Short Test that assesses students' ability to make sense of and make connections among the themes and topics taught.

A Sample Student Project from GE1220: Bus-Tracking App

Below is an example of a *bus-tracking app* (see Fig. 1) developed by students of GE1220 in 2013. The apps allow passengers to type in certain bus numbers, direction, and bus stop location to track the incoming bus. Students used free app builder to build a prototype which is shown below. The apps are not only interesting but useful to serve the public.

Fig. 1 Bus-tracking app

Highlight of GE1218: The Challenge of Social Entrepreneurship in a Globalized World

Social entrepreneurship (SE) is an important type of organizations in the US and UK civil society. However, social enterprises are relatively new to Hong Kong and even newer to Greater China (Chandra and Wong 2014). Our GE1218 is the first course of its kind in Hong Kong and Chinese universities that offers a serious treatment on social entrepreneurship, from theoretical and practical lenses. Our curriculum approach was unique. It combines the expertise of three persons. The team comprises the course leader Yanto Chandra, who has a decade of experience in research and teaching in entrepreneurship, plus nearly 7 years of corporate experience; Linda Wong, who is an expert in social welfare and China studies; and Timothy Ma, who has decades of experience in NGOs and was the CEO of the biggest social enterprise in Hong Kong offering home safety and support service to senior citizens. At the start, Joan Leung, an expert in politics and public adminis-tration, also contributed to the course design and teaching. This rich combination was critical in our delivery of the course, which has now run on its 4th semester. The annual enrolment is always close to capacity.

We infused many real-life cases on social entrepreneurs, readings, and content (e.g., the biography of social entrepreneurs, the innovation strategies in social entrepreneurship, social business models) into the GE1218. We have also adapted the "Dragon's Den" approach (a popular British TV show where entrepreneurs pitch to get funding from investors) to GE1218, where students need to complete a social business plan and present it in front of judges, who are a mix of real social entrepreneurs and faculty members. These novel approaches have been instrumen-tal in the GE1218's popularity and success.

Some key highlights of the course include:

1. In-class game in solving a social problem (e.g., using old newspapers as a resource to solve social problems) as a way to build students' creativity and awareness that social entrepreneurs do not accept to be constrained by economic, legal, and institutional constraints, an approach known as "social bricolage" (Domenico et al. 2010; Chandra 2014b).
2. Laying out the conceptual boundaries of social entrepreneurship and the differ-ences between conventional change-making practices such as charity/philan-thropy, corporate social responsibility, bottom of the pyramid, non-profit organizations, for-profit organizations, benefit corporation, and social enter-prises. Biography of social entrepreneurs is also an important part of the course.
3. Tools for social entrepreneurs including social innovation methods (from brico-lage, exaptation, to design thinking), social business plan, and storytelling and linguistic skills (Chandra 2014a) for social entrepreneurs.
4. Guest speakers who are celebrated social entrepreneurs, such as Doris Leung (founder of Diamond Cab), Ricky Yu (founder of Light Home), and Wendy Cheung (founder of Green Ladies). Company visits are organized for every class.
5. Social business plan presentation, where groups of students researched on an idea to solve a social problem and packaged it as a social enterprise.
6. Dragon's Den approach where four to five judges are invited to the final social business plan presentation to challenge, ask questions, and refine students' social enterprise plan. Our Dragon's Den approach has been very successful in helping students refine their ideas and make them real and novel.

Our teaching approach addresses and corrects some common mindsets of young people in Hong Kong. First, there is the tendency to be afraid of failure. Second is the inclination to embrace a "single model answer." There is also a "rote memori-zation" approach to learning. In addition, many lead a comfortable life and are not willing to step outside their comfort zone. We believe this will not benefit the society over the long term. For Hong Kong and China to succeed in a sustainable way, we need a more entrepreneurial society who also cares about the social problems surrounding them. This course asks them to learn by trial and error, to take risks, to try thinking of new ideas, to be caring about the social problems, to see that social problems can be addressed using entrepreneurial tools. Being entrepreneurial is what entrepreneurs do (Chandra et al. 2015), what scientists and engineers do. It is what successful leaders do. There is no "template" to follow to make a change in the world. There are real judges in life – employers, colleagues, clients, the general public – whom an entrepreneur needs to deal with. As teachers, what we can do is to nurture young people and give them guidance along the process of discovery and innovation. In the last 2 years, we have spent countless hours outside the classroom to coach them, to help them refine their ideas, and to get them to think out of the box.

We hope that our efforts are not wasted. None have taken the step to start a social business. We do hope that they will remember that it is the mindset that matters – the belief that everyone can be a change maker and create positive externalities to the society no matter how small they are. We know that many have become inspired. The launch of the new minor will allow the really committed to venture further into the path of social entrepreneurship.

Sample Student Project in GE1218

In GE1218, students have also successfully proposed interesting ideas and refined them. One of the projects called "Transfriendly" focused on developing a *vibrator stick* to help the elderly and disabled to walk and wait for public transport (see Fig. 2). With a programmable device on the stick, it allows users to type in the bus number and location, and the stick will vibrate when the requested bus is approaching. It helps the elderly to stay vigilant and not miss a single bus. The project has recently won CityU My Own Discovery Contest in March 2014. This was an open tournament attended by many students and judged by professors from engineering, science, creative media, business/management, and social sciences. One group built a prototype app that lets people trade in used goods. Another group built a prototype app that aims to replace paper receipt with digital receipts. Still another group built a prototype video camera on glasses that tells direction by voice for the blind users. In 2014, we have received good media coverage in 12 newspapers in Hong Kong and two radio interviews with local stations. We also received a number of inquiries from businesspeople who showed interest in manufacturing these prototypes. The students are currently working with the Education Development and Gateway Education Office and the Office of Technology Transfer to explore if their invention could be patented or funding could be sought.

One recent success is a group of students in Semester A, 2014/2015, called "Sonus," which developed a social business plan that aims to transform finger movement into verbal speech via the use of fake fingernails that are equipped with Bluetooth and text-to-speech converter (see Fig. 3). This group pitched in the Project Flame Social Innovation Contest held at CityU Hong Kong in early

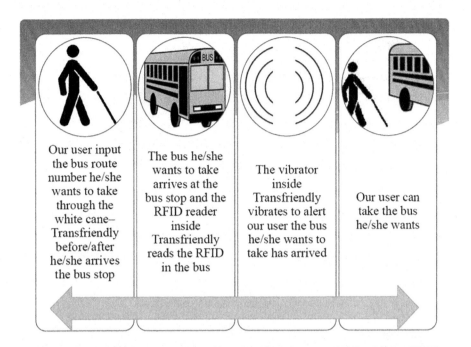

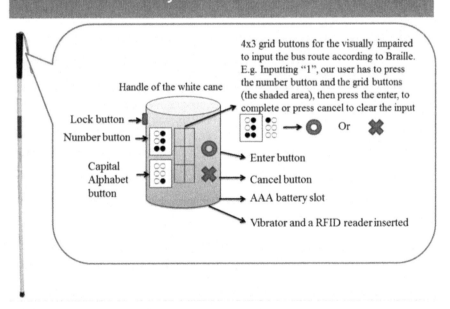

Fig. 2 Transfriendly: a walking-stick vibrator for the elderly and disabled (winner of CityU My Own Discovery Contest, March 2014)

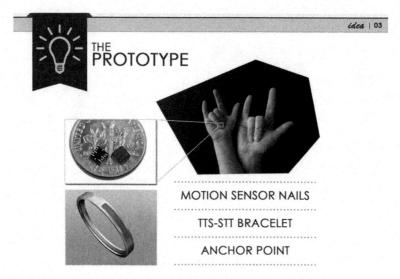

Fig. 3 Sonus: turning finger motion into speech for the disabled using fake nails and ring (champion of Project Flame Social Innovation Contest, October 2014)

November 2014 and won the first prize, out of many contestants, some of which are already social enterprises running for 5 years.

Conclusion

City University's experimentation in service leadership and social entrepreneurship has achieved good results in the last 2 years. One measure is positive student feedback. We continue to attract good students to our courses and are launching a new minor in social entrepreneurship. In corollary, we offer students and faculty a rich platform to engage in curricular, co-curricular, and extracurricular activities alongside opportunities to do research, to innovate new ideas, and to make forays into entrepreneurial ventures. Our work is still in its early stage. We will evaluate the effectiveness of our programs continuously in order to achieve better outcomes and social impact. With our continuous refinement in our design and delivery of the course, backed by serious scholarly research efforts, we hope to continue to be the innovator in empowering young people in Hong Kong. We also aspire to be a pioneer in social entrepreneurship education and research.

In hindsight, what we have done in the two exemplary courses described above is among the most interesting and successful application of the discovery-enriched learning adopted by City University of Hong Kong. Although some laments that Asia is crippled by a lack of innovation as a result of its "memorization-approach to learning" – an extension of the annual scholars' examination that focused on rote memorization in ancient China for a few 1,000 years – our experience with the two

Gateway Education courses revealed that university students have plenty of creative potential and are trainable to be discoverers in their own way. Ideally the process should start in an earlier age. It is definitely not too late to unleash students' creative and innovative potentials during their time in university. This requires a paradigm shift in how we nurture their learning process. Obviously, this calls for creativity in course design, clever management of the learning process, and readiness for "coaching" throughout the learning process as we apply a positive psychology approach to empowering students to pursue "the extra miles" in whatever they do.

Our experimentation in integrating service leadership with social innovation and entrepreneurship has been valuable. It has led us to this conclusion: universities must play a bigger role in sharpening and unleashing the creative/innovative potential of their students and give a greater focus on discovery-enriched learning to make their graduates more relevant to the fast-changing world. We hope the experience and insight we made all along on each individual who took our courses at City University of Hong Kong will add up and create a bigger impact in the future. We want our young people to play their part in shaping a better world in a creative, sustainable, and compassionate way.

References

Chandra, Y. (2014a, July). *Toward a meta-linguistic model of social entrepreneurship: Insights from computational linguistics*. In 74th academy of management annual conference, Philadelphia.

Chandra, Y. (2014b). *A unified innovation models in social entrepreneurship: Evidence from award winning social entrepreneurs* (Working Paper). City University of Hong Kong.

Chandra, Y., & Wong, L. (2014). *Social entrepreneurship in the greater China: Policy, process and cases*. Accepted, Routledge.

Chandra, Y., Styles, C., & Wilkinson, I. F. (2015). Opportunity portfolio: Moving beyond single opportunity explanations in international entrepreneurship research. *Asia Pacific Journal of Management, 32*(1), 199–228.

Chung, P. (2012). *Service reborn: The dignity, design, and desire of service companies*. San Francisco: Lexingford Publishing.

Dacin, M. T., Dacin, P. A., & Tracey, P. (2011). Social entrepreneurship: A critique and future directions. *Organization Science, 22*(5), 1203–1213.

Domenico, M. L. D., Haugh, H., & Tracey, P. (2010). Social bricolage: Theorizing social value creation in social enterprises. *Entrepreneurship Theory & Practice, 34*(4), 681–703.

Grönfeldt, S., & Strother, J. (2006). *Service leadership: The quest for competitive advantage* (Chapter 1–2). New York: SAGE Publication.

Hong Kong Government. (2013). *Hong Kong: The facts.* Information Services Department, Hong Kong SAR Government. Retrieved from http://www.gov.hk

Moss, T. W., Short, J. C., Payne, G. T., & Lumpkin, G. T. (2011). Dual identities in social ventures: An exploratory study. *Entrepreneurship Theory and Practice, 35*(4), 805–830.

Zeithaml, V., Bitner, M. J., & Gremler, D. D. (2013). *Services marketing: Integrating customer focus across the firm* (6th ed.). New York: McGraw-Hill.

Nurturing Leadership and Changing Student Mindset Through Meaningful Community Service: The HKU Service Leadership Internship

Jessie Mei-ling Chow and Shui-fong Lam

Abstract Service-learning and leadership education research has suggested that service-learning projects enhance students' leadership skills, in turn nurturing leaders with social responsibility for the twenty-first century. The Service Leadership Internship (SLI) of the University of Hong Kong, sponsored by the Victor and William Fung Foundation, fosters leadership in college students through community service. The SLI is a credit-bearing course that spans 6–8 weeks, beginning in the summer of 2012. The students from different disciplines worked as a team to generate innovative solutions. Typically, students from the Faculty of Social Sciences ran services in collaboration with nongovernment organizations, whereas students from the School of Business provided consultation services to small and medium enterprises. To equip students with the basic knowledge, skills, and attitudes, a series of pre-internship workshops with ongoing support was offered to them. Multiple assessment methods were used to assess students' learning outcomes and to evaluate the program. Results indicated acquisition of shared-leadership skills, change of growth mindset, enhancement of social responsibility, and improvement of personal and social competencies among the students.

The authors would like to express their gratitude to Prof. Samson Tse for his insightful comments to this chapter.

J.M.-l. Chow (✉)
Faculty of Social Sciences, The University of Hong Kong, Pokfulam Road, Hong Kong, Hong Kong
e-mail: jmlchow@hku.hk

S.-f. Lam
Department of Psychology, The University of Hong Kong, Pokfulam Road, Hong Kong, Hong Kong

© Springer Science+Business Media Singapore 2015
D.T.L. Shek, P. Chung (eds.), *Promoting Service Leadership Qualities in University Students*, Quality of Life in Asia 6, DOI 10.1007/978-981-287-515-0_5

Service-Learning and Leadership

Service-learning is an instructional method incorporating meaningful community service into the curriculum (Dipadova-Stocks 2005). As Giles Jr and Eyler (1994) point out, service-learning emphasizes experience, inquiry, and reflection. Learning should not be restricted to the four walls of the classroom; learning needs to be applied to the real world. Service-learning provides ample opportunities for the integration of academic knowledge and real-world experiences. It offers students the platform to experience and validate the provisional truths they have acquired from the classroom and textbooks (Beatty 2010). As it is a time for testing and validation of what has been learned, self-reflection is a significant component in the process of service-learning. Self-reflection encourages students to incorporate thinking with experience for further development and change (Kenworthy-U'ren and Peterson 2005). Another significant component of service-learning is problem solving (Hecht 2003). Students are required to tackle real-life problems in authentic settings. They have to engage in a continuous process of analyses, planning, implementation, and evaluation.

Service-learning can be performed individually or in a group. In the former situation, students are assigned individually to different agencies in the community, whereas in the latter situation, students are sent as a team. Recently, team-based project in service-learning has received much attention. Papamarcos (2005) describes it as a new service-learning approach in which students are able to overcome the inherent uncertainty of real-world problems. This collaborative learning process promotes structural changes of mindset among students.

Research has demonstrated a wide range of positive influences of service-learning on students' moral development, social responsibility, and leadership (Eyler et al. 2001; Lester et al. 2005). In the learning process of service-learning, students develop academic knowledge and skills, respect for others, and commitment to the common good. Students acquire critical knowledge and relate it to the curriculum. This learning process is also helpful in raising social conscience among students and prepares students to be truly effective leaders (Dipadova-Stocks 2005). In addition, collaborating with others in service-learning projects facilitates their team skills, leadership skills, and conflict resolution skills (Beatty 2010).

Service-learning highlights the application of academic knowledge that is context dependent. There is a growing trend urging higher education to connect academic knowledge to real-world experiences and address social problems by developing engaged citizenship (Boyte 2008; Reynolds and Vince 2004). Service-learning can supplement the acquirement of knowledge, thus overcoming the limitations of the traditional classroom. As Kenworthy-U'ren and Peterson (2005) put it, service-learning is often unattainable in the regular lecture format. With a person-centered approach, service-learning creates opportunities for students to be responsible for their own learning in authentic tasks and real-wold setting.

Leadership Development in Team-Based Community Service

Traditional leadership development focuses on leaders with formal positions and their roles to lead followers. To cope with the challenges in the twenty-first century, the traditional model is inadequate. It is important to develop self- and shared leadership in team-based projects (Pearce and Manz 2005). Distinct from the transactional or charismatic leadership approach where the leaders exert top-down influence (Avolio et al. 2009), the self- and shared leadership approach focuses on self-initiation and mutual support at a collective group work level.

Based on the concept that everyone can lead and manage oneself, self-leadership involves managing one's behaviors to meet the existing goals. The process of developing self-leaders involves intrinsic motivation, self-influenced skill development, and strategic-oriented cognitions (Pearce and Manz 2005). Shared leadership highlights the interactive influence process within a group with shared or organizational goals (Pearce and Sims 2002). Social support is also an integral part of the team environment that facilitates shared leadership. Strong efforts should be made to provide emotional and psychological support to one another by team members so that the team can work together toward the same goals (Carson et al. 2007). By engaging all members of a team, shared leadership recognizes everyone's unique contribution (Hernandez et al. 2011).

The Service Leadership Internship at the University of Hong Kong

The Service Leadership Internship (SLI) at the University of Hong Kong (HKU) is an endeavor employing service-learning to develop self- and shared leadership among college students. With funding from the Hong Kong Institute of Service Leadership and Management (HKI-SLAM) and the Victor and William Fung Foundation, the SLI provides the students in social sciences and business a precious opportunity to hone their leadership skills in authentic services to the community. This program was first launched in the summer of 2012 as a credit-bearing course that spans 6–8 weeks. The enrollment is approximately 100, half from the School of Business and half from the Faculty of Social Sciences. The students are organized in teams of three to five members. Each team is sent to an agency in the community and designated to work on an assigned project under the supervision of a staff from the agency concerned.

It is often difficult to learn leadership, social awareness, and social responsibility within the regular lecture setting of a traditional classroom. Students cannot acquire these skills by simply sitting in a lecture hall listening to the experts. It takes an experiential learning process for the students to practice, consolidate, and master the skills learned in the classroom. In this process, students are required to actively integrate the academic component in the curriculum with their frontline experience. To develop students' self- and shared leadership, students in the SLI are placed in the community to undertake different service tasks. They are expected to learn the values, knowledge, and skills involved in leadership with hands-on experience in a real-world setting.

The Objectives of the SLI

With reference to the advantages of community involvement in leadership training, the SLI at the University of Hong Kong aims to achieve the following four objectives:

1. To strengthen the students' sense of social responsibilities in leadership
2. To assist the students to acquire the personal competencies required in leadership through the enhancement of:

    (a) Self-efficacy and abilities in tackling novel challenges and ill-defined issues
    (b) Resilience to setbacks
    (c) Critical thinking skills and problem-solving skills
    (d) Self-reflection on personal and professional growth

3. To help the students acquire the social competencies needed in leadership by enhancing their

    (a) Collective efficacy and team building skills
    (b) Collaboration and conflict resolution skills
    (c) Communication skills

4. To enable the students to hone their leadership skills in authentic services to the community. These skills include:

    (a) Organization and management skills
    (b) Planning and decision-making skills
    (c) Skills in exerting positive influence on others

These four objectives are in line with the core beliefs of the curriculum framework proposed by the HKI-SLAM. That being said, leadership is a service to the people who are being led. This service must be for the common good of the community. Therefore, the uppermost important objective of leadership training is the cultivation of social responsibility among the students as future leaders. In the SLI, students are expected to work for the betterment of human conditions through their services to the community. To do so, they need both personal and social competencies.

The SLI adopts a social-cognitive approach in motivation (Dweck 2006) as the theoretical basis for the enhancement of self-growth and personal competencies.

Emphasis is placed on changing the mindset and promoting self-efficacy and self-resilience. Mindset denotes the implicit but powerful belief about the malleability of ability. Students with a growth mindset believe that ability is malleable, whereas students with a fixed mindset believe that ability is a fixed entity that is rarely changed. According to Dweck (2006), students with a growth mindset have stronger resilience after setbacks because they believe that failures cannot define them. They will continue to seek challenges to see continuous growth in themselves. In contrast, students with a fixed mindset tend to give up after setbacks because they believe that they cannot do much to enhance their ability and redeem themselves. In the pre-internship workshops, students are introduced to the concepts of growth and fixed mindsets. They are encouraged to examine their own mindset and the differential consequences of alternative mindsets.

A strong sense of social responsibility and sound personal competencies are the necessary, but not sufficient, conditions for reliable leadership. Effective leaders need to have social competencies and adequate skills in organization, management, and decision-making. Therefore, the third objective of the SLI is to promote social competencies of the students and the fourth objective is to hone the students' skills in leadership. A team-based project provides an exceptional learning practice to achieve these two objectives because it requires collaboration. Indeed, the students have to work together for the same goals and resolve any interpersonal conflicts that deter them from task completion. A social-cognitive approach in motivation is adopted to aid the students to cope with interpersonal conflicts. In the pre-internship workshops, students are introduced to two attribution styles in interpersonal conflicts: situation-based attribution and trait-based attribution (Weiner 2001). People tend to attribute their own mistakes to situational factors and other people's mistakes to personality factors. This fundamental attribution error is not conducive to conflict resolution. To avoid fundamental attribution error, students are encouraged to see interpersonal conflicts from other people's perspectives. Past research has shown that a growth mindset can facilitate situation-based attribution and forgiveness in interpersonal conflicts (Chiu et al. 1997; Levy and Dweck 1998). Personal competencies and social competencies are not isolated. What students learn from the instruction on personal competencies is also related to social competencies.

Unlike individual internships, team-based internships offer a unique opportunity for students to hone their leadership skills. An intern who is attached individually to an agency in the community is usually the most inexperienced and junior person. As the animal at the bottom of the totem pole, the intern can rarely assume a leadership role. In contrast, when interns are sent to the agency as a team and designated to work on a specific project, they must become responsible leaders in order to complete the task. In the process of working together as a team for a shared vision and mission, they master the skills of collaboration and instinctively improve their social competencies. Most importantly, they have a chance to sharpen their leadership skills through experiential learning in real community services.

Types of Projects

One core feature of the SLI at HKU is the integration of academic knowledge and practical work in experiential learning. Throughout the summer, the interns are organized into teams of three to five members to initiate, develop, and implement service tasks for their community partners. By making advantageous use of their multidisciplinary knowledge, the interns contribute as shared leaders to help their community partners to generate innovative solutions to authentic problems. Although the nature of the service varies across projects, all the tasks involved are realistic.

Sample Projects of the School of Business

The SLI teams from the School of Business are engaged in consultation services for small and medium enterprises or nongovernment organizations (NGO). Some sample consultation projects are listed below:

Promotion of fair trade. By comparing and analyzing fair trade and non-fair trade products, a team of interns suggested ways for a social enterprise to improve market competitiveness.

Advertising strategies. A team of interns used a wide range of marketing tools (e.g., marketing mix, PEST analysis, segmentation, targeting, and positioning) to understand the current trend and challenges of a company and to recommend a future marketing strategy.

Funeral planning services. To help an NGO that provided funeral services, a team of interns conducted comprehensive marketing research on the perception of pre-funeral planning and innovative funeral products, pricing, and choices. They also worked on a promotional plan for the current services of this NGO.

Sample Projects of the Faculty of Social Sciences

For the SLI teams from the Faculty of Social Sciences, all projects are organized in terms of five different themes: (1) clinical and educational services; (2) communication, media, and culture; (3) corporate social responsibility; (4) community or social services; and (5) research and policy analysis. During the summer of 2014, 57 students worked on 22 SLI projects involving 19 different community partners. Some examples are presented below:

Clinical and educational services. One team of interns supported young adult cancer patients by compiling a positive psychology program manual and creating a website with online resources and materials. Another team worked on an evaluation plan of a project supporting students with autistic spectrum disorder by conducting focus group interviews with different stakeholders.

Communication, media, and culture. A team of interns supported the cookbook project of a food bank by working on the liaison between professional chefs and nutritionists for recipe submission and publication.

Corporate social responsibility. Through preparation and participation in different programs, a team of interns promoted social enterprise development and devised a comprehensive program plan for the following year.

Community or social services. One team of interns conducted outreach interviews, distributed newsletters, and organized activities for the sex workers who often work in isolation. The purpose was to promote mutual support among them and enlighten awareness toward their uninformed rights. An additional team of interns were involved in an outreach program for drug prevention. The interns prepared the promotional and educational materials for the outreach program.

Research and policy analysis. One team of interns conducted a research analysis of working poverty. They reviewed relevant statistics and conducted a fieldwork survey with the low-income workers in Hong Kong. Another team of interns worked on an in-depth research project that involved data collection from various sources and comprehensive analysis. On the basis of the analysis, the interns advised the community partner about the immediate needs of the youth.

Preparation

Arranging SLI projects for 100 students over the summer requires careful preparation. Although the internship is launched in summer, preparatory work has to be undertaken 9 months prior. As early as September and October, the academic tutors of the SLI pay visits to different organizations and identify the appropriate community partners that would offer suitable internship sites. It is important to match the skills and interest of the interns with the projects offered by the community partners. The list of community partners is reviewed and revised every year. Feedback from the interns plays an important part in the review process.

The list of community partners is usually confirmed by the beginning of the spring semester. An internship fair is organized in January in order to notify the students of what internship opportunities are available. The internship fair is a highly interactive process where prospective interns can receive useful information regarding different projects. Past interns and community partners are on site to share information and past experiences as well as clarify any concerns or questions. The nature of the various projects and the requirements from different community partners are displayed on exhibition boards. Each prospective intern is provided with a brochure containing information about the available projects.

Three weeks after the internship fair, the students apply for their preferred projects using an online system. They indicate their preferences by means of a priority list. From March to May, the supervisors of the community partners contact the interns directly for interviews in several rounds of matching. If some students do not receive an offer in the first round of interviews, the academic tutors will meet with them and provide advice about how to proceed with their priority list and the next round of interviews. The academic tutors will help every student to secure an offer as the total number of posts available outnumbers the total number of applicants. In other words, all the students will be able to find a job by the end of May.

Learning Process

Pre-internship Workshops

Five mandatory pre-internship workshops are organized to equip students with the basic knowledge, skills, and values before commencing with project teams.

Workshop 1. The first workshop focuses on team building. In this kickoff activity, students form into teams and learn how to play African drums. This is a playful and energizing start-up that most students enjoy. For some teams, it is the first time the members meet each other.

Workshop 2. The second workshop focuses on service-learning and leadership. After watching videos of companies and social enterprises, the students are asked to reflect on the significance of social responsibility and how it is related to transactional leadership, transformational leadership, shared leadership, servant leadership, and self-leadership.

Workshop 3. The third workshop focuses on personal competencies within the theoretical framework of social-cognitive approaches in motivation. Through interactive activities, the students learn how different goal orientations and mindsets influence their self-efficacy and resilience to setbacks. Students also reflect on their own mindsets after exposure to different scenarios.

Workshop 4. The fourth workshop focuses on social competencies in leadership. Through a series of simulated games, students learn how attribution affects interpersonal interactions. They also learn how to resolve conflicts.

Workshop 5. The last workshop focuses on academic outcomes; support is provided to students so that they can integrate academic knowledge with experiential learning.

The five workshops offer the necessary provision to the students before they embark upon their internship. It is noteworthy that the themes in Workshops 2, 3, and 4 are social responsibility, personal competencies, and social competencies, respectively. They are in correspondence with the objectives of the SLI described earlier.

Ongoing Support

In addition to the pre-internship training, ongoing support and guidance are provided to students throughout the internship. Each team of students is assigned a supervisor from the community partner and an academic tutor from the university. Regular meetings are held among these three parties. The supervisor monitors their progress at work and provides feedback to the team. The academic tutors pay visits to the internship site and observe how the students are performing their service tasks.

The students are invited to come back to the campus to share their experiences with the other teams. This provides an opportunity for problem solving and alternative perspectives. The academic tutors are available for further consultation.

Assessment for Learning Outcomes

Multiple assessment methods are structured in the program for evaluation of achievement relative to the expected learning outcomes. In the first 2 weeks of internship, students are required to submit a background report of the organization and a project proposal. A self-reflection journal is required along with the submission of an integrated report, which is to be completed by the end of the internship. A poster conference is held a week after the internship is completed in celebration of the students' accomplishments. This presentation allows the students to share the valuable knowledge they have gained with the other teams. The students' achievement is evaluated by community partners, academic tutors, peers, and the students themselves.

Program Evaluation

In general, the students find their involvement in the SLI rewarding. The followings are comments from some students

> This SLI was honestly one of the best internships I have ever done … Along the way, I learned an enormous amount about project management, effective communications both within the team and with external parties. I also had fun working with a great team. I have learned many new cooking tips, and discovered numerous new restaurants! (Comment from an intern in the food bank)
>
> It was an inspiring and fulfilling journey. It provided me with ample opportunities in understanding the true nature of the sex industry and sex workers … Another valuable gain for me from the SLI was the experience of teamwork. We worked closely and solved problems effectively. The process and experience of shared leadership let me further explore my strengths and weaknesses. (Comment from an intern in an NGO for sex workers)

The above anecdotal comments may illustrate how some students felt about their experience in the SLI. However, the students were not well positioned to provide objective feedback about the effectiveness of SLI in achieving its program aims. Therefore, an evaluation study was conducted with the students who took the SLI in summer, 2013. Change in mindset and attribution styles, gains in social responsibility, personal competencies, social competencies, and shared-leadership skills were investigated.

Participants

The experimental group consisted of 98 students who participated in the SLI group matched with the control group consisting of 99 students who participated in another internship provided in the Faculty of Social Sciences during the same period. The latter internship also required the students to work in the community for 8 weeks; however, they did not work as a team and a leadership component was not involved. The interns in the control group were sent individually to the community partners. Most of the students within both groups were students who had just finished their first year of college study. Females made up 63 % and 75 % of the experimental group and control group, respectively. The difference was not significant: $\chi^2 = 3.23$, df $= 1$, $p = .07$

Procedures

Before and after the internship, students from both groups completed a questionnaire that measured their mindset, attribution style, tendency to forgive in social conflicts, and perception of gains from the internship. In the fourth week of the internship, the students in the SLI also completed a peer evaluation questionnaire on shared-leadership skills.

Measures

Mindset

The students' mindset was measured by six items of the implicit theories scale developed by Dweck, Chiu, and Hong (1995). Students were asked to indicate their agreement to the items (e.g., "Everyone is a certain kind of person and there is not much that can be done to really change that") on a 6-point scale (1 = strongly disagree, 6 = strongly agree). A high score indicated a high endorsement for a person's intelligence and personality being fixed entities that would not alter significantly due to the experiences of the internship ($\alpha = .87$).

Attribution Style

The students' attribution style was measured by their responses to four scenarios of social conflicts (e.g., "A friend betrayed the trust you had in her/him"). The students were asked to indicate how much they thought each scenario was caused by the personality of this friend on a 6-point scale (1 = not at all, 6 = very much). A high score indicated a high tendency to adopt a trait-based attribution ($\alpha = .70$). They were also asked to indicate how much they thought each scenario was caused by many factors in the situation on the same rating scale. A high score indicated high tendency to adopt situation-based attribution ($\alpha = .70$).

Forgiveness

The students' tendency to forgive was also measured by their responses to the above scenarios. They were asked to indicate how likely they would forgive this friend (1 = not likely, 6 = very likely). A high score indicated a high tendency to forgive ($\alpha = .76$).

Social Responsibility and Personal and Social Competencies

At the end of the internship, the students evaluated how much they gained from the internship regarding social responsibility, personal competencies, and social competencies. The scale of social responsibility was composed of six items (e.g., "I had an opportunity to develop social responsibility and citizenship skills"), $\alpha = .84$. The scale of personal competencies was composed of six items (e.g., "I had an opportunity to experience personal growth"), $\alpha = .86$. The social competencies scale was composed of four items (e.g., "I had an opportunity to enhance my interpersonal skills"), $\alpha = .84$. The students were asked to indicate their agreement to these items on a 6-point scale (1 = strongly disagree, 6 = strongly agree).

Shared Leadership

In the fourth week of the internship, the students in the SLI were asked to evaluate the shared-leadership skills of them and their peers in the same team with the scale developed by Small and Rentsch (2010). The scale consists of 12 items (e.g., "Member X treated all group members as his/her equals; acknowledged and considered suggestions from all team members"). The students were asked to evaluate each team member including themselves on a 5-point scale (1 = never, 5 = always). A high score indicated a high evaluation of shared-leadership skills ($\alpha = .93$).

Results

Mindset

To test whether the SLI had changed the mindset of the students, a mixed-model ANOVA was performed on the mindset scores with time as the within-subject variable (pre vs. post) and condition as between-subject variable (experimental vs. control). A significant interaction effect between time and condition was found, $F(1,143) = 6.49, p = .012, \eta^2 = .043$. To decompose the interaction effect, two post hoc t tests were performed. As shown in Fig. 1, the two groups were not different in their fixed mindset scores (3.30 vs. 3.32) before the internship, $t = -.14$, df $= 143$, $p = . 87$. However, the experimental group had lower scores in the fixed mindset $(M = 3.08, SD = .86)$ than the control group $(M = 3.32, SD = .89)$ after the internship, $t = 2.33$, df $= 143, p = .02$.

Attribution Style and Forgiveness

Students with a less-fixed mindset at the end of the program tended to be more forgiving $(r = -.30, p = .02)$. They also tended not to attribute their friends' minor transgressions to a personality trait $(r = .29, p = .02)$. In addition, students who attributed the transgressions of their friends to a personality trait tended to be less forgiving $(r = -.42, p = .001)$. In contrast, students who attributed the transgressions of their friends to factors in the situation tended to be more forgiving $(r = 31, p = .02)$.

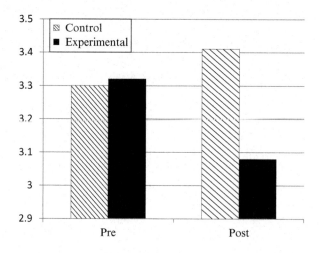

Fig. 1 The fixed mindset of the control and experimental groups before and after the internship

Social Responsibility, Personal and Social Competencies, and Shared Leadership

There was no significant difference between the experimental group and the control group in their perceived gains in social responsibility ($M_{Exp} = 4.50$, $SD_{Exp} = .67$; $M_{Con} = 4.51$, $SD_{Con} = .82$; $t = .03$, df $= 143$, $p = .97$), personal competencies ($M_{Exp} = 4.78$, $SD_{Exp} = .56$; $M_{Con} = 4.80$, $SD_{Con} = .84$; $t = .15$, df $= 143$, $p = .89$), and social competencies ($M_{Exp} = 4.85$, $SD_{Exp} = .61$; $M_{Con} = 4.76$, $SD_{Con} = .82$; $t = -.71$, df $= 143$, $p = .48$). Nevertheless, the students in the experimental group received a high evaluation from their teammate on shared leadership ($M = 4.25$, $SD = .43$). One sample t-test indicated that it was significantly higher than 3, the midpoint ($t = 27$, df $= 86$, $p < .001$).

Future Directions

The SLI at the University of Hong Kong has contributed to the field by integrating service-learning into leadership training in the Hong Kong context. Instead of lecturing the students about leadership skills and social responsibility in the classroom, the SLI involves students in authentic team-based project work. They initiate, develop, and implement service tasks for different organizations in the community contributing as shared leaders. The program evaluation indicated positive changes among students in shared-leadership skills, growth mindset, and forgiving behaviors that are conducive to conflict resolution.

Although the program evaluation indicated positive results, there is room for improvement of the study. First, the program evaluation procedure can be improved by including more control groups. The SLI should not only be compared to another internship that does not involve team projects but also to other different modes of instructions, e.g., lectures. Second, as the SLI provides a platform for students to work as shared leaders, it would be beneficial for future studies to study the team environment (Carson et al. 2007) and investigate the factors contributing to the developmental cycles of teams. Last but not least, as the SLI aims at nurturing responsible leaders with social awareness, it will be instrumental in conducting a longitudinal study to scrutinize the long-term impact of the experience across different aspects of students' lives.

As for the future development for SLI at the University of Hong Kong, one possible direction is to go beyond the territory of Hong Kong. To nurture global leaders, it is worthwhile to send students to community development projects beyond the border of Hong Kong. Through authentic team-based service-learning in developing countries, students will acquire not only knowledge related to being an integral part of a real context but also the social awareness that arises through interconnectedness across countries. Service-learning is different from volunteering because it promotes the highest ideal of social change (Morton

1995). The social change is not restricted to Hong Kong. Another possible direction is the involvement of students from more disciplines other than those in the Faculty of Social Sciences and the School of Business. The skills acquired in an interdisciplinary team will be helpful for the students in their future endeavors.

Conclusion

The SLI at the University of Hong Kong sheds light on leadership training in higher education by using community-based service-learning to nurture future leaders. With the support of community partners from different service sectors, students have the opportunity to enhance both their personal and social competencies. Students are able to become competent leaders through the team-based platform and the application of academic knowledge in real-life arenas utilizing self- and shared leadership skills. Most importantly, they work together for the betterment of human conditions through their service to the community.

References

Avolio, B. J., Walumbwa, F. O., & Weber, T. J. (2009). Leadership: Current theories, research, and future directions. *Annual Review of Psychology, 60*, 421–449. doi: 10.1146/annurev.psych.60.110707.163621

Beatty, J. E. (2010). For which future? Exploring the implicit futures of service-learning. *International Journal of Organizational Analysis, 18*(2), 181–197. doi: 10.1108/19348831011046254

Boyte, H. C. (2008). Against the current: Developing the civil agency of students. *Change, 40*(3), 9–15. doi: 10.3200/CHNG.40.3.8-15.

Carson, J. B., Tesluk, P. E., & Marrone, J. A. (2007). Shared leadership in teams: An investigation of antecedent conditions and performance. *Academy of Management Journal, 50*(5), 1217–1234. doi: 10.2307/AMJ.2007.20159921.

Chiu, C. Y., Hong, Y. Y., & Dweck, C. S. (1997). Lay dispositionism and implicit theories of personality. *Journal of Personality and Social Psychology, 73*(1), 19–30. doi: 10.1037/0022-3514.73.1.19.

Dipadova-Stocks, L. N. (2005). Two major concerns about service-learning: What if we don't do it? And what if we do? *Academy of Management Learning & Education, 4*(3), 345–353. doi: 10.5465/AMLE.2005.18122424.

Dweck, C. S. (2006). *Mindset: The new psychology of success.* New York: Random House.

Dweck, C. S., Chiu, C. Y., & Hong, Y. Y. (1995). Implicit theories and their role in judgments and reactions: A world from two perspectives. *Psychological Inquiry, 6*(4), 267–286. doi: 10.1207/s15327965pli0604_1.

Eyler, J., Giles Jr, D. E., Stenson, C. M., & Gray, C. J. (2001). *At a glance: What we know about the effects of service-learning on college students, faculty, institutions, and communities, 1993–2000.* Scotts Valley: Learn and Serve America's National Service-Learning Clearinghouse.

Giles, D. E., & Eyler, J. (1994). The theoretical roots of service-learning in John Dewey: Toward a theory of service-learning. *Michigan Journal of Community Service Learning, 1*(1), 77–85.

Hecht, D. (2003). The missing link: Exploring the context of learning in service-learning. In S. H. Billig & J. Eyler (Eds.), *Deconstructing service-learning: Research exploring context, participation, and impacts.* (pp. 25–49). Greenwich: Information Age Publishing.

Hernandez, M., Eberly, M. B., Avolio, B. J., & Johnson, M. D. (2011). The loci and mechanisms of leadership: Exploring a more comprehensive view of leadership theory. *The Leadership Quarterly, 22*(6), 1165–1185. doi: 10.1016/j.leaqua.2011.09.009.

Kenworthy-U'ren, A. L., & Peterson, T. O. (2005). Service-learning and management education: Introducing the 'WE CARE' approach. *Academy of Management Learning & Education, 4*(3), 272–277. doi: 10.5465/AMLE.2005.18122417.

Lester, S. W., Tomkovick, C., Wells, T., Flunker, L., & Kickul, J. (2005). Does service-learning add value? Examining the perspectives of multiple stakeholders. *Academy of Management Learning & Education, 4*(3), 278–294. doi: 10.5465/AMLE.2005.18122418.

Levy, S. R., & Dweck, C. S. (1998). Trait- versus process-focused social judgment. *Social Cognition, 16*(1), 151–172. doi: 10.1521/soco.1998.16.1.151.

Morton, K. (1995). The irony of service: Charity, project, and social change in service-learning. *Michigan Journal of Community Service Learning, 2*(1), 19–32.

Papamarcos, S. D. (2005). Giving traction to management theory: Today's service-learning. *Academy of Management Learning & Education, 4*(3), 325–335. doi: 10.5465/AMLE.2005. 18122422.

Pearce, C. L., & Manz, C. C. (2005). The new silver bullets of leadership: The importance of self- and shared leadership in knowledge work. *Organizational Dynamics, 34*(2), 130–140. doi: 10. 1016/j.orgdyn.2005.03.003.

Pearce, C. L., & Sims, H. P. Jr. (2002). The relative influence of vertical vs. shared leadership on the longitudinal effectiveness of change management teams. *Group Dynamics Theory Research and Practice, 6*(2), 172–197.

Reynolds, M., & Vince, R. (2004). Critical management education and action-based learning: Synergies and contradictions. *Academy of Management Learning & Education, 3*(4), 442–456. doi: 10.5465/AMLE.2004.15112552.

Small, E. E., & Rentsch, J. R. (2010). Shared leadership in teams: A matter of distribution. *Journal of Personnel Psychology, 9*(4), 203–211. doi: 10.1027/1866-5888/a000017.

Weiner, B. (2001). Intrapersonal and interpersonal theories of motivation from an attribution perspective. In F. Salili & C. Y. Chiu (Eds.), *Student motivation: The culture and context of learning.* Plenum series on human exceptionality (pp. 17–30). Dordrecht: Kluwer Academic Publishers.

The Construction of Student Leadership Development Model in HKIEd: Based on Service Leadership Core Beliefs Advocated by HKI-SLAM

Loretta M.K. Leung

Abstract This paper aims at explaining the construction of the student leadership development model, under the operation of the Student Affairs Office (SAO) in the Hong Kong Institute of Education (HKIEd). The office consolidates and shares our unique experiences in service leadership development at HKIEd in the cocurricular context and examines how this approach could be further developed and enhanced to benefit other experiential learning programs in future.

The model has three distinctive features. To start with, it demonstrates how service leadership core beliefs can be incorporated into self-directed cocurricular activities. Moreover, it provides an individualized learning experience unique to each participant, relevant to fulfilling one's own personal development goals, based on self-understanding. Last but not least, the project consists of different interlocking phases of guided learning experiences, including acquiring knowledge on service leadership concepts, developing one's own service leadership goals, balancing the needs of self and others, and examining how skills of effective service leadership can be applied in different social contexts.

This model suggests a road map for student leadership development. Students under this road map will develop a clearer picture on understanding themselves (including personality strength and weakness), so that they have the knowledge to set primary developmental goals and to design their own developmental paths during the course of their studentship at HKIEd.

This paper bases on the materials of Dr. Tom Wing Ho Fong, Ms. Carmen Wing Yee Ng, and Prof. Richard Yip Fat Tsang and Ms. Loretta Mee Kuen Leung, presented at the international conference on "Service Leadership Education for University Students: Experience in Hong Kong" (May 14–15, 2014).

L.M.K. Leung (✉)
Student Affairs Office, The Hong Kong Institute of Education, 1/F, Block A, 10 Lo Ping Road, Tai Po, N.T., Hong Kong, Hong Kong
e-mail: lmkleung@ied.edu.hk

© Springer Science+Business Media Singapore 2015

D.T.L. Shek, P. Chung (eds.), *Promoting Service Leadership Qualities in University Students*, Quality of Life in Asia 6, DOI 10.1007/978-981-287-515-0_6

Introduction

This paper aims at explaining the construction of the student leadership development model, under the operation of the SAO in HKIEd. Our institute attempts to strike the balance of the student leadership development between the concept of the provider (SAO) and the needs of the recipients (students). This model is a structure of programs for student leadership development. It provides a road map for students who can design their own leadership development paths according to their needs and interests. Students may amend their choice of program from time to time, as they understand themselves deeper and deeper through the course of the road map. This road map comes into existence after the launching of a special cocurricular learning project named "Achiever" in 2012 by SAO.

In this paper, the Achiever Project will be introduced, including its background, concept, program design, users' participation, and feedbacks (II). Developmental processes of various training model, based on the achiever's project, targeting various service learning programs in HKIED (III) will then be described.

The Achiever Project

With the support of Victor and William Fung Foundation and HKI-SLAM, the year-round cocurricular learning project Achiever was launched by SAO service leadership training in 2012–2013. The name "Achiever" is an abbreviation of the Prospective Service Leaders Enhancement Project and is composed of three interlocking phases, namely, foundation, self-advancement, and integration.

This project serves as a pilot-run attempt to provide feedback and assessment on how the core beliefs, key principles, and learning outcomes as outlined in HKI-SLAM Curriculum Framework can be fully incorporated and applied in the contexts of student development projects of the SAO in HKIEd and in the communities for the coming second and third years, respectively. With "leadership is a service" as the basic understanding among all core beliefs of the HKI-SLAM Curriculum Framework, the Achiever Project focuses more on (1) everyone is a leader, (2) the server is the service, and (3) quality service leadership = competency + character + care (3C).

Besides the three foci mentioned above, this project also has three distinctive features: (1) It demonstrates how the key service leadership core beliefs and principles can be incorporated into self-directed cocurricular activities fully operated outside an academic faculty and adopting an experiential-learning approach and continued self-reflection. (2) It provides an individualized learning experience, which is unique to each participant relevant to fulfilling his/her own personal development goals based on self-understanding within the HKI-SLAM Curriculum Framework. (3) It consists of three interlocking phases of guided learning experiences for participants, with all phases serving to assist participants achieving various goals, including knowledge acquisition on service leadership concepts, developing their own service leadership goals, balancing needs of self and others, and examining how skills of effective service leadership are applied in different contexts and situations.

In each of the interlocking phases, there is one specific focus of the three core beliefs.

Phase 1: Foundation

Phase 1 included students who participated in various projects launched by SAO, including the Study Tour Organizer Award Competition, Leadership Enhancement and Development (LEAD) Program, WoFoo Community Service 5 Takes Service Leaders Competition, and Campus Life Advising Scheme. The intended learning outcomes of phase 1 for participating students are (1) acquiring a basic understanding of concepts of service leadership, (2) discovering developmental strength and weakness, and (3) setting personal goals and developing plans towards enhancing effective service leadership on 3Cs.

A talk on service leadership was organized as the launching of the project. Most students could grasp the foundation concepts of service leadership thereafter, which includes three core beliefs: "everyone is a leader," "server is a service," and "the three Cs." These core beliefs are focused in phases 1, 2, and 3, respectively.

Core Belief One: Everyone Is a Leader

In the past, "leader" was defined by their position and power. Today, we hold a strong belief that everyone is a leader. Everyone leads themselves and has ownership over their lives. They can create their own enjoyable relationships, build up their own healthy communities, and more. Everyone has the potential to enhance their leadership skills and abilities, so that they can have a better performance in leading their lives in any position. Bryant and Kazan (2013) found that people with a strong sense of self are more likely to be both self-actualizing and self-transcending. The belief that everyone is a leader is a strong foundation for self-leadership.

Based on this belief, we provide a variety of leadership training. All students are encouraged to join us, so they can have the opportunity to clearly visualize and choose their developmental path and develop their potential according to their needs, interest, strength, and pace. As Albert Einstein said, "Everybody is a genius. But if you judge a fish by its ability to climb a tree, it will live its whole life believing that it is stupid." Any mismatch could be disastrous to a person's development. To achieve our ideal, we adopt self-directed learning and experiential learning as two key learning strategies.

1. *Self-Directed Learning*: In self-directed learning, learners/students take up the responsibility of their learning. The main purpose of the training is to develop their learning attitude and skills. Students should take the initiative to proactively make use of resources, rather than simply react to resources. This enables them to go on acquiring new knowledge easily and skillfully in the rest of their lives to come. To empower students' learning, we provide four stages to self-directed learning: (i) being ready to learn, (ii) setting learning goals, (iii) engaging in the learning process, and (iv) evaluating learning.
2. *Experiential Learning*: Most people adhere to the notion of "trial and error" learning. Ancient Chinese wisdom suggested that expressed experiential learning is more effective:

  I HEAR AND I FORGET
  I SEE AND I REMEMBER
  I DO AND I UNDERSTAND

  Others may like Sophocles' idea (400 BCE), "One must learn by doing the thing, for though you think you know it – you have no certainty, until you try." Experiential learning is participative, interactive, and applied. As such, students have to leave their comfort zone and face uncertainty ahead. The students' learning involves the whole person; learning takes place on the affective and behavioral dimensions as well as on the cognitive dimension.

  One of the foci in this phase is self-leadership, which means taking control for our own lives. Self-leaders will not take over responsibility for other people's goals or lives, but will offer empathy, quality attention, and focused effort to help. In preparation for this learning mode, all participating students received training in phase 1, which comprises of the following three workshops:

1. *Talk on Service Leadership*
  Students are expected to have an overview on the core concept and beliefs of service leadership and the 12 dimensions in service leadership development so that they can apply the theories into real lives.
2. *Workshop on Self-Understanding*
  Students have to be able to lead themselves before they can really lead others. Our project adopts MBTI personality inventory, which uncovers student's preferences within four dichotomies, namely, extraversion/introversion, sensing/intuition, thinking/feeling, and judging/perceiving. After the workshop, students understand their personality strength and the area of improvement on one hand and to appreciate differences of others on the other. Self-understanding is vital for them to design their leadership development plans.
3. *Workshop on Goal Setting: Well-Formed Outcome Model*
  Fail to plan is planning to fail. Every student learns how to use the well-formed outcome model to set their personal goal related to their specific projects. Their goals are set under the five criteria: positive, specific and evidence based, ownership, ecology check, and resource. At the end of the project, students will evaluate their achievement relating to their personal goals.

Phase 2: Self-Advancement

In phase 2, we selected approximately 20 students for further training, focusing on self-advancement. It aims at developing participants' self-leadership, providing a basis for them to deepen their reflection on knowledge and their concept of service leadership.

Core Belief Two: Server Is a Service

Chung and Bell (2012) share the idea of "leadership is a service." Life is about providing service to people around oneself; this is particularly true in Hong Kong as 90 % of jobs are in the service industry. Leadership itself should be considered as a service also; its quality depends on the quality of the server. The concept of service is not just to serve others, but to satisfy the needs of self of the server, from which the server may further serve others, groups and communities.

In phase 2, we provide activities including adventure-based trainings, life education: my life, understanding death tour, experiential learning in dialogue in the Dark, company visits, as well as consolidation group. These training activities aim at equipping students with service leadership knowledge, skill, and enhancing self-understanding. Intended learning outcomes for the experiential training activities are formulated for assessment purposes, as described below:

1. *Adventure-Based Training Camp and Adventure-Ship Program*
   To enhance the development of self-confidence through facing uncertainties and challenges and increasing self-understanding on own competency areas, character, and caring disposition by finishing challenging tasks and cooperation in team.
2. *Life Education: My Life, Understanding Death Tour*
   To identify the limitation of life and realizing the importance of setting priorities for lives and understanding of strengths and weaknesses to achieve goals in self-enhancement and serving others.
3. *Dialogue in the Dark*
   To display appropriate actions and nonverbal cues that foster positive social relationships to satisfy own and others' needs.
4. *Company Visit*
   Students are divided into four groups to conduct interviews with awardees of one out of four enterprises as recommended by the Community Caring Shop Recognition Scheme organized by the Social Welfare Department. It is hoped that students can learn about the shops' managing principles, core beliefs, and philosophies to compare and contrast with those of service leadership initiatives (SLI). After the interviews, students need to apply one of the themes of SLI to analyze their findings and observations. During the debriefing presentation, most students agree that the core beliefs of SLI could be reflected in local community to some extent. They have discovered new perspectives on the definition of a

successful leader, not only measured by the profit made but also their caring to others and services provided to the community. These were reflected to be common characteristics of successful leaders in their business operation.

5. *Consolidation Group*

   Consolidation groups are organized to provide a platform for students to deeply reflect and receive feedback from others on their performance in their own projects based on service leadership principles under the guidance of professional mentors. Participants are divided into two groups, and a total of six sessions are conducted for each group from March to May 2013. In each session, some core beliefs and concepts of SLI are discussed, including competence, character, and care. Besides, two to three participants are required to share their own experiences in fulfilling leadership roles, progress on reaching their own goals, and how SLI core beliefs affect their leadership style. A personal consultation session conducted by professional mentor is also offered to participants to assist in their preparation work. After presenting the case, other group members provide feedback and raise comments or suggestions for improving leadership style. All members agree that it is a valuable opportunity for them, not only to increase mutual understanding and support but also to deepen their scope of view towards service leadership as they could have a platform to share about their own learning. As a whole, they agree with SLI core beliefs, and to a great extent, they could apply the core beliefs in different contexts in daily lives and future planning on personal development.

Phase 3: Integration

Phase 3 is the final phase of the project and focuses on integration. Students are required to apply core beliefs of SLI in their own enrolled projects. Such integration is important because it enhances the quality of service leadership of our students. Gronfeldt and Strother (2006) emphasized that service leadership is the culture that empowers the organization to strategize its promises, design its process, and engage its people in a proactive quest for competitive advantage.

Core Belief Three: The Three Cs

These three Cs of the quality service leadership are competency, character, and care. We regard them as quintessence and incorporate them in the last phase of our Service Learning Development Project. A brief description is provided:

Competency – Other than particular competencies specifically related to the tasks at hand, students should also cultivate those transferable competencies such as communication, problem solving as well as time management skills, etc.

Character – Character building is a process in nurturing one's moral authority. The leader with moral authority has the ability to establish trust and respect and attract followers.

Care – While both competency and character are individual qualities, care is the quality to link up individuals and build an interdependent community.

In order to develop competency, to nourish the character, and to express the caring attitude, we offer various opportunities to students to apply and develop their service leadership.

International work camps are arranged to further motivate students to plan for a self-directed learning experience through involving in voluntary service tours. Participants form pairs to join work camps during summer based on their interests and aspirations. Various international organizations are invited as working partners, locating in Poland, Spain, Iceland, Ukraine, Sweden, Turkey, Taiwan, Sri Lanka, and Vietnam. These organizations themselves are involved in projects related to environmental protection, education with children, service for people with disabilities, and more. Each pair of students has to work with volunteers in various host organizations coming from different cultures or countries and form into teams to serve people in need. They are required to demonstrate service leadership skills and evaluate its effectiveness in different cultural contexts. This is undoubtedly an eye opening opportunity for participants to broaden their international horizons and enhance leadership development. After completing these work camps, they have to present their learning experiences by the use of an e-portfolio.

Besides international work camps, participants are required to further apply service leadership skills to other service projects, including the Study Tour Organizer Award Competition, Leadership Enhancement and Development Program, WoFoo Community Service 5 Takes Service Leaders Competition, and Campus Life Advising Scheme.

The summary of the pilot-run achievements in 2012–2013 and 2013–2014 is attached in the Appendix at the end of this paper for references.

The Construction of the Student Leadership Development Model

The Achiever Project provided valuable experiences and reflections that contribute to the gradual evolution of our framework of student leadership program and further the new concept of the road map for student development.

Framework of Student Leadership Program

We have discussed thoroughly the pilot-run Achiever Project in 2012–2013. Now we describe what we have been doing in the following 2 years (2013–2015).

With the positive feedback and experience from the pilot run of the Achiever Project in the first year, the SAO further modified the program content to best fit students' needs in the following years. Since phase 1 helps a lot in identifying and setting goals for students' own developmental needs, most of the students participating in SAO's leadership training programs have to attend the talk on service leadership and workshop on self-understanding and goal setting as prerequisite in order to proceed to phases 2 and 3. It is now suggested that the development of any current or future long-term student leadership development projects run by the SAO should incorporate training components of service leadership, self-understanding, and goal setting. Please refer to Table 1 for the framework of student leadership program.

Phase 1 is a common prerequisite to all participants of various student development programs. Different student development programs have different phase 2 and phase 3 activities designed according to the program needs; these are extended to students joining designated cocurricular projects through incorporated various enhancement initiatives into their program design. In phase 2, each program would design on its own training activities, according to their specific program objectives so as to fulfill participants' own developmental needs.

Lastly, instead of arranging international work camps for each participant, all students joining phase 3 are encouraged to integrate their learned service leadership concepts into their own enrolled platforms or projects and reflect on their personal gains as well as its limitations at the end of their program.

Table 1 Framework of student leadership program

Phase 1	Phase 2	Phase 3
1. Talk on service leadership	1. Interview with personnel or company visit	1. Application of core beliefs in each service project
2. Workshop on self-understanding (a) MBTI (b) Personality dimension (c) Self-directed search	2. One tailor-made adventure activity of each program (a) Adventure-based training day camp (b) Crossroads foundation experiential program (c) Dialogue in the Dark	2. Assessment methods (a) Group presentation (b) Learning journal (c) Sharing session (d) Service Leadership Initiative (SLI) framework evaluation
3. Workshop on goal setting	(d) Life education program (e) Student leadership challenge (f) Wild cooking	

Road Map of Students' Service Leadership Development

Through consolidating the experiences gained from adopting the above student development framework in HKIEd, we have further enhanced and constructed our student leadership development model and cocurricular education framework, which emphasize self-directed service learning, reflection, and consolidation within the different contexts of learning experience.

Based on the conception of "everyone is a leader," we have expanded the concept of "service" towards coaching student leaders to satisfy needs of self, others, groups, communities, and global contexts ethically. We also emphasize the balanced development of the dimensions of the "3C" (competency, character, and care), through acquiring appropriate knowledge and skills, cultivating values, and developing attitudes as effective and caring leaders. We further adopt the six approaches to develop students' service leadership capabilities (modeling, empowering, coaching, transforming, mentoring, and supporting).

According to our experiences in the Achiever Project, we group these six approaches and present them in three groups:

1. *Modeling and Empowering*: Social learning theory, which provides the foundation for behavior modeling, asserts that most behaviors are learned by observation and modeling. In our programs, the facilitators act as a good models for the participants, and they cultivate a reciprocal learning culture through observation, collaboration, and sharing of good practices. To empower students in the development of skills, resources, authority, opportunity, and motivation while holding them responsible and accountable for outcomes of their actions will contribute to their competence and satisfaction.

2. *Coaching and Supporting*: Trainers of the program provide support for a person or a group of students to do a specific task, achieve a goal, or develop certain skills. Coaching always targets on high performance and improvement at work, and it focuses on specific skills and goals. The kind of coaching and supporting may also have an impact on an individual's personal attributes, such as social interaction and confidence.

All our student development programs are student oriented and outcome based. We support students to pursue high performance and monitor their personal growth.

3. *Mentoring and Transformation*: Mentoring is a relationship built on trust, and one of its primary goals is to make a young person (or people new to a field of endeavor) more confident in their abilities and talents.

In some of our higher level of leadership programs, we have developed mentorship training. Some experienced students will be selected as peer mentors for new participants. A more experienced student uses his or her greater knowledge and understanding of the project to support the development of new participants. It is usually a more personal relationship, based on shared experiences. As the new-comer grows, the mentoring relationship evolves. With the support of SAO staff, peer mentors help the mentees both with concrete skill-related guidance and with psychological guidance, usually focusing on developing the mentees' self-esteem and habits of responsibility. In the process, SAO staff tries to assess all the possibilities and resources available to help both mentors and mentees fulfill their potential in spite of their difficulties. The mentors and the mentees will become more competent and caring in this mentoring relationship. They will undergo a change in character. We call this a transformation, which brings into a more effective leadership.

Leadership capacity is a developmental process. Students can choose their own development pathways according to their interests and abilities. We believe it is more effective to develop the leadership skills through the collaboration with others through group projects.

In such a routing for learning experiences, the SAO of HKIEd gradually emerges the idea of a road map for service leadership development and develops a variety of programs under each level of learning. Under this road map, we articulate a picture that students could be responsible for designing their own leadership developmental paths, shown in Fig. 1.

Legend for Fig. 1:

Service Alumni Network – To build up a support and resource network for further development
Transforming – To become a competent and conscience leader in the community
Consolidating – To initiate new projects through own initiatives based on past learning experience
Mentoring – To serve as peer mentor to the participants
Organizing – To learn how to organize activities under the guidance of SAO staff
Participating – Available to all students, especially first-year

Scope of the Learning Experience

Leadership cannot be developed in vacuum. Students can become competent, positive, and caring professionals with intellectual enthusiasm, social commitment, and global awareness only through gaining experiences in diverse real-life contexts. Lai (2009) stressed that as a multicultural service-learning cocurricular activity, participants can acquire new knowledge, change attitudes, and develop constructive behaviors through a genuine and caring environment and reflection.

As shown in Fig. 1, programs in different contexts were organized, from campus, community to globe-wide projects. It is expected that all participants will be leaders at different levels, hence the multifacet program immersions and the potential to migrate between different programs. For example, please see Fig. 2.

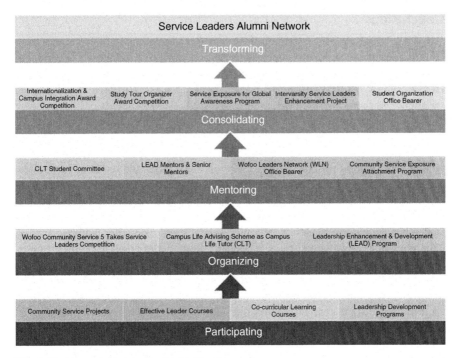

Fig. 1 Road map for service leadership development

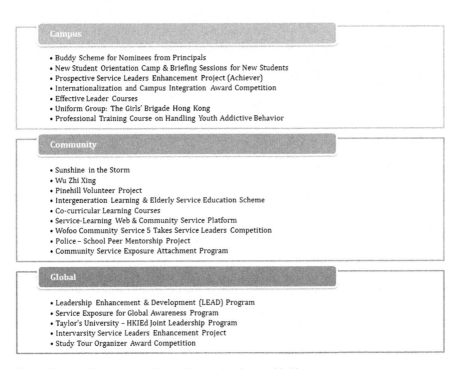

Fig. 2 Scope of learning experiences intended to be provided by programs

Conclusion

HKIEd aims at educating our younger generation, both academics and cocurricular, to become future leaders of our society and of the world at large. The SAO of HKIEd shares the task of whole-person development. We have been striking excellence in providing the best training programs to our students.

With the support of the Victor and William Fung Foundation and HKI-SLAM, the Achiever Project was launched by SAO in 2012–2013. This project enhanced the excellence of the SAO to develop the road map for student leadership development. We adopt three core beliefs (everyone is a leader, the server is the service, and quality service leadership = competency + character + care) to design our program activities into three phases (foundation for basic knowledge, self-advancement, and integration). All this constitutes to our road map in student leadership development model. The model has three distinctive features. Firstly, it demonstrates how key service leadership core beliefs and principles can be incorporated into self-directed cocurricular activities operated outside an academic context and adopting an experiential-learning approach with continuous self-reflection. Secondly, it provides an individualized learning experience unique to each participant and relevant to fulfilling one's own personal development goals based on self-understanding. Thirdly, the project consists of different interlocking phases of guided learning experiences, including acquiring knowledge on service leadership concepts, developing one's own service leadership goals, balancing the needs of self and others, and examining how skills of effective service leadership can be applied in different social contexts and situations.

Students under this road map may thus have a clear picture on understanding themselves (including but not limited to personality and personal strength and weakness), so that they have the necessary tools and knowledge to set their developmental goals and design their own developmental paths during the course of their studentship at HKIEd. As the service provider to student development professionals, SAO staffs are also benefited during the course of constructing such a road map, in particular, their knowledge on service leadership and concept in developing students for their betterment.

Appendix: Summary of Achievements in 2012–2013 Pilot Run and 2013–2014

It is realized that students who participated in the abovementioned three phases have learned about the basic concepts of service leadership, applied what they learned, and enhanced competencies in various settings. The extent of their achievements and alignments with the curriculum and learning outcomes are summarized in the following table, and the numbers of students involved in various training programs in the three phases are also illustrated in the tables.

Achievements in 2012–2013 Pilot Run

A. Participants

Program name	No. of participants
Talk on service leadership	268
Self-understanding workshops	241
Workshops on goal setting	223
Adventure-based training camp	33
Company visit	20
Life education	15
Dialogue in the Dark	16
Presentation for company visit	20
Adventure-ship program	42
Consolidation group	17
International work camp	14
Other service projects	178

B. Key findings of feedback questionnaires and learning outcomes assessment

Training/activity	Key findings of feedback questionnaires and learning outcomes assessment
Talk on service leadership	64.2 % ($N = 156$) of respondents either disagree or strongly disagree that leadership effectiveness is only dependent on possessing power and a minimum level of expertise
	60.5 % ($N = 147$) of respondents either disagree or strongly disagree that service is only performed to satisfy the needs of someone else
Workshop on self-understanding – MBTI assessment	98.2 % ($N = 214$) of respondents agreed that they can understand their personality in strengths and potential areas for growth after the workshop
	97.7 % ($N = 213$) of respondents agreed that they can appreciate people who differ from them after the workshop
Workshop on goal setting	95.9 % ($N = 210$) of respondents agreed that they realized the importance of setting goals for their lives after the workshop
Adventure-based training camp	Students agreed that the training camp can develop their self-understanding (4.20), problem-solving skills (4.27), building trust with others (4.47), and respond to others' needs (4.00) (1 = strongly disagree, 5 = strongly agree)
Company visit	After interviewing caring shop awardees, students are able to learn from awardees and consolidate their learning by using SLI framework during their presentations
Life education: my life, understanding death tour	71.4 % of respondents agreed that they could realize their own priorities, strengths, and weaknesses after the tour

(continued)

Training/activity	Key findings of feedback questionnaires and learning outcomes assessment
Dialogue in the Dark	Students reflected that good body language skills with clear instructions can enhance communication
Adventure-ship	100 % of respondents agreed that this program empowered their self-confidence in facing challenge
	100 % of respondents agreed that they can demonstrate active listening to other points of view in completing tasks after activity
Consolidation group	100 % of respondents agreed that this program empowered their self-understanding
	100 % of respondents agreed that personal character, task competency, and caring disposition affected one's quality on leadership
	100 % of respondents agreed that understanding on other's needs contributed to the effectiveness of leadership
International work camp	Students are required to practice and take up a leadership role in their projects or work camp

Achievements in 2013–2014

A. Participants

Workshop name	No. of participants
Talk on service leadership	303
Self-understanding workshops	268
Workshops on goal setting	293
Service project name	
Campus Life Advising Scheme (CLAS)	165
Community Service Exposure Attachment Program	13
Intergeneration Learning and Elderly Service Academy	20
Leadership Enhancement and Development (LEAD) Program	163
Pinehill Volunteer Project	24
Service Exposure for Global Awareness (SEGA) Program	24
Study Tour Organizer Award Competition	45
Sunshine in the Storm	29
WoFoo Community Service 5 Takes Service Leaders Competition	45

B. Key findings of feedback questionnaires and learning outcomes assessment

Training/activity	Key findings of feedback questionnaires and learning outcomes assessment
Workshop on self-understanding	96.6 % ($N = 168$) of respondents agreed that they can understand their personality in strengths and potential areas for growth after the workshop
	94.8 % ($N = 165$) of respondents agreed that they can appreciate people who differ from them after the workshop
Workshop on goal setting	98.1 % ($N = 202$) of respondents agreed that they realized the importance of setting goals for their lives after the workshop
Interview with a role model	After interviewing with someone who is taking leadership role, students reported that caring and compassion are the most important personal qualities to be a successful service leader after the interview

C. Key findings of other service projects

Name of program	Key findings of the program
Campus Life Advising Scheme (CLAS)	100 % of Campus Life Tutors (CLT) found that the CLAS could help them to equip with basic guidance and leadership skills to support their respective tutees
Leadership Enhancement and Development (LEAD) Program	Participated mentors reported in the regular mentors' meeting and group discussion that the program enhanced their (1) leadership ability, (2) communication and interpersonal skills, (3) crisis-management ability, (4) collaboration skills, and (5) problem-solving skills
	In the academic year of 2013–2014, students' contributions in Ethiopia, India, and Sri Lanka were reported by the media in Hong Kong and host country to share their learning experiences
Study Tour Organizer Award Competition	84.4 % of participants reported that the "talk on service leadership," "workshop on self-understanding," and "workshop on goal setting" are helpful to their leadership development
	100 % of participants recommended that the project should be conducted in the next year
Sunshine in the Storm	100 % of participants recommended that the project should be conducted in the next year

References

Bryant, A., & Kazan, A. L. (2013). *Self-leadership: How to become a more successful, efficient, and effective leader from the inside out.* New York: McGraw-Hill.

Chung, P., & Bell, A. (2012). *Service reborn: The knowledge, skills and attitudes of service companies.* New York/Hong Kong: Lexingford Publishing.

Gronfeldt, S., & Strother, J. (2006). *Service leadership: The quest for competitive advantage.* Thousand Oaks: SAGE.

Lai, K. H. (2009). Developing leadership and cultural competency through service exposure attachment program. *New Horizons in Education, 57*(3), 105–118.

The Service Leadership Initiative at Lingnan University

Robin Stanley Snell, Maureen Yin Lee Chan, Carol Hok Ka Ma, and Carman Ka Man Chan

Abstract We explain six aspects of the service leadership initiative for undergraduates at Lingnan University. The first comprises co-curricular service leadership through service-learning projects that we have embedded within seven different credit-bearing courses. The second is a comprehensive infrastructure for setting up and supporting such projects. The third is a set of templates that we developed as resources for students to undertake self-, peer-, and team-review exercises of their attempts to practice ten attributes of service leadership during the projects or practicums. We provide illustrative extracts from two completed templates. The fourth aspect is an eight-facet model of the process of developing service leaders through the projects, which we developed on the basis of formative evaluation studies. The fifth comprises sponsored opportunities for students to conduct extracurricular service leadership practicums with community or noncommercial organizations, mainly during the summer recess. The sixth involves discipline-based quantitative and qualitative research into service leadership in commercial settings.

Introduction

Lingnan University (LU) provides liberal arts education, which is based on close faculty-student and student-student relationships, and is guided by the motto of "Education for Service." LU adopts a whole-person approach and aims to instill a sense of civic duty and cultivate generic skills, competences, and sensibilities in undergraduates that equip them for rapidly changing service habitats. Undergraduate students from across LU are encouraged to take at least one credit-bearing course in service-learning mode during their studies. Service-learning involves integrating community services with academic curricula to help benefit partner organizations and the wider community while enhancing the participating students'

R.S. Snell (✉) • M.Y.L. Chan
Department of Management, Lingnan University, SEK102/11, Simon and Eleanor Kwok Building, Tuen Mun, N.T., Hong Kong, New Territories, Hong Kong
e-mail: robin@ln.edu.hk

C.H.K. Ma • C.K.M. Chan
Office of Service-Learning, Lingnan University, LBY-101/1, B. Y. Lam Building, Tuen Mun, N.T., Hong Kong, New Territories, Hong Kong

© Springer Science+Business Media Singapore 2015
D.T.L. Shek, P. Chung (eds.), *Promoting Service Leadership Qualities in University Students*, Quality of Life in Asia 6, DOI 10.1007/978-981-287-515-0_7

academic experience and graduate attributes. Prior research has shown that if students are given opportunities to tackle real problems and make a difference through service-learning, they derive significant benefits in terms of self-insight, self-efficacy, self-esteem, and social, political, and relationship-building skills (Eyler et al. 2001; Kendrick 1996; Mitton-Kükner et al. 2010; Waterman 1993). In this chapter, we shall explain and illustrate how LU has woven five aspects of the service leadership initiative into service-learning project and practicum experiences for students while also pursuing a sixth aspect, discipline-based research, to enhance the body of knowledge about service leadership. These aspects are represented in Fig. 1.

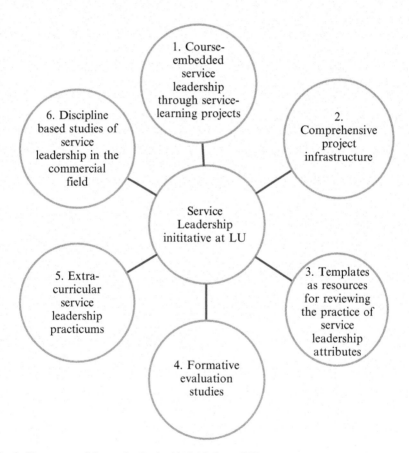

Fig. 1 Six aspects of the service leadership initiative at LU

Cocurricular Service Leadership Through Service-Learning Projects

Since its inception in 2006, the Office of Service-Learning (OSL) at LU has established a collaborative network of more than 150 nongovernmental organizations (NGOs), social enterprises, and government agencies. The OSL has also built an internal network of LU-based academics, who incorporate service-learning projects into courses that they teach. Mutual trust and understanding, built up over the years across LU's networks, have opened access to diverse community-based problems and opportunities that can be addressed through service-learning projects while enabling OSL to match particular courses that are run at LU with real problems and needs in the community. A key principle is that student teams should draw on course-related theories and techniques as conceptual tools for analyzing and solving real problems and for identifying and meeting real needs, thereby furthering the mission of the respective partner organizations and aligning with LU's "Education for Service" motto.

Under the service leadership initiative, we have built on this platform to enable students to practice service leadership attributes while undertaking co-curricular service-learning projects. Since September 2012, in addition to the standard service-learning provision across the rest of the university, service leadership through service-learning projects has been incorporated into seven credit-bearing courses.

The seven focal courses bear the titles, *Corporate Social Responsibility*, *Strategic Management*, *Leadership and Teamwork*, *Introduction to Business*, *Service Leadership*, *Social Marketing*, and *Services Marketing*. In conjunction with these courses, 673 students in 112 teams have participated in service leadership through service-learning projects (hereafter referred to as "projects"), serving a total of 30 partner organizations, mostly social enterprises or non-governmental organizations. Students have applied knowledge and skills from these courses, and from their broader programs of study, to guide the processes of delivering various services, such as market surveys, consultancy reports, publicity campaigns, and training sessions. The projects have addressed diverse problems and issues in the community, such as the sustainability of social enterprises, environmental protection, active aging, fair trade, and social inclusion. Alignment between the focal courses and expertise required to address community needs has enabled and empowered students to practice service leadership.

Project Infrastructure

We have been operating infrastructure that spans three phases of the life of each project: the preparatory phase, the service phase, and the review phase, as shown in Fig. 2.

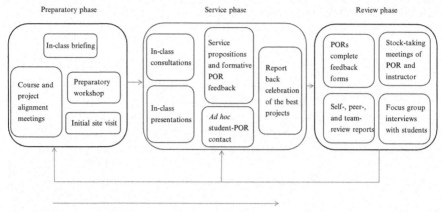

Preparatory phase   Service phase   Review phase

Project Timeline for a semester of about 3.5 months

Fig. 2 Project infrastructure

Preparatory Phase

The key infrastructural elements during the preparatory phase comprise course and project alignment meetings between partner organization representatives (PORs) and instructors, along with in-class briefings, preparatory workshops, and initial site visits for the students.

Course and Project Alignment Meetings

Prior to the semester commencement, a field coordinator based in the OSL convenes course and project alignment meetings with the PORs and the respective course instructors. These meetings have four broad aims. The first aim is to ensure close alignment between the projects that the students will undertake and the real needs of the partner organization. To that end, the field coordinator establishes that the PORs are willing to disclose important problems, challenges, and needs that the partner organizations face in pursuing their respective missions and goals and are willing to allow teams of students to address these genuine issues through their projects.

The second aim is to ensure that the PORs are committed to supporting the students throughout the projects. The field coordinator asks the PORs to keep in contact with the students, to provide access to necessary sources of primary and secondary data for the projects, and to open doors to key stakeholders whenever necessary. The third aim is to confirm that the instructors regard the envisaged projects as relevant to the contents, goals, and grading requirements of the respective courses. The fourth aim is to deepen inter-institutional trust and reciprocity-based learning relationships over time, so that successive teams of students, supported by instructors, will provide valuable services to the partner organizations, while the PORs will gain cumulative insights into effective ways of collaborating with students.

In-Class Briefings and Initial Site Visits

Early in the semester, the OSL field coordinator briefs the participating students, in their respective classes, about the scope and requirements of their projects and facilitates the project team formation process. Normally, she then leads a site visit for each class to the partner organization, during regular class time.

Preparatory Workshops

Each participating student attends a mandatory 3-h orientation workshop, held outside the scheduled class time. Besides introducing the general mission of non-governmental organizations and social enterprises in Hong Kong, the workshop aims to encourage students to make a difference through their projects and to prepare them to take the initiative, rather than waiting for instructions. During the workshop, in their project teams, students discuss case vignettes of problems faced by previous project teams and are asked to identify alternatives and solutions.

The preparatory workshop also addresses team issues (Falk 2012). Students receive explanations about the intended role of the team convenors and the distributed nature of service leadership. While each team elects a convenor, this role involves bringing the team together for meetings and liaising with the PORs and is not supposed to be the only leadership position within the team. Under distributed leadership, each team member is expected to practice service leadership attributes as appropriate, to the best of their ability. These are unfamiliar leadership concepts. The dominant, centralized, or hierarchical mindset models of leadership are very difficult to supplant. As an initial step, students are introduced to ten attributes of service leadership and reminded that everyone will be expected to practice them during the project.

The preparatory workshop also introduces the concept of stakeholders, as in Fig. 3. According to the model, students should take account of their impact on all stakeholders and be mindful of diverse stakeholder expectations. We share our assumption that if the students develop their service leadership attributes while addressing stakeholder needs, society as a whole will benefit.

Service Phase

The key infrastructural elements during the service phase include in-class consultations and presentations, ad hoc student-POR contact, service propositions and formative POR feedback, and a report-back celebration of the best projects.

Fig. 3 Multiple
stakeholder considerations
during the projects

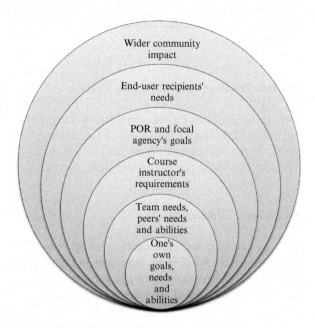

In-Class Presentations and Consultations and Ad Hoc Student-POR Contact

Students make interim and final in-class oral project presentations. Normally, instructors also arrange two or three in-class project consultations across the semester. During these meetings, the instructor, POR, and OSL field coordinator rotate among the student teams to discuss project-related issues. Teams are expected to maintain close contact with their respective POR outside the classroom, and besides telephone or e-communication, they typically initiate special consultation meetings with him or her.

Service Propositions and Formative Feedback

Project teams are encouraged to keep their objectives and terms of reference under constant review, since exposure to stakeholder perspectives can imply modifications. In such cases, teams must present new service propositions to the POR for approval or adjustment.

Some projects involve structured arrangements for submitting service propositions and obtaining formative feedback. For example, projects undertaken in conjunction with *Leadership and Teamwork*, or *Service Leadership*, typically involve designing and providing training sessions for children or for the elderly, and teams are required to send each lesson plan as a service proposition to the respective POR for consideration and feedback. At the micro level, students delivering training or other direct services are expected to present realistic service propositions to end users and to adjust the services actually provided in the light of end-user reaction and feedback.

Report-Back Celebration

For consultancy projects undertaken in conjunction with *Strategic Management*, instructors invite the best teams, chosen for in-class presentations, to make reprise presentations at a "celebration," held at the end of the semester and attended by respective instructors and PORs.

Review Phase

The review phase comprises several elements. Besides sending feedback forms to solicit written comments from PORs, the OSL field coordinator convenes bilateral stock-taking meetings between instructors and PORs. These are channels for evaluating student teams' contributions and for identifying aspects of the project experience, such as any miscommunications or misunderstandings, that require improvement in any future projects.

The OSL field coordinator also arranges individual and focus group interviews with a sample of students to identify perceived problems and achievements, both in terms of processes and outcomes, with special attention given to factors influencing the effectiveness of their attempts to practice service leadership attributes. Typically also, as required items of coursework and as described in the next section, students submit self-reflection reports regarding their own attempts to practice service leadership, peer-review reports regarding their teammates' attempts, and team-review reports, which are collectively completed.

These elements within the review phase facilitate formative evaluation, by yielding information to inform improvements in subsequent cycles of the preparatory and service phases, as represented by the feedback loops in Fig. 2. In the following section, we shall provide illustrations of data and insights that have emerged during our formative evaluation studies.

Templates as Resources for Self-, Peer-, and Team-Review

Based on pioneer work (Chung 2012; HKI-SLAM 2014) and in conjunction with our formative evaluation work, we developed three review templates to guide students in reporting their practice and development of ten selected service leadership attributes. These attributes are active listening, anticipating and solving problems, caring disposition, showing originality in expressing opinions, contributing to cohesiveness and close relationships, committing to continuous improvement, undertaking delegated responsibilities, civic engagement, influencing others, and project coordination skills.

Students' template-based reports contribute to some of their coursework requirements and are graded for completeness, clarity, and depth. One template guides students in compiling their individual self-review reports, as illustrated in Table 1,

Table 1 Extracts from the individual self-reflection report of one student on the *Service Leadership* course

Aspects of Service Leadership	Examples of your attempts to practice	Your further learning needs and how you became aware of your further learning needs
1. Actively listening to others (paying close attention to what others are saying or trying to say, demonstrating that you are paying attention)	When my team members were giving suggestions on the activity plans for the workshops, I listened carefully and showed my understanding constantly. I also asked for more details of their suggestions	I think I have to smile more when I am listening to the sharing given by the service recipients. When the representative (G) was talking with the children, she kept smiling during the whole conversation. Therefore, I think keeping smiling during the conversation is another good way to demonstrate that I am listening carefully. Also, I realized that my facial expression will affect the willingness of the speaker to share his/her story...
	In addition, I paid close attention when my mentee shared her stories and worries. For example, she told me things about her dreams and busy school life. During her sharing, I nodded and kept good eye contact with her, so as to show that I was listening actively. This helped encourage her to express herself more freely	
3. Caring disposition (discovering other people's needs and taking positive action to address those needs)	Through the sharing of my mentee, I know her dream is to be a policewoman when she grows up. However, she did not know much information about the criteria for being a policewoman. Thus, I searched information with her. As she was only in primary three, there were some specific terms that she did not know on the websites. Therefore, I also explained the information to her. By letting her know more information on how to be a policewoman, it helped her pursue her dream...	In my opinion, I need to learn to be more sensitive to the needs of different service recipients. In the service leadership project, the mentee I was responsible for was very active and outgoing. In the first workshop, I only focused on getting along with her. However, after hearing the feedback of my team members in the evaluation meeting, I found that I neglected that there was a boy who was quiet and might require extra care. Instead of talking in a group, the boy would be more willing to share if I asked him questions individually. Thus, in order to provide service according to the needs of service recipients, I need to have careful observation and learn to be sensitive to others' needs

(continued)

Table 1 (continued)

Aspects of Service Leadership	Examples of your attempts to practice	Your further learning needs and how you became aware of your further learning needs
5. Contribution to cohesiveness and close relationships (helping to build positive relationships among team members and/or with service recipients)	At first, I did not understand much about my team members. Therefore, I suggested to have lunch together after Friday class. Then, we gradually knew more about each other and had a closer relationship. We were able to cooperate well	In fact, I need to learn about how to build a close relationship with the service recipients. Honestly speaking, I thought the mentees would be able to build a harmonious relationship among themselves after one or two workshops as they would play ice-breaking games together. However, I found that I was wrong. They were not very close to each other, especially the boys. Sometimes, boys and girls may even have little conflicts. If the mentees had a closer relationship, then they would cooperate well with each other and perform better in the group works of Workshop 3 and 4. Thus, there is a need for me to learn about how to build close relationships among the service recipients. This would help increase cohesiveness and a more harmonious atmosphere could be built
	In order to build positive and trustful relationships with the mentees, we played games that they are interested in. Also, I searched information about the popular cartoons, so that I could have a common topic with the mentees. What's more, I shared a lot of my stories that happened in primary school, such as what I did with my friends during recesses and the games we played. This motivated to share more about themselves and the differences between their childhood and mine	
6. Committing to continuous improvement (working to improve your self-leadership and self-management competencies)	After completing each workshop, I reflected on my own performance in the workshop, in order to identify improvements. For example, I helped lead several games in the project. I reflected on my performance of leading the games by thinking of whether the atmosphere was well set and whether the mentees enjoyed playing the games. Also, I compared my performance in different workshops, so as to see whether I had made improvements	In my opinion, I have to learn to use different methods to evaluate my performance, so that I can make improvements continuously and effectively. One of the team members told me that my time management was not very good when I was leading the game in Workshop 2. Since then, I realized that I actually can ask my team members for opinions and advice on how to improve my performance. By learning to use various means to evaluate myself to make improvements, I believe that I can be a more successful service leader

(continued)

Table 1 (continued)

Aspects of Service Leadership	Examples of your attempts to practice	Your further learning needs and how you became aware of your further learning needs
8. Civic engagement (striving to maximize the value of your project to the service recipients/community)	I do service because I care. I understand that the mentees are not from a rich family. Therefore, they may have less opportunity to use computers and have limited computer skills. Thus, I tried my best to teach them how to use software like Microsoft Word, so that they will not be less competitive than their classmates...	I think I have to learn to take the initiative to serve the community. Before taking part in this project, I have limited understanding about the partner organizations. Since engaging in the project, I have realized that I should join more voluntary services organized by different non-governmental organizations, in order to give a helping hand to the community

Further comments:

After engaging in this service leadership project, I learnt to be more mature. When the mentees relied on me, I felt like I was their elder sister. Also, I like the process of building trusting and close relationships with the mentees. It was so magical and I enjoyed it a lot. I hope that I will have a long-lasting relationship with my mentee

in which the middle column exemplifies the consciously competent usage of service leadership attributes (Robinson 1974), while the right-hand column illustrates some perceived areas of conscious learning need (Wilhelm 2011).

A second template provides the format for collectively written team-review reports, as illustrated in Table 2. A third template (not illustrated here) guides students' peer-review reports about their teammates' contributions. Blank templates are available from the authors on request. Besides guiding students in meeting some coursework requirements and providing data for formative evaluation, we also regard the templates as vehicles to help students plan their further development of service leadership attributes.

The illustrations in Tables 1 and 2 feature students from the *Service Leadership* course, whose projects supported a Hong Kong-wide interagency initiative, which has aimed to bridge the "digital divide" for primary school children from poor families. This initiative has been driven by an IT-oriented social enterprise and has been supported by other social enterprises, charities, universities, and schools. In autumn 2014, students from the *Service Leadership* course formed six teams to serve as mentors to children from a nearby housing estate. In addition to the standard preparation, they received training in mentorship and programming skills and an orientation about the needs of children from deprived backgrounds. Over a 6-week period, each team designed and delivered four 90-min training sessions for the mentees on information literacy skills, including how to develop e-portfolios. They also collaborated in arranging a joyful closing ceremony at the university, aimed at inspiring the mentees to strive for educational achievement.

Table 2 Extracts from an interim team-review report from one of the teams on the *Service Leadership* course

Indicate to what extent the following statements describe your team as a whole	Always	Often	Sometimes	Rarely	Never	Illustrations (areas of achievement/for improvement)
1. Our team has realistic goals	✓					*List all of your team's major goals*
						Have a good relationship with the kids
						Introduce various types of use of the Internet to kids
						Facilitate the kids to have a better understanding of themselves and develop an e-portfolio for future use
						Everyone contributes his/her own part and is a good team player
						Have good time management
8. Our team works cooperatively toward its goals.	✓					*Provide some examples of how the team works together to review its progress toward its goals*
						We have set regular dates at the very beginning to ensure all members can attend the meeting. We do evaluation about the learning and performance of students and our work. Sometimes, we ask the kids opinions about the workshop and try to modify it for next time. This helps to fulfill their learning needs. We use Google Drive to share documents so everyone knows about our progress. We monitor each other and have a better time management system

(continued)

Table 2 (continued)

Indicate to what extent the following statements describe your team as a whole	Always	Often	Sometimes	Rarely	Never	Illustrations (areas of achievement/for improvement)
10. Our team seeks for excellence and continuous improvement	✓					*Provide vivid illustrations*
						We have a meeting after each session with the kids and evaluate our preparation work and performance. We look for both things done well and things done badly. We keep the good things and discuss how to improve the bad things. We try our approaches and will review their effectiveness at the next meeting. We would also try to understand what the other groups are doing and take up their good points
11. Our team strives to make a difference to the community through this project		✓				*Provide vivid illustrations*
						We aim to equip the children with various uses of the Internet. By doing that, we hope that they will use the Internet widely to learn something and get themselves ready for the future challenges. We hope that after the four workshops, they can continue to explore the world curiously with the assistance of the Internet

Learning from this team-review exercise:

It is a good opportunity for us to review our team. We have identified some things that we are doing well and should be continued. We need to spend some more time building closer relationships with each other. Reviewing the different aspects has helped us to be more organized, set goals, and identify improvements

Formative Evaluation Studies of the Project Experience

Based on our analysis of data from students via individual and focus group interviews and written self-reflection, team-review, and peer-review reports and from some PORs via interviews, we developed an eight-facet model of how the project experience can encourage and empower students to practice as service leaders (see Fig. 4). The model is part of a bigger "road map" (Snell et al. 2014).

First, a legitimate role in providing services aimed at meeting real needs motivates and empowers students to practice service leadership. In order to be meaningful, this role requires that the project is perceived by students and the POR as addressing a genuine problem or need for the partner organization and that it is feasible to make a meaningful contribution toward solving the problem or meeting the need within the one-semester duration of the project.

Second, the project should be relevant to the associated course. Unless the students perceive significant alignment between their project activities and the curriculum of the course within which the project is embedded, they are likely to feel overburdened and will lack sufficient energy for the project.

Some key mediating factors ensue. The third factor in the model is POR commitment and support, based on the belief that the students will be able to make a positive contribution to the partner organization's mission. Fourth is the students' commitment and willingness to take the initiative. These two factors appear to be crucial inputs to the fifth factor, which is constructive student-POR learning relationships, involving mutual trust, open dialogue, and two-way formative feedback.

Students' commitment and willingness to take the initiative foster the development of performance norms within the project team that support distributed

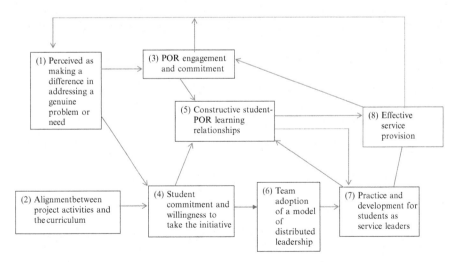

Fig. 4 Facets of the service-learning context and experience that encourage and empower students to practice as service leaders

leadership, with every member sharing responsibility for monitoring and ensuring prompt and effective project progress. In successful projects, these factors fuel and feed upon one another, enabling and empowering the students to practice as service leaders while also supporting effective service provision. Effective service provision by the students encourages enthusiastic POR engagement and increases inter-organizational confidence and trust between the university and the partner organization, yielding more service leadership opportunities for future students.

Practicing service leadership through project work for NGOs and social enterprises appears to have had a transformational impact on some students, who are contemplating future careers as social entrepreneurs or managers within social enterprises or are envisaging other contributions, such as volunteering to help people in need, as expressed by the student in the "civic engagement" row of Table 1 above.

Extracurricular Service Leadership Practicums

Under the service leadership initiative, the OSL has used its external network to arrange some extra-curricular (non-credit-bearing) service leadership practicums for selected students. In the summers of 2013 and 2014, a total of 28 students were placed full time with 13 host organizations, mainly NGOs, social enterprises, or government agencies. Two private firms also participated. Besides the opportunity to practice and benefit from the application of service leadership attributes, a further incentive for the students and partner organizations was that the university paid each student a small stipend. We conducted formative evaluation studies, based on students' and PORs' experiences and perceptions of the practicums, and identified key issues that we shall mention as we explain the associated infrastructure next.

Practicum Infrastructure

The practicum infrastructure comprised the following elements: student and partner organization selection and matching processes, appropriate "mini-missions," length of the practicum period, the preparatory workshop, the self-reflection template, plenary review meetings, and coaching by PORs and/or placement supervisors.

Selecting and Matching Students and Partner Organizations

We adopted a systematic screening and selection process. Key criteria were satisfactory prior service-learning experience and apparent readiness to practice the ten service leadership attributes. Our selection process was far from perfect, and we discovered, in practice, that the students varied considerably in terms of their actual readiness to practice service leadership during the subsequent practicum. Some were willing to work independently, initiate actions and plans, and build collaborative relationships with coworkers, while others were relatively passive.

We selected the partner organizations on the basis of the effectiveness of their prior service-learning partnerships with the university and the apparent availability of realistic and meaningful mini-missions for students to accomplish during the practicum. In addition, students were matched with available practicum places on the basis of their own preferences while taking their undergraduate major into account.

Establishing Appropriate Mini-Missions

Analysis of the summer 2013 placements revealed that some practicums did not provide the necessary opportunities for meaningful project work. In such cases, the PORs mainly allocated traditional "internship" tasks, such as filing, updating mailing and telephone lists, and other clerical activities and small tasks that the students did not find challenging. Some students accepted this, while others asked around for supplementary assignments, which nonetheless constituted insufficient substitutes for an appropriate mini-mission.

Our analysis also indicated that practicum assignments comprising a balance of day-to-day office work plus a challenging mini-mission gave rise to the greatest satisfaction for students and PORs alike. When setting up practicum places for 2014, the field coordinator encouraged PORs to arrange for such a balance. The most fruitful mini-missions involved discrete projects, to which students applied knowledge acquired from their academic programs of study and which allowed them to initiate ideas and use their own judgment while aligning their efforts with the broader mission of their respective host organization.

For example, one student, placed at a charitable NGO, conducted a questionnaire survey of recipients of food donations organized by that NGO about the usefulness of the donations and their impact on the recipients' household expenditure on food. Two students, placed at an NGO, whose mission aims to support the elderly, jointly developed and delivered some training programs for the elderly on using information technologies and produced some accompanying IT-user manuals. One student, who was placed at a social enterprise, shared responsibility with colleagues for selecting the enterprise's products for sales exhibitions at various venues, for setting up the booths, and for selling the products. We noted also that some PORs offered student(s) a choice of mini-missions to be completed within the time frame of the practicum, which appeared to be a good practice.

The Length of the Practicums

In the summer of 2013, the practicums were 6 weeks in duration. On review, it was found that students tended to spend the first fortnight settling in and finding their feet. Accordingly, the practicum length was extended to 8 weeks in the summer of 2014.

Preparatory Workshop and Self-Reflection Templates

The selected practicum students attended a preparatory 3-h workshop. The content resembled that of the preparatory workshops for course-embedded projects. The students were introduced to the ten service leadership attributes and to the template for the self-reflective diaries in which they record their learning experiences and which they were required to submit regularly during the practicum. Again, the template is available from the authors. In 2013, students completed the diaries weekly, but as a result of student feedback, this interval was changed to a fortnightly basis in 2014.

Plenary Review Meetings

The practicum students joined an interim plenary review meeting that we organized half way through the practicum experience in 2013 and 2014. Students expressed that there was an encouraging and motivating atmosphere at the meetings and indicated that they found it useful to share lessons and advice with other practicum students.

There was no final plenary review meeting in 2013, but in the summer of 2014, a final 2-h-long plenary review meeting was held with the practicum students, at which each placement individual or team made a 15-min PowerPoint presentation about their practicum experience. Many brought along resources that they had created as part of their practicum, for example, a poster or handbook. The students appeared to appreciate this opportunity to share and reflect together.

Coaching by PORs or Placement Supervisors

This factor varied considerably between placements. Some PORs or placement supervisors held weekly performance review meetings with practicum student(s), who found that such meetings were a major source of satisfaction in identifying areas of achievement and improvement. However, those students, who did not have similar access to such review meetings, were less sure about their own effectiveness and appeared less confident about what they were achieving.

Discipline-Based Studies of Service Leadership in the Commercial Field

Our team has been studying service leadership, practiced by serving managers, and its impact on service recipient satisfaction. For example, Wong, Liu, and Tjosvold (2014) conducted a quantitative field study of 113 customer service team leaders and 285 team members from consumer electronics retailing firms in Beijing. They found that service leadership by customer service team leaders, manifest as promoting service values, listening to service recipients, and encouraging service improvements, helped team members to become more effective in adopting adaptive approaches to selling their services, resulting in better customer orientation, better performance outcomes, and better recovery of service shortcomings. Further quantitative studies are in progress, with the aim of building a body of evidence about service leadership effectiveness based on systematic model testing.

We are also in the process of designing a qualitative interview-based study of around 16 practicing managers, who are perceived by others as effective service leaders. Our focus in this study will be on the acquisition, use, and further self-improvement of the ten service leadership attributes that we have identified earlier in this chapter.

The purpose of our quantitative research is to strengthen the body of evidence about the need for, and effectiveness of, service leadership as a distinctive alternative to the traditional top-down leadership model, while our qualitative work will seek to provide positive exemplars and role models for encouraging and guiding students to practice service leadership.

References

Chung, P. Y. (2012). *Service reborn: The knowledge, skills and attitudes of service companies.* Hong Kong: Lexingford.

Eyler, J., Giles Jr., G. E., Stentson, C. M., & Gray, C. J. (2001). *At a glance: What we know about the effects of service-learning on college students, faculty, institutions and communities, 1993–2000* (3rd ed.). Nashville: Vanderbilt University.

Falk, A. (2012). Enhancing the team experience in service learning courses. *Journal of Civic Commitment, 18*, 1–16.

HKI-SLAM. (2014). *Essential skills strands.* Retrieved from http://hki-slam.org/index.php?r=article&catid=3&aid=43

Kendrick, J. R. (1996). Outcomes of service-learning in an introductory sociology course. *Michigan Journal of Community Service Learning, 3*(1), 72–81.

Mitton-Kükner, J., Nelson, C., & Desrochers, C. (2010). Narrative inquiry in service learning contexts: Possibilities for learning about diversity in teacher education. *Teaching and Teacher Education, 26*(5), 1162–1169.

Robinson, W. L. (1974). Conscious competency: The mark of a competent instructor. *Personnel Journal, 53*, 538–539.

Snell, R. S., Chan, M. Y. L., Ma, C. H. K., & Chan, C. K. M. (2014). A road map for empowering undergraduates to practice service leadership through service-learning in teams. *Journal of Management Education*, 1–28. doi: 10.1177/1052562914545631.

Waterman, A. (1993). Conducting research on reflective activities in service-learning. In H. C. Silcox (Ed.), *A how-to guide to reflection: Adding cognitive learning to community service programs* (pp. 90–99). Philadelphia: Brighton Press.

Wilhelm, J. D. (2011). Outgrowing the current self: A case for cultivating conscious competence and a sense of possibility. *Voices from the Middle, 18*(4), 52–55.

Wong, A., Liu, Y., & Tjosvold, D. (2014). Service leadership for adaptive selling and effective customer service teams. Accepted for publication, *Industrial Marketing Management.*

Service Leadership Education and Research at The Hong Kong Polytechnic University of Hong Kong (PolyU): An Overview

Daniel T.L. Shek, Rachel C.F. Sun, Lu Yu, Cecilia M.S. Ma, Andrew M.H. Siu, Hildie Leung, and Moon Y.M. Law

Abstract Several credit-bearing subjects have been developed at The Hong Kong Polytechnic University (PolyU), including a 2-credit "service leadership" subject, a 3-credit "service leadership" subject in the Cluster Area Requirement, a free elective 3-credit "service leadership" subject, and a 3-credit "service leadership through serving children and families with special needs" subject. Noncredit-bearing service leadership programs including the Global Youth Leadership Program and Wofoo Leaders' Network have also been designed. Different evaluation mechanisms including objective outcome evaluation, subjective outcome evaluation, process evaluation, and qualitative evaluation were carried out to evaluate the credit-bearing subjects. Results

The service leadership project and the preparation for this paper are financially supported by the Victor and William Fung Foundation.

D.T.L. Shek, Ph.D., S.B.S., J.P (✉) • H. Leung, Ph.D.
Department of Applied Social Sciences, The Hong Kong Polytechnic University, HJ407, Hunghom, Hong Kong, China
e-mail: daniel.shek@polyu.edu.hk

R.C.F. Sun, Ph.D.
Division of Learning, Development and Diversity, Faculty of Education, The University of Hong Kong, C606, Pokfulam Road, Hong Kong

L. Yu, Ph.D.
Department of Applied Social Sciences, The Hong Kong Polytechnic University, HJ430, Hunghom, Kowloon, Hong Kong

C.M.S. Ma, Ph.D.
Department of Applied Social Sciences, The Hong Kong Polytechnic University, HJ431, Hunghom, Kowloon, Hong Kong

A.M.H. Siu, Ph.D.
Department of Applied Social Sciences, The Hong Kong Polytechnic University, QT502, Hunghom, Kowloon, Hong Kong

M.Y.M. Law, MSW
Department of Applied Social Sciences, The Hong Kong Polytechnic University, V1214, Hunghom, Kowloon, Hong Kong

© Springer Science+Business Media Singapore 2015
D.T.L. Shek, P. Chung (eds.), *Promoting Service Leadership Qualities in University Students*, Quality of Life in Asia 6, DOI 10.1007/978-981-287-515-0_8

generally revealed that students showed positive change in service leadership qualities and well-being after they took the subjects and they gave very positive feedback about the subjects. Research and publication programs have also been carried out at PolyU.

Introduction

In terms of economic and social development, the contemporary world is gradually transforming from an industrial society to a post-industrial society. While manufacturing is dominant in the industrial society, service characterizes a post-industrial society or service economy. With particular reference to Hong Kong, service industries contribute to more than 93 % of the gross domestic product. Service economies feature several interesting attributes. First, besides satisfying the service providers' needs such as the maximization of profits, concern about others and the community, such as sustainability, is a value cherished in service economies. Second, besides possessing professional skills, intrapersonal skills (e.g., creativity and emotional intelligence) and interpersonal competencies (e.g., conflict resolution and communication skills) are needed (Shek et al. in press-a). Third, there are specific requirements for effective service leaders. In contrast to industrial economies where directive, autocratic, and top-down leadership attributes are emphasized, service economies focus on collaborative, democratic, and bottom-up involvement in leadership attributes. Hence, the presence of these attributes raises one important question – how can we nurture students to be effective leaders in a service economy?

In addition, the question of nurturing students is important when we realize that there are developmental issues in university students in Hong Kong. Shek (2010) pointed out that mental health problems, overemphasis on examination, lack of training in psychosocial skills, and political apathy were issues commonly observed in university students in Hong Kong. A recent study by Shek and Cheung (2013) reported that there were four developmental concerns in university students. Those included problematic behavioral and lifestyle issues (such as drinking, Internet addiction, Internet pornography consumption, sleeping problems, and dating violence), mental health problems (emotional and internalizing problems), self-determinism and life choice issues (lack of life goals), and egocentrism in students. In sum, taking the demands of the service economy and well-being issues of university students into account, one important question that should be addressed is how we can nurture leadership skills in a service economy to promote the well-being of university students (Shek and Wong 2011).

Development of Credit-Bearing Subjects and Noncredit-Bearing Subjects

To promote service leadership education in Hong Kong, the Victor and William Fung Foundation launched the Fung Service Leadership Initiative in collaboration with the Hong Kong Institute of Service Leadership and Management. In this initiative, eight universities funded by the University Grants Committee (UGC) in Hong Kong were invited to join the project. In each UGC-funded institution, service leadership subjects, curriculum, programs, and education materials were developed. With reference to the Fung Service Leadership Initiative, two main areas of work have been conducted at The Hong Kong Polytechnic University, which include the development of credit-bearing subjects and noncredit-bearing leadership training programs. Besides, basic and evaluation research has been carried out.

Since the inception of the Service Leadership Initiative at The Hong Kong Polytechnic University, several credit-bearing subjects have been developed. Primarily, a 2-credit service leadership subject was developed and offered to the students studying the 3-year undergraduate curriculum (i.e., old curriculum for A-level students). This subject aims to achieve several intended learning outcomes. After the students complete the subject, it is expected that they will be able to (a) gain knowledge and integrate theories and concepts on service leadership, particularly the theoretical bases, core beliefs, and curriculum content strands of the framework proposed by the Hong Kong Institute of Service Leadership and Management, (b) learn service leadership skills and appreciate the attitudes and values underlying the service leadership curriculum, and (c) understand the role of service leadership in the well-being of oneself and others, including one's personal development and the wellness of other people and the society (particularly the connection between learning in the subject and one's own life). Details of this subject can be seen in Shek et al. (2013b). This subject was offered to three batches of students in the 2012/2013 and 2013/2014 academic years.

Modeled after the 2-credit subject, another 3-credit service learning subject entitled "Service Leadership" in the Cluster Area Requirement has been developed for students of the 4-year program (i.e., the new 4-year curriculum for graduates of the Diploma of Secondary Education Examination). The subject attempts to help students learn the basic models of leadership with reference to the service sector; understand the basic leadership attributes intrinsic to effective service leaders including leadership competences, moral character, and caring disposition; reflect on their own service leadership qualities (leadership competences, moral character, and caring disposition); and learn to develop and apply the basic qualities of an effective service leader. After taking this subject, students are expected to understand the contemporary models of leadership with reference to the service sector, including their assertions, strengths, and weaknesses, demonstrate understanding of the basic leadership attributes intrinsic to effective service leaders, reflect upon the need for developing the qualities of effective service leaders and their own leadership qualities, and appreciate the potential application of knowledge on effective service leadership gained in this subject to themselves. To enhance the English proficiency of students, this study also includes a component on English reading and English writing requirement. The lecture content of this subject can be seen in Appendix 1.

Based on the above subject, a free elective 3-credit service leadership subject was developed for students studying in the 4-year programs. The subject is offered by the Department of Applied Social Sciences. This free elective subject includes an additional component on the critical appraisal of the service leadership model proposed by the Hong Kong Institute of Service Leadership and Management and other major leadership models. Essentially, additional topics on the strengths and weaknesses of different leadership models with reference to the service leadership model are discussed.

In addition to the above credit-bearing subjects, which are "classroom-based" subjects, a service learning subject on service leadership utilizing both classroom and outside classroom teaching and learning strategies has been developed. In the subject entitled "Service Leadership through Serving Children and Families with Special Needs," the subject is designed to enable students to know the core attributes of service leaders, apply the service leadership concepts and skills through the engagement of community-based service activities, develop self-awareness of sharing and empathy with others and the community, and reflect on their service leadership qualities, particularly intrapersonal and interpersonal competencies. Regarding the learning outcomes of the subject, it is expected that students will be able to achieve the following outcomes: addressing the needs of the service recipients through service delivery, linking the service experiences with course materials, respecting people with different backgrounds, integrating service leadership knowledge and service project, demonstrating empathy and care, applying the knowledge and skills in service project setting, reflecting on their service leadership qualities through service learning, and working effectively with different parties. To date, several service sites have been employed in the subject. Those include special schools admitting boys with behavioral and emotional problems (Society of Boys' Centres), a nongovernmental organization providing service for preschool children with developmental disorders and mental retardation (Heep Hong Society), a drug rehabilitation agency (Christian Zheng Sheng College), and schools admitting students with social and economic deprivation (schools in Project WeCan). The course content and teaching methods for this subject can be seen in Appendix 2 and Appendix 3, respectively.

Besides credit-bearing subjects, noncredit-bearing service leadership programs have also been designed. A modified version of the service leadership subject (4.5 days) was offered to students joining the Global Leadership Program jointly organized by The Hong Kong Polytechnic University and Peking University in Beijing in July 2013. The curriculum can be seen in Appendix 4. Several service leadership training workshops have been developed and offered to members of Wofoo Leaders' Network.

Research on Service Leadership

Evaluation research is a hallmark of the Fung Service Leadership Initiative at The Hong Kong Polytechnic University. In the credit-bearing subjects and noncredit-bearing programs, systematic evaluation mechanisms including objective outcome evaluation, subjective outcome evaluation, process evaluation, and/or qualitative evaluation were carried out where appropriate.

Objective Outcome Evaluation

For objective outcome evaluation, an assessment tool was used to understand the change in the students by collecting data at the beginning and at the end of the subject. This objective assessment tool is composed of several parts. In the first part, 31 modified items from the Chinese Positive Youth Development Scale (CPYDS) were selected. Positive youth development attributes in the areas of social competence, emotional competence, cognitive competence, behavioral competence, moral competence, self-determination, clear and positive identity, belief in the future, spirituality, and resilience were included. Since previous studies showed that there were four higher-order factors in the items of the CPYDS, pretest and posttest scores were tested on those measures. Those higher-order factors included cognitive-behavioral competencies, positive identity, general positive youth development qualities, and positive youth development total score. Besides positive youth development attributes, the second part of the scale includes the 5-item Satisfaction with Life Scale. Basically, the items assess the subjective evaluation of one's satisfaction with life. In the third part of the study, based on the service leadership model proposed by the Hong Kong Institute of Service Leadership and Management, items on self-leadership, caring disposition, and character strengths were developed and beliefs of service leadership were also assessed.

Objective outcome evaluation was carried out in several credit-bearing subjects. For example, pretest and posttest data were collected from 60 students in the 2012/ 2013 academic year using measures of positive youth development, life satisfaction, and service leadership qualities (Shek et al. 2014d). Results showed that students showed positive changes after taking these subjects in the areas of behavioral competence, moral competence, character strengths, general positive youth development qualities, and overall service leadership qualities. In the study of the Global Youth Leadership, findings similarly showed that students had changed from baseline to posttest and the changes persisted until the posttest (12 days after posttest 1).

Subjective Outcome Evaluation

As far as subjective outcome evaluation is concerned, subjective views of the students on the subject, instructor, and benefits of the subject are assessed by a validated measure of subjective outcome evaluation at the end of the course. The scale is composed of several parts. Part 1 includes 10 items which are concerned with satisfaction with the course content (arrangement of the course content, curriculum objectives and design, classroom atmosphere, peer interaction, and student participation). Part 2 includes 10 items related to the perceptions of the lecturers (professional attitude, teaching skills, involvement, and interaction). Part 3 includes 18 items assessing the benefits of the course (e.g., promotion of critical thinking, intrapersonal competencies, overall personal development, and realization of intended learning outcomes). In the next two parts, the participants are invited to indicate whether they would recommend the subject to other people and whether they would take the subject again. Finally, four open-ended questions regarding the participants' perceptions of the positive and negative aspects of the subject are asked.

Shek et al. (2014a) showed that students generally displayed positive perceptions of the subject content and teachers, and most of them regarded the subject as being beneficial to the development of their service leadership qualities. While the three dimensions of subjective outcome were significantly correlated, perceived program qualities but not perceived instructor qualities predicted perceived effectiveness of the program.

Process Evaluation

Process evaluation examines the program implementation quality as well as the degree of adherence to the program content. In the study by Shek et al. (2014b), a process evaluation was carried out for ten lectures, with each lecture being observed by two independent observers who were registered social workers. Inter-rater reliability across the two observers was high, suggesting the observations were reliable. Results showed that program adherence was high in these lectures (mean = 97.7 %) and ratings on the implementation quality of the subject were also high. Some of the qualities of program implementation were significant predictors of the overall quality and success of the program.

Qualitative Evaluation

Concerning qualitative evaluation, students are invited to give some qualitative comments on the subject by using some "descriptors" and "metaphors." Through these qualitative materials, we will know more about the subjective and inner views of the students (Shek et al. 2014c).

For the qualitative evaluation component, students were invited to participate in a qualitative study where they used three descriptors and a metaphor to describe their experiences about the subject. For example, based on the reflections of 50 students, results showed that 96.1 % of the descriptors and 90 % of the metaphors used by the students were positive (Shek et al. 2014c). For example, a student remarked, "even if we don't have vitamin pills, we still can live. But with this pill, we will be better. Just like this course, after I studied this course, I strengthened my own competence."

Besides, Shek et al. (in press-b) conducted two focus groups to understand the views and experiences of students taking the 2-credit service leadership subject.

This qualitative study showed that students generally had positive views of the subject, instructor, and benefits of the subject. Some translated narratives are as follows:

- "In ordinary courses—no matter General Education or other pre-assigned subjects, we just gained some knowledge after learning, whereas the present subject not only offers knowledge, but also helps to enhance our personal qualities... In my view, it doesn't matter whether you remember many models. The most important point is that you really care and maintain good relationships with others after taking this course. Hence, it is very special to me, which I think is a mind-oriented course."
- "University students today are quite egocentric, so I think this course can teach them that you are not the only person living in the society, so you need to be empathetic to others. Only through collaborative efforts... can the contribution to the society be maximized."

For the noncredit-bearing service leadership training programs, evaluation based on the subjective outcome evaluation approach similarly revealed that the participants had very positive perceptions of the training programs.

Research on Service Leadership

Besides evaluation research, several research initiatives have been carried out. First, a scale assessing service leadership knowledge and qualities has been developed to assess changes in the students taking this subject (Shek et al. 2014d). Second, a research project on the relevance of Confucian virtues to service leadership was carried out. An assessment instrument on Confucian virtues has been developed, and data have been collected from more than 1,000 students (Shek et al. 2013a). Third, besides the English version of the curriculum, a Chinese version of the curriculum has also been developed. Besides, some Chinese papers were also published.

Fourth, three papers on the key concepts and curriculum materials were presented in the Third International Congress on Pediatric Chronic Diseases, Disability and Human Development held on December 2–5, 2012, in Jerusalem, Israel. Fifth, a Service Leadership Roundtable was held on March 22, 2013, at The Hong Kong Polytechnic University, Hong Kong. In that roundtable, our research team gave multiple presentations about service leadership education and curriculum development at PolyU. Sixth, two papers were presented in the International Conference on Service Leadership Education for University Students: Experience in Hong Kong held on May 14–15, 2014 at The Hong Kong Polytechnic University. In the first paper, credit-bearing subjects and noncredit-bearing programs were described. In the second paper, evaluation studies were covered. The related references can be seen in Appendix 5.

Finally, two special issues of the *International Journal on Disability and Human Development* documenting the curriculum of the service leadership model, including the distinction between manufacturing and service economies and comparison between the service leadership model and existing major leadership models in the scientific literature, are in press. The papers in the two special issues can be seen in Appendix 5.

In conclusion, with the financial support of the Victor and William Fung Foundation, the service leadership program at The Hong Kong Polytechnic University has been gradually established. Several credit-bearing and noncredit-bearing subjects have been developed and implemented; evaluation findings are generally favorable suggesting that the service leadership attributes and well-being of the students were promoted after joining the subject or the program. As far as research is concerned, besides evaluation research, several projects on assessment and book projects have been developed. Looking into the future, it is suggested that more basic research on service leadership and evaluation of the developed education programs should continue.

Appendices

Appendix 1: Course content of the 3-credit "Service Leadership" subject

Topic	Subject content
1.	*Introduction*
	Definitions and conceptions of service leadership; nature and rationales of service leadership; service sector and service leadership; relevance of service leadership to university students and graduates in Hong Kong; differences between manufacturing economy and service economy; desired leadership attributes under manufacturing and service economies; three realms of service leadership
	Required readings:
	Yammarino, F. (2013). Leadership: Past, present, and future. *Journal of Leadership & Organizational Studies, 20*(2), 149–155.
	Shek, D. T. L., Chung, P. P. Y., Leung, H. (in press). Manufacturing economy versus service economy: Implications for service leadership. *International Journal of Disability and Human Development.*
2.	*History and contemporary leadership models*
	Review of contemporary models of leadership: leadership in a historical perspective; contemporary models of leadership, including top-down and bottom-up leadership models, charismatic leadership, authentic leadership, spiritual leadership, transformational leadership, and servant leadership; strengths and limitations of existing leadership models
	Required reading:
	Avolio, B. J., Walumbwa, F. O., & Weber, T. J. (2009). Leadership: Current theories, research, and future directions. *Annual Review of Psychology, 60*, 421–449.

(continued)

Topic	Subject content
3.	*Core beliefs and components*
	Seven core beliefs about service leadership: service leadership as a function of competences of leadership, moral character and care [E (effective service leadership) $= MC^2$ (moral character $\times$ competence $\times$ care)], ultimate goals of service leadership education, essential knowledge, skills, attitudes, and value strands
	Required reading:
	Sendjaya, S., & Sarros, J. C. (2002). Servant leadership: Its origin, development, and application in organizations. *Journal of Leadership & Organizational Studies, 9*(2), 57–64.
4.	*Basic leadership competences: Intrapersonal competences*
	IQ (task-relevant knowledge, problem solving, and decision making); EQ (understanding and managing emotion effectively); AQ (adversity quotient); SQ (spiritual quotient)
	Required readings:
	Dulewicz, C., Young, M., & Dulewicz, V. (2005). The relevance of emotional intelligence for leadership performance. *Journal of General Management, 30*(3), 71–86.
	Emmons, R. A. (2000). Is spirituality and intelligence? Motivation, cognition, and the psychology of ultimate concern. *International Journal for the Psychology of Religion,* 10(1), 3–26.
5.	*Basic leadership competences: interpersonal competences*
	Communication skills; positive social relationship building; conflict resolution
	Required readings:
	Guo, K. L., & Anderson, D. (2005). The new health care paradigm: Roles and competencies of leaders in the service line management approach. *International Journal of Health Care Quality Assurance incorporating Leadership in Health Services, 18*(6–7), 12–20.
	Ma, H. K. (2006). Social competence as a positive youth development construct: Conceptual bases and implications for curriculum development. *International Journal of Adolescent Medicine and Health, 18*(3), 379–385.
6.	*Character strengths and service leadership*
	The server is the service; moral character; basic character strengths (love of learning, honesty, courage, perseverance, humility, and gratitude)
	Required reading:
	Peterson, C., & Park, N. (2006). Character strengths in organizations. *Journal of Organizational Behavior, 27,* 1149–1154.
7.	*Character strengths in Chinese philosophies*
	Relevance of Confucian virtues to service leadership: integrity (lian), shame (chi), loyalty (zhong), filial piety (xiao), benevolence (ren), affection (ai), trustworthiness (xin), righteousness (yi), propriety (li), wisdom (zhi), harmony (he), and peace (ping)
	Required readings:
	Shek, D. T. L., Yu, L., & Fu, X. (2013). Confucian virtues and Chinese adolescent development: A conceptual review. *International Journal of Adolescent Medicine and Health,* 25(4), 335–344. doi: 10.1515/ijamh-2013-0031.
	Zhang, G., & Veenhoven, R. (2008). Ancient Chinese philosophical advice: Can it help us find happiness today? *Journal of Happiness Studies, 9*(3), 425–443.

(continued)

Topic	Subject content
8.	*Caring disposition and service leadership*
	Universal dimensions of social cognition (warmth and competence); love; servant leadership
	Required readings:
	Fiske, S. T., Cuddy, A. J. C., & Glick, P. (2007). Universal dimensions of social cognition: Warmth and competence. *Trends In Cognitive Sciences, 11*(2), 77–83.
	Waterman, H. (2011). Principles of 'servant leadership' and how they can enhance practice. *Nursing Management, 17*(9), 24–26.
9.	*Factors leading to creation, development and maintenance of positive social relationship*
	Trust, fairness, respect, care, behavioral consistency, and loyalty
	Required reading:
	Wieselquist, J., Rusbult, C. E., Foster, C. A., & Agnew, C. R. (1999). Commitment, pro-relationship behavior, and trust in close relationships. *Journal of Personality and Social Psychology, 77*(5), 942–966.
10.	*Self-leadership and service leadership*
	Everyone is a leader; optimization of one's operating systems; personal branding; importance of self-monitoring and self-improvement
	Required reading:
	Stewart, G. L., Courtright, S. H., & Manz, C. C. (2011). Self-leadership: A multilevel review. *Journal of Management, 37*, 185–222.
11.	*Developmental assets and service leadership*
	Self-esteem, self-efficacy, purpose in life, and optimism about future
	Required readings:
	Chemers, M. M., Watson, C. B., & May, S. T. (2000). Dispositional affect and leadership effectiveness: A comparison of self-esteem, optimism, and efficacy. *Personality and Social Psychology Bulletin, 26*(3), 267–277.
	Dhiman, S. (2007). Personal mastery: Our quest for self-actualization, meaning, and highest purpose. *Interbeing, 1*(1), 25–35.
12.	*Review of effective service leadership qualities*
	Comparisons with the existing models of leadership; critical evaluation of the HKI-SLAM model; potential application of service leadership knowledge to oneself: possibilities and difficulties
	Required reading:
	Shek, D. T. L., Chung, P. P. Y., & Leung, H. (in press). How unique is the service leadership model? A comparison with contemporary leadership approaches. *International Journal on Disability and Human Development.*

Appendix 2: Course content of the 3-credit "Service Leadership through Serving Children and Families with Special needs" subject

Topic	Subject content
1.	Concept of service learning
	Principles, concepts, and myths of service learning
	Benefits of service learning to students, the university, and the community
	Ethical issues in service learning
	Proper attitudes and behaviors in service delivery
	Reflection as a tool for learning
2.	Subject-specific concepts, issues, and skills
	Nature and rationales of service leadership
	Core beliefs about service leadership
	Major components of service leadership (i.e., leadership competencies, moral character, and care: the SLAM model)
	Three realms of leadership (i.e., self-leadership, team leadership, and service habitats)
	Importance of service leadership in Hong Kong
3.	Project-specific concepts
	Understanding children with special needs
	Application of knowledge obtained in leadership and intrapersonal development subjects (i.e., leadership competencies and interpersonal skills) through service delivery
	Development of service leadership through serving children with special needs and their families
	Collaborative learning and problem-solving in service delivery
	Health, safety, and other issues related to service activities
	Moral and ethical concerns in serving children with special needs

Appendix 3: Teaching/learning methodology of the 3-credit "Service Leadership through Serving Children and Families with Special needs" subject

Topic	Subject content
1.	E-learning module
	Students are required to attend the 10-h e-learning module, which is developed by the Office of Service Learning at PolyU, within the first 4 weeks of the semester
2.	Lecture, seminar, and workshop
	Discipline-specific knowledge and skills, such as concepts and nature of service leadership, the Service Leadership and Management Model (SLAM Model), and positive youth development model, will be delivered through lectures
	Students are asked to complete several assessment tools to raise their awareness of leadership competencies, moral character, and caring disposition
	Project-specific knowledge and skills, such as methods to communicate with service recipients, ways to create a positive and safe learning environment, and generic skills in planning and designing service-learning projects, will be delivered through seminars
	Workshops will be organized by agencies and professionals to guide students for designing service-learning projects
3.	Service learning project
	Students will be divided into small groups with each group comprising students from different faculties, thus pulling together expertise from multidisciplines and enabling the provision of all-rounded service to children, adolescents, and their families in need
	Through collaborative learning, students will be assigned with different roles (e.g., group leader, group coordinator, etc.). They will be asked to rotate roles within the group in order to work together as a team to solve a problem, complete a task, and achieve a common goal
	Collaborative skills and leadership competencies (e.g., caring, group accountability) will be assessed through peer assessment and ongoing reflective journals
	Teachers will be present in order to provide a safe and orderly learning environment throughout the service delivery process
4.	Ongoing reflective journals
	Students will be asked to reflect and analyze their service learning experience (e.g., examine the meaning and impact of their services personally and academically, evaluate the effectiveness of cooperative learning activities, review their strengths and weaknesses based on the results of the self-assessment tools, leadership qualities demonstrated in teamwork and service provision, the relationship between their experience and learning objectives and concepts covered in class, their role in the society) by writing reflective journals

Appendix 4: Content of the 4.5 day (30-h) intensive course on service leadership

- *Lecture one:* Service leadership characteristics and attributes of effective service leadership
- *Lecture two:* Introduction of the service leadership model and the core beliefs of service leadership (model proposed by the Hong Kong Institute of Service Leadership and Management): history, background, and emphases of the service leadership model
- *Lecture three:* Intrapersonal competencies and service leadership: competencies within effective service leaders, intelligence quotient (IQ), emotional quotient (EQ), spiritual quotient (SQ), and adversity quotient (AQ)
- *Lecture four:* Moral character as an attribute of effective leader; character strengths in Chinese philosophies; character strengths and service leadership
- *Lecture five:* Factors leading to creation, development, and maintenance of positive social relationship; role of interpersonal competencies (e.g., communication, conflict resolution skills) in effective service leadership
- *Lecture six:* Caring for others and service leadership; becoming a caring service leader
- *Lecture seven:* Developmental assets and service leadership; positive and healthy identity; different types of developmental assets
- *Lecture eight:* Leaders as mentors; mentorship role of an effective service leader; teacher-student relationship in leadership
- *Lecture nine:* Self-leadership and service leadership; leading oneself before leading others; revisit of service leadership curriculum and its core beliefs

Appendix 5: Publications arising from the Fung Service Leadership Initiative at The Hong Kong Polytechnic University

Papers Presented at the International Conference on Service Leadership Education for University Students: Experience in Hong Kong, Held on May 14–15, 2014 at The Hong Kong Polytechnic University, Hong Kong

- Shek, D. T. L., Sun, R. C. F., Yu, L., Ma, C. M. S., Siu, A. M. H., Lin, L., Leung, H., & Law, M. Y. M. (2014, May 14–15). *Service leadership education and research at The Hong Kong Polytechnic University: An overview.* Paper presented at the international conference on service leadership education for university students: Experience in Hong Kong, Hong Kong.
- Shek, D. T. L., Lin, L., Leung, H., Law, M. Y. M., & Li, X. (2014, May 14–15). *Evaluation of service leadership programs using multiple evaluation methods.* Paper presented at the international conference on service leadership education for university students: Experience in Hong Kong, Hong Kong.

Papers Presented at the Third International Congress on Paediatric Chronic Diseases, Disability and Human Development Held on December 2–5, 2012 at Jerusalem, Israel

- Ma, C. M. S., Shek, D. T. L., & Liu, T. T. (2012, December 2–5). *Caring dispositions and positive youth development: Relevance to service leadership in university students.* Paper presented at the Third International Congress on Paediatric Chronic Diseases, Disability and Human Development, Jerusalem, Israel organized by Cincinnati Children's Hospital Medical Centre, Hadassah-Hebrew University Medical Centre, and National Institute of Child Health and Human Development, Israel.
- Shek, D. T. L., Sun, R. C. F., Yu, L., Ma, C. M. S., & Siu, A. M. H. (2012, December 2–5). *Promotion of holistic development of university students in Hong Kong: Development of a service leadership course.* Paper presented at the third international congress on paediatric chronic diseases, disability and human development, Jerusalem, Israel organized by Cincinnati Children's Hospital Medical Centre, Hadassah-Hebrew University Medical Centre, and National Institute of Child Health and Human Development, Israel.
- Yu, L., & Shek, D. T. L. (2012, December 2–5). *Confucian virtues and positive youth development: Insights for service leadership.* Paper presented at the third international congress on paediatric chronic diseases, disability and human development, Jerusalem, Israel organized by Cincinnati Children's Hospital Medical Centre, Hadassah-Hebrew University Medical Centre, and National Institute of Child Health and Human Development, Israel.

Papers Presented at the Service Leadership Roundtable Held on March 22, 2013 at The Hong Kong Polytechnic University, Hong Kong

- Law, M. Y. M., & Shek, D. T. L. (2013, March 22). *Development of a non-credit-bearing service leadership program for university students in Hong Kong: Some initial experience.* Paper presented at the service leadership roundtable, The Hong Kong Polytechnic University, Hong Kong.
- Leung, H., & Shek, D. T. L. (2013, March 22). *The development of service leadership models and its implications for university education in Hong Kong.* Paper presented at the service leadership roundtable, The Hong Kong Polytechnic University, Hong Kong.
- Lin, L., & Shek, D. T. L. (2013, March 22). *A good service leader, a good mentor.* Paper presented at the service leadership roundtable, The Hong Kong Polytechnic University, Hong Kong.
- Liu, T. T., & Shek, D. T. L. (2013, March 22). *Developmental assets of service leaders.* Paper presented at the service leadership roundtable, The Hong Kong Polytechnic University, Hong Kong.

- Ma, C. M. S., & Shek, D. T. L. (2013, March 22). *Caring disposition and service leadership among Hong Kong university students.* Paper presented at the service leadership roundtable, The Hong Kong Polytechnic University, Hong Kong.
- Munley, A. (2013, March 22). *What can we learn from the service leadership literature?* Keynote speech presented at the service leadership roundtable, The Hong Kong Polytechnic University, Hong Kong.
- Shek, D. T. L., Sun, R. C. F., & Siu, A. M. H. (2013, March 22). *Helping university students to thrive: The service leadership initiative at The Hong Kong Polytechnic University.* Keynote speech presented at the service leadership roundtable, The Hong Kong Polytechnic University, Hong Kong.
- Yu, L., & Shek, D. T. L. (2013, March 22). *Character strengths in Chinese philosophies: Confucian virtues and service leadership.* Paper presented at the service leadership roundtable, The Hong Kong Polytechnic University, Hong Kong.

Journal Articles

- Shek, D. T. L., Law, M. Y. M., & Liu, T. T. (in press). Focus group evaluation of a service leadership subject in Hong Kong. *International Journal on Disability and Human Development.*
- Shek, D. T. L., Lin, L., Liu, T. T., & Law, M. Y. M. (2014a). Process evaluation of a pilot subject on service leadership for university students in Hong Kong. *International Journal on Disability and Human Development, 13*(4), 531–540. doi 10.1515/ijdhd-2014-0351.
- Shek, D. T. L., Lin, L., & Liu, T. T. (2014). Service leadership education for university students in Hong Kong: Subjective outcome evaluation. *International Journal on Disability and Human Development, 13*(4), 513–521. doi: 10.1515/ ijdhd-2014-0349.
- Shek, D. T. L., Lin, L., Liu, T. T., & Law, M. Y. M. (2014b). Service leadership education for university students in Hong Kong: Qualitative evaluation. *International Journal on Disability and Human Development, 13*(4), 523–529. doi: 10.1515/ijdhd-2014-0350.
- Shek, D. T. L., Yu, L., & Fu, X. (2013). Confucian virtues and Chinese adolescent development: A conceptual review. *International Journal of Adolescent Medicine and Health, 25*(4), 335–344. doi: 10.1515/ijamh-2013-0031.
- Shek, D. T. L., Yu, L., & Ma, C. M. S. (2014). The students were happy but did they change positively? Yes, they did. *International Journal on Disability and Human Development, 13*(4), 505–511. doi: 10.1515/ijdhd-2014-0348.
- Shek, D. T. L., Yu, L., Ma, C. M. S., Sun, R. C. F., & Liu, T. T. (2013). Development of a credit-bearing service leadership subject for university students in Hong Kong. *International Journal of Adolescent Medicine and Health, 25*(4), 353–361. doi: 10.1515/ijamh-2013-0033.

Special Issues on Service Leadership Articles (Editors: Daniel T. L. Shek, Chung Po and Lu Yu)

- Shek, D. T. L., Chung, P. P. Y., & Leung, H. (in press-a). How unique is the service leadership model? A comparison with contemporary leadership approaches. *International Journal on Disability and Human Development*.
- Shek, D. T. L., Chung, P. P. Y., & Leung, H. (in press-b). Manufacturing economy versus service economy: Implications for service leadership. *International Journal on Disability and Human Development*.
- Shek, D. T. L., Chung, P. P. Y., Yu, L., & Merrick, J. (in press). Editorial: Service leadership education for university students: Experience of Hong Kong. *International Journal on Disability and Human Development*.
- Shek, D. T. L., Law, M. Y. M., & Liu, T. T. (in press). Focus group evaluation of a service leadership subject in Hong Kong. *International Journal on Disability and Human Development*.
- Shek, D. T. L., & Li, X. (in press-a). Nurturing students to be caring service leaders. *International Journal on Disability and Human Development*.
- Shek, D. T. L., & Li, X. (in press-b). The role of caring disposition in service leadership. *International Journal on Disability and Human Development*.
- Shek, D. T. L., & Lin, L. (in press-a). Core beliefs in the service leadership model proposed by the Hong Kong Institute of Service Leadership and Management. *International Journal on Disability and Human Development*.
- Shek, D. T. L., & Lin, L. (in press-b). Factors leading to creation, development and maintenance of positive social relationship. *International Journal on Disability and Human Development*.
- Shek, D. T. L, & Lin, L. (in press-c). Intrapersonal competences and service leadership. *International Journal on Disability and Human Development*.
- Shek, D. T. L., & Lin, L. (in press-d). Leadership and mentorship – service leaders as mentors of the followers. *International Journal on Disability and Human Development*.
- Shek, D. T. L., & Lin, L. (in press-e). Nurturing university students to be social entrepreneurs: Relevance of service leadership education. *International Journal on Disability and Human Development*.
- Shek, D. T. L., Ma, C. M. S., & Liu, T. T. (in press). Adolescent developmental assets and service leadership. *International Journal on Disability and Human Development*.
- Shek, D. T. L., Ma, C. M. S., Liu, T. T., & Siu, A. M. H. (in press). The role of self-leadership in service leadership. *International Journal on Disability and Human Development*.
- Shek, D. T. L., Sun, R. C. F., & Liu, T. T. (in press-a). Character strengths in Chinese philosophies: Relevance to service leadership. *International Journal on Disability and Human Development*.

- Shek, D. T. L., Sun, R. C. F., & Liu, T. T. (in press-b). Evolution and realms of service leadership and leadership models. *International Journal on Disability and Human Development.*
- Shek, D. T. L., & Yu, L. (in press). Character strengths and service leadership. *International Journal on Disability and Human Development.*
- Shek, D. T. L., Yu, L., & Siu, A. M. H. (in press). Interpersonal competence and service leadership. *International Journal on Disability and Human Development.*

References

Shek, D. T. L. (2010). Nurturing holistic development of university students in Hong Kong: Where are we and where should we go? *The Scientific World Journal, 10,* 563–575.

Shek, D. T. L., & Cheung, B. P. M. (2013). Developmental issues of university students in Hong Kong. *International Journal of Adolescent Medicine and Health, 25*(4), 345–351.

Shek, D. T. L., & Wong, K. K. (2011). Do adolescent developmental issues disappear overnight? Reflections about holistic development in university students. *The Scientific World Journal, 11,* 353–361.

Shek, D. T. L., Yu, L., & Fu, X. (2013a). Confucian virtues and Chinese adolescent development: A conceptual review. *International Journal of Adolescent Medicine and Health, 25*(4), 335–344. doi: 10.1515/ijamh-2013-0031.

Shek, D. T. L., Yu, L., Ma, C. M. S., Sun, R. C. F., & Liu, T. T. (2013b). Development of a credit-bearing service leadership subject for university students in Hong Kong. *International Journal of Adolescent Medicine and Health, 25*(4), 353–361.

Shek, D. T. L., Lin, L., & Liu, T. T. (2014a). Service leadership education for university students in Hong Kong: Subjective outcome evaluation. *International Journal on Disability and Human Development, 13*(4), 513–521. doi: 10.1515/ijdhd-2014-0349.

Shek, D. T. L., Lin, L., Liu, T. T., & Law, M. Y. M. (2014b). Process evaluation of a pilot subject on service leadership for university students in Hong Kong. *International Journal on Disability and Human Development, 13*(4), 531–540. doi: 10.1515/ijdhd-2014-035.

Shek, D. T. L., Lin, L., Liu, T. T., & Law, M. Y. M. (2014c). Service leadership education for university students in Hong Kong: Qualitative evaluation. *International Journal on Disability and Human Development, 13*(4), 523–529. doi: 10.1515/ijdhd-2014-0350.

Shek, D. T. L., Yu, L., & Ma, C. M. S. (2014d). The students were happy but did they change positively? Yes, they did. *International Journal on Disability and Human Development, 13*(4), 505–511. doi: 10.1515/ijdhd-2014-0348.

Shek, D. T. L., Chung, P. P. Y., & Leung, H. (in press-a). Manufacturing economy versus service economy: Implications for service leadership. *International Journal on Disability and Human Development.*

Shek, D. T. L., Law, M. Y. M., & Liu, T. T. (in press-b). Focus group evaluation of a service leadership subject in Hong Kong. *International Journal on Disability and Human Development.*

Why Is Service Leadership Important in Higher Education?

Catherine Zhou, Ben Y.B. Chan, and Neil C. Mickleborough

Abstract Service leadership is a skill set with which people present a more active and proactive attitude towards study, work, and life. The development and application of service leadership is not restricted by disciplines, space, or time. It is a positive perception that people living in the modern society should possess in order to make them more competitive and serve others more effectively. This study examines the different definitions of service, leadership, servant leadership, service leadership, and service-learning and points out that people should possess service leadership skills no matter what their job is, where they live, or when they are requested to offer service, which strengthens the necessity and importance of service leadership training in higher education.

Introduction

Since the service leadership initiative started, service-learning, service, leadership, and servant leadership have attracted a lot of attention. Education researchers have raised questions such as: Is service leadership a simple combination of service and leadership? What is the difference between service leadership and servant leadership? These questions require us to identify the characteristics of service leadership in order to provide a solid theory foundation for building a service leadership community in Hong Kong. By studying the definitions of these terms through literature review, it is obvious that the development of service leadership is an effective way for students to establish an active and proactive attitude towards their study, future career, and life as a whole, which is not restricted by disciplines, space, or time. Service leadership should be a key professional skill set and be integrated into the curriculum of higher education.

C. Zhou, Ph.D. (✉) • B.Y.B. Chan • N.C. Mickleborough
Center for Engineering Education Innovation, The Hong Kong University of Science and Technology, Clear Water Bay, Kowloon, Hong Kong
e-mail: egcatherine@ust.hk

© Springer Science+Business Media Singapore 2015   135
D.T.L. Shek, P. Chung (eds.), *Promoting Service Leadership Qualities in University Students*, Quality of Life in Asia 6, DOI 10.1007/978-981-287-515-0_9

Service-Learning

In higher education, service-learning is always used for leadership skills development. Three popular service-learning definitions follow:

> Service-learning is a teaching and learning strategy that integrates meaningful community service with instruction and reflection to enrich the learning experience, teach civic responsibility, and strengthen communities. (Groh et al. 2011, p. 400)
>
> Service-learning is a teaching method, which combines community service with academic instruction as it focuses on critical, reflective thinking and civic responsibility. Service-learning programs involve students in organized community service that addresses local needs, while developing their academic skills, sense of civic responsibility and commitment to the community. (Lavery 2008, p. 8)
>
> Service-learning is a teaching pedagogy used in primary and secondary schools, and in universities, to enhance traditional modes of learning . . . . . . Service-learning is a teaching method where classroom learning is deepened and extended through service to others. (Lavery 2009, p. 1)

Obviously, service-learning is an instruction channel through which such skills as leadership can be developed. It emphasizes the combination of classroom learning and commitment to community service and aims at meeting "specific learning goals and community needs" (Lavery 2008). Therefore, leadership skills can be developed through service-learning. However, different forms of leadership require educators and trainers to tailor the training programs so as to achieve different learning outcomes.

Leadership, Servant Leadership, and Service Leadership

Many definitions of leadership have emphasized that leadership is an influence process to achieve a common goal (Avolio et al. 2003; Blanchard 1998; Houghton et al. 2003; Locke 2003; Manning and Curtis 2012). Some literatures also define leadership as "a relationship between those who aspire to lead and those who choose to follow" (Kouzes and Posner 2006, p. 52; Kouzes and Posner 2012, p. 20). Chung (2010) redefines leadership by including "satisfying the needs of self, others, groups, communities, systems, and environments." Leadership has a variety of forms, among which are servant leadership and service leadership. It is important to state that different forms of leadership do not exclude each other but emphasize different aspects.

Servant leadership emphasizes leadership as service and "servant-leader is servant first" (Spears 1998, p. 1). As Manning and Curtis (2012) mention, "servant leadership is a calling to serve" (p. 147). "Servant leaders do not view leadership as a position of power; rather they are coaches, stewards, and facilitators" (Manning & Curtis 2012, p. 148). According to Lavery (2008), the heart of such leadership is the wish to "make sure that other people's highest priority needs are being served" (p. 5). According to Chung (2010), the traditional definition of service is "about delivering high quality, one-size-fits-all service propositions to customers." In Chung (2010) this definition is extended to "improving one's competencies, abilities, and willingness to help satisfy the needs of others." Comparing Chung's definitions of leadership and service, both present an active and proactive attitude that modern society expects from service providers and leaders.

Service leadership is not the simple combination of leadership and service. It has its own unique characteristics, requiring educators and service leadership trainers to tailor service-learning programs to ensure the achievement of learning outcomes. Gronfeldt and Strother (2006) define service leadership as "the culture that empowers the organization to strategize its promises, design its processes, and engage its people in a proactive quest for competitive advantage" (p. 5). Edvinsson (1992) describes service leadership as "a collective leadership mindset" (p. 34) including the thought leader, process leader, and commercial leader. When a person possesses the skills of all the three roles, that person has developed service leadership skills. Different from servant leadership, service leadership emphasizes everybody, everywhere, and every day. It encourages the provision of service to everyone that they come into contact with (Chung 2010). The unique characteristics of service leadership can also be reflected by the fact that it provides personal service according to the needs of each person encountered, which is different from the traditional one-size-fits-all service. More importantly, service leadership requires a person to consistently provide "the highest quality service one can afford" (Chung 2010). These aspects together form the uniqueness of service leadership, which proves that service leadership is not the simple combination of service and leadership but a more active and proactive skill set. This skill set is not restricted by the specialization of whoever is involved, when it happens, or where it happens. Students in engineering, science, social science, and business can all adopt it as part of their professional skill set.

References

Avolio, B. J., Sivasubramaniam, N., Murry, W. D., Jung, D., & Garger, J. W. (2003). Assessing shared leadership: Development and preliminary validation of a team multifactor leadership questionnaire. In C. L. Pearce & J. A. Conger (Eds.), *Shared leadership: Reframing the hows and whys of leadership* (pp. 143–172). Thousand Oaks: Sage Publications.

Blanchard, K. (1998). Servant-leadership revisited. In L. C. Spears (Ed.), *Insights on leadership: Service, stewardship, spirit, and servant-leadership* (pp. 21–28). New York: Wiley.

Chung, P. (2010). *Transformative paradigm shift*. Retrieved from http://hki-slam.org/index.php?r=article&catid=3&aid=34

Edvinsson, L. (1992). Service leadership: Some critical roles. *International Journal of Service Industry Management, 3*(2), 33–36.

Gronfeldt, S., & Strother, J. B. (2006). Introduction. In S. Gronfeldt & J. B. Strother (Eds.), *Service leadership: The quest for competitive advantage* (pp. 5–15). Thousand Oaks: Sage Publications.

Groh, C. J., Stallwood, L. G., & Daniels, J. J. (2011). Service-learning in nursing education: Its impact on leadership and social justice. *Nursing Education Perspectives, 32*(6), 400–405.

Houghton, J. D., Neck, C. P., & Manz, C. C. (2003). Self-leadership and superleadership: The heart and art of creating shared leadership in teams. In C. L. Pearce & J. A. Conger (Eds.), *Shared leadership: Reframing the hows and whys of leadership* (pp. 123–140). Thousand Oaks: Sage Publications.

Kouzes, J. M., & Posner, B. Z. (2006). Leadership is personal. In J. M. Kouzes & B. Z. Posner (Eds.), *A leader's legacy* (pp. 50–55). San Francisco: Wiley.

Kouzes, J. M., & Posner, B. Z. (2012). When leaders are at their best. In J. M. Kouzes & B. Z. Posner (Eds.), *The leadership challenge: How to make extraordinary things happen in organizations* (pp. 9–40). San Francisco: Jossey-Bass.

Lavery, S. D. (2008). Developing student leadership through service-learning. *Journal of Catholic School Studies, 80*(2), 5–12.

Lavery, S. D. (2009). Service-learning: Promoting leadership in young people. *Principal Matters, 80*, 28–30.

Locke, E. A. (2003). Leadership: Starting at the top. In C. L. Pearce & J. A. Conger (Eds.), *Shared leadership: Reframing the hows and whys of leadership* (pp. 271–284). Thousand Oaks: Sage Publications.

Manning, G., & Curtis, K. (2012). *The art of leadership*. New York: McGraw-Hill.

Spears, L. C. (1998). Tracing the growing impact of servant-leadership. In L. C. Spears (Ed.), *Insights on leadership: Service, stewardship, spirit, and servant-leadership* (pp. 1–12). New York: Wiley.

Impacts of Learning Through Experience: An Application of Service Leadership in Whole-Person Development

Susanna Chui, Paula Hodgson, and Alice Wong

Abstract This chapter sheds light on how a leadership general education (GE) course, called "Leadership in Sustainability", which adopted a mixed pedagogy and andragogy approach, succeeded in facilitating students' leadership development. Upon conceptualisation of the course, research was conducted on learning approaches and two areas of knowledge domains—namely, leadership and sustainability. Finally, the course design adopted a mixed learning approach to maximise students' learning experience. "Leadership in Sustainability" was the first GE course in Hong Kong that combined the two knowledge domains of leadership and sustainability in one module. It was launched in September 2013 for a class of 38 students for one semester at Hong Kong Baptist University, which has a long history of providing "whole-person education".

This chapter is divided into four parts. It begins with a literature review, which yielded the course design rationale based on theories of learning approaches and the two knowledge domains. Conceptual propositions based on six areas of the reviewed literature became the principles for designing the course content. Next, descriptions of the course and the different course activities are provided. Following that, the students' evaluations of the course are presented; they reveal how the course affected students' learning in the areas of leadership and sustainability. Finally, the conclusion discusses the lessons learned and the implications for future leadership development education.

Introduction

Underpinning the development of individuals in tertiary education has two main considerations: learning and relationship building within a context in which learners can develop meaningful sense-making. University students who are

S. Chui (✉)
Durham Business School, Doctoral Researcher, Durham University, Durham, UK
e-mail: s.l.m.chui@durham.ac.uk

P. Hodgson • A. Wong
General Education Office, Hong Kong Baptist University, Kowloon, Hong Kong

© Springer Science+Business Media Singapore 2015
D.T.L. Shek, P. Chung (eds.), *Promoting Service Leadership Qualities in University Students*, Quality of Life in Asia 6, DOI 10.1007/978-981-287-515-0_10

entering the adult world need to be given an opportunity to develop the skills and knowledge that will help them pursue lifelong learning. These considerations aim to achieve an important purpose—growth in adulthood through whole-person development of learners. Whether a learner learns by going through an active classroom process of knowledge acquisition or by interacting with other learners to pursue common goals, learning serves a natural part of the learner's impetus to grow, to flourish, and to achieve self-actualisation.

Leadership development is an area of knowledge that cannot be built solely through classroom learning. Leadership in action involves not just personal strength, but also practical intelligence, emotional control, and team cooperation (Day et al. 2004). Leadership development is seen as an important area of whole-person development because, like adult development, it covers the entire lifespan and requires the evolution of cognitive, emotional, and team processes and a variety of practical skills (Day et al. 2009).

Sustainability is a timely topic that affects both daily human life and business operations. In many cities around the world, challenges related to air, water, and environmental quality are posing serious issues for existing and up-and-coming leaders. As this subject is relevant to every individual, it was thought that the integration of sustainability and leadership would create an inspiring course that would allow students to combine knowledge, action, and imagination in pondering their potential roles as change agents to help build a better world in their future careers. Facilitating university students in self- and leadership development directed toward community development was, therefore, the main spirit that guided the design of the course known as "Leadership in Sustainability".

Adult Learning in Tertiary Education

This section begins with a discussion of the difference between pedagogy and andragogy. This exploration paves the way for the explanation of why a mixed approach was adopted for designing the general education (GE) leadership course, "Leadership in Sustainability". In conjunction with the clear objective of nurturing university students to become change agents who demonstrate the pragmatism needed to tackle issues related to sustainability, it was recognised that learners needed to be stimulated to embrace a proactive learning process that could be applied throughout their future careers.

While the course "Leadership in Sustainability" was being conceptualised, there was a vision that this course would differ in important ways from any knowledge- or skill-imparting modules. It had one single and clear goal: to nurture and prepare students to be future change agents. With this goal in mind, the traditional teacher-centred approach to delivering knowledge was perceived as inadequate. Therefore, a journey of exploring a mixed learning approach combining both pedagogy and andragogy was conducted.

Pedagogy and Andragogy

Pedagogy is derived from the Greek words *paid*, meaning "child", and *agogus*, meaning "leader of". Thus, the word *pedagogy* literally refers to the art and science of teaching children. This concept encompasses the notion of providing education through the presence of teachers or having teachers to steer and conduct the education process. Within this context, a body of teacher(s) makes all decisions on the content, method, timing, and evaluation of learning. Such a method is evident in the formal education systems practised in most educational institutions. Learning, however, is not confined within classrooms or institutions. According to Knowles (1990), the pedagogy perspective assumes that the needs of learners are controlled by teachers; in turn, the learners' self-concept is one of dependent personality from the teachers' perspective. Nevertheless, a different approach to adult education has been recognised since 1949, when Harry Overstreet's (1984) *The Mature Mind* was published.

From the 1950s through the 1970s, developmental and social psychologists searched for and discussed the purpose of adult education. According to these scholars, adult education serves a different purpose from youth education. This perception sparked a social movement toward developing a different sort of adult education, accompanied by emerging philosophical assertions and theory development. While Bischof (1969), Goulet and Baltes (1970), and Havighurst (1973) focused on identifying the developmental aspects associated with different stages of growth, Etzioni (1961), Lewin (1951), and Knowles (1972) discussed the environmental influences on this process, including culture, race, population characteristics, and population density, and advocated an innovative approach that would facilitate the "self-directing inquiry" of learners. A descriptor for this unique approach—namely, *andragogy*—was introduced in 1957 by a book published by a German teacher, Franz Poggeler (1957), entitled *Introduction to Andragogy: Basic Issues in Adult Education*. Adult education was recognised to be important and different from youth education. More importantly, it should be learner centred rather than teacher centred, because adult education is closely linked to problem-solving related to work or self-development in adulthood. Therefore, learning new knowledge and skills for application to tackle practical issues requires a different approach to suit the needs of learners.

Andragogy, according to Knowles (1990), is based on the assumption that learners have the capacity to take on learning actively and independently because their basic human needs (Ryan and Deci 2002) are closely linked to the development of the self in terms of competence, autonomy, and growth. Learning can be motivated intrinsically and extrinsically. Intrinsic motivation involves a person to take on the learning for personal enjoyment, while extrinsic motivation requires instrumentalities such as endorsement by other people or future benefits or career advancement. One way or another, if the right environment is provided, then, adult education can trigger the learning motivation within learners. As the learners adopt a proactive approach to learning, taking it into their own hands, they will take their experience to heart. Collectively, these impulses contribute to a more effective and fruitful learning process. Compared to pedagogy, andragogy emphasises facilitation of the learning process in learners rather than directly steering the learning process.

Knowles' (1990) six fundamental assumptions of andragogy portray why adult learners need a differentiated approach from pedagogy. To Knowles, adult learners can (1) be nurtured and facilitated to evaluate their own need to learn; (2) develop the capability of self-direction in learning; (3) learn through their own discussion, interpretation, and reflection based on their own experiences; (4) move from one developmental stage to another through a "readiness to learn"; (5) be conscious of an "orientation to learning" because of the practical requirement to deal with problems in real-life situations; and (6) be motivated by both positive and negative environmental factors to learn or not to learn. Knowles assumed that adult learners, if placed in a motivating and positive environment, could pursue learning through their own self-initiative. In contrast, in pedagogy, "readiness to learn" is decided by the teacher or an authority, such as parents, institutions, or government policy. Adult learning can also impact the deep-structure development of the learner by orienting him or her to capitalise on learning as a means of tackling problems in life. This kind of learning can foster long-term memory of what is learned. In pedagogy, the learners usually go through a "subject-matter" learning process that does not necessarily find much application in everyday life. The adult learning approach, however, is learner centred and can create a long-lasting impact on learners because the learning is internalised. This is achieved as the learner creates new meaning from an area of knowledge, a process, or simply an experience, which allows the learning to be understood, owned, shared, and applied.

Andragogy also takes into consideration the dynamic cognitive processes happening within an active learning self. Mischel and Morf (2003) have described the self as "an organised dynamic cognitive–affective–action system and an interpersonal self-construction system" (p. 23). Learning is a psychodynamic process that is especially important for the transition into adulthood. Recognising the individual needs and the dynamic complexity competence of the "cognitive–affective–action system", the andragogy approach gives each learner the autonomy and freedom to learn according to his or her own unique personality, personal history, and personal and practical needs. What the learning self needs is immersion into a learning process based on intrinsic motivation, rather than detailed instructions and didactic imparting of knowledge by teachers. Respecting the self-development of the learner is a core belief in adult education.

Proposition 1 Combining the learner-centred andragogy approach with the pedagogy approach will maximise students' learning, which will in turn lead to more effective internalisation of what is learned by students.

Learning and the Development of Self

As theorists embraced the notion that adult education is closely linked to the development of self, the transformative nature of learning became apparent and was more widely recognised by contemporary psychologists. According to Illeris (2009), learning is defined as "any process that in living organisms leads to permanent capacity change and which is not solely due to biological maturation or ageing" (p. 3). Piaget and Cook (1952) asserted that learning could create new impulses within the mental patterns of the brain and could stimulate new mental organisation depending on the types of learning involved.

Put simply, different types of learning can stimulate the brain differently. Indeed, Illeris (2009) identified four types of learning based on the specific mental processes involved. First is *cumulative* or mechanical learning. This kind of learning results in an isolated mental process that does not necessarily have any connection to any context or personal meaning. Teaching a child how to play a musical instrument that the child does not like, for example, can be a kind of mechanical learning. In such a case, the playing of the instrument may be perceived as a kind of mechanical skill rather than as a source of artistic enjoyment. Learning a new personal identification number (PIN) is another example of mechanical learning; that is, the learning is useful only when the same condition requires the same piece of information to be recalled by the learner.

The second type of learning identified by Illeris (2009) is *assimilative* learning, also called learning by addition. Learning of this type is a sequel to an existing mental pattern. A typical example is when a learner embarks on an advanced level of the same subject learned before—for example, advanced mathematics.

Of course, learners can also acquire knowledge and engage in a process of learning that is not directly linked to existing mental patterns or prior experience. In such a case, the learners may be driven by a "purpose" or a "self-initiated interest". Illeris (2009) called this third type *accommodative* or transcendent learning, in recognition of the fact that it might require the learner to unlearn existing schemas and reconstruct new schemas to form new mental patterns. When an individual wants to go beyond his or her limitations and reach new heights in a certain domain of knowledge, this kind of learning can bring huge satisfaction but require substantial efforts. For example, learners who are motivated by their own interests to pick up computer programming or music composition without guidance may engage in accommodative learning. This kind of learning requires the learner to be adaptable and to exercise constant processes of evaluation and adjustment.

Finally, *transformative* learning is the process in which the learner changes his or her perspectives and frames of reference for certain topics through self-reflection on existing assumptions, validation of beliefs, new actions to act on new insights, and evaluation of the steps taken. According to Illeris (2009), this fourth type of learning demands a great deal of mental energy. The first three types of learning involve mental and memory processes that involve aggregation of information and knowledge, whereas transformative learning demands a slightly different cognitive process.

Transformative learning is about altering one's perspective on meaning. The way we perceive ourselves and our relationships affects how we determine values, set priorities for actions, and define directions. Along the way, the meaning of our success (Mezirow 1978) can be restructured or even reconstructed. We can learn to "negotiate and act upon our own purposes, values, feelings and meanings rather than those we have uncritically assimilated from others" (Mezirow 2000, p. 8). For example, a successful business entrepreneur might decide to drop his or her profit-making pursuits and start a new non-profit social enterprise devoted to addressing a social issue. This change in direction, which may be a consequence of the individual's change in perspective regarding his or her purpose in life, relies on the cognitive ability to differentiate and integrate meaning. In a way, this process creates new meaning or knowledge unique to the self because of the individual's interpretation based on critical thinking, which is in turn affected by the learner's personality and personal experiences. As the learner is capable of "reforming meaning" through learning, Kegan (2009) describes this shift as moving from a socialised to a "self-authoring" epistemology. From an educational perspective, it is considered transformative learning; from a psychological perspective, it is "constructive developmentalism" (Kegan 2009, p. 45).

Experience is always linked to human learning and human development. Therefore, transformative learning cannot happen in a vacuum. Experiential learning, as explored in the works of modern scholars and psychologists including Kurt Lewin, Jean Piaget, and Carl Rogers, can be a very effective way of learning, especially in terms of transformative learning. Kolb and Kolb (2005, p. 194) summarise experiential learning by introducing six propositions:

1. Learning is best considered as a process and not in terms of outcomes.
2. All learning is relearning. What is learned must be reconciled and integrated with current ideas and beliefs.
3. Conflicts, differences, and disagreement drive the learning process. A learner moves back and forth between "dialectically opposed modes of adaptation to the world", such as reflection–action and thinking–feeling.
4. Learning is a holistic process of adaptation to the world (and involves more than cognition).
5. Learning results from "synergetic transactions between the person and the environment".
6. Learning is the process of creating or constructing knowledge.

Moreover, learning from experience has a pragmatic impact on learners. This relationship has been confirmed by Elkjaer (2009), who has embraced the earlier work of John Dewey, an American pragmatist philosopher and educator. Elkjaer (2009) posits that development and learning can be drawn from disruption on habitual routines, especially in difficult and new situations that cause dissonance.

This kind of interference triggers closer examination of situations (usually problematic ones), inquiry into problems, search for solutions, application of solutions, and evaluation before the dissonance can be finally resolved. Of course, not all experiences will necessarily lead to knowledge. Some of the experiences never enter a thorough cognitive process or lead to action; rather, they remain at the emotional or subconscious level. According to Elkjaer (2009), "if experience is to become a learning experience in the sense that experience can inform future experience, experience has to get out of the bodily and non-discursive field and into the cognitive and conscious field of experience" (p. 82). Brown (2004) agrees, noting that "[by] exposing candidates to information and ideas that they may resist and by assisting them to stretch beyond their comfort zones, a critique and transformation of hegemonic structures and ideologies can occur" (p. 78). Therefore, learners who are learning from experience must be given the opportunity to reflect, discuss, share, and transform their experience into new learning. Through such a process, the learners put their learning into practice with a new frame of reference.

For students, both sustainability and leadership may be new knowledge domains that are abstract and difficult to grasp without direct personal experience. Stimulating transformative learning through direct experience will, therefore, help students embark on their initial learning of sustainability and leadership.

Proposition 2 To facilitate the development of the self, adopting experiential learning and enhancing direct and personal experience will facilitate students in thinking and reflecting more intensively compared to learning purely from textbooks.

Leadership Development as Adult Development

The trajectory of leader development overlaps with that of adult development, according to Day et al. (2009), as both of them stretch across the entire lifespan. Leadership development, like adult development, is an area of learning that should be closely linked to practice and experience to allow learners to become better leaders. Three specific elements link the two kinds of development. First, both kinds of development happen within individuals and share commonalities in development. Second, such development can bring about between-person differences in terms of outcomes in leadership style and behavioural patterns. Third, both kinds of development show within-person plasticity in development.

Baltes, Staudinger, and Lindenberger (1999) describe leader development as a kind of adult development—that is, as "a process of selective adaptation and transformation" (p. 483). As individuals face challenges in life, they learn to adapt through three common coping strategies. First, the selection of goals and the identification of outcomes are established to manage the challenge. Second, the leveraging and optimisation of goal-relevant means and resources are achieved through active acquisition. Third, a compensation strategy is used to respond to loss functioning when goal-relevant means or resources are not available. This selection–optimisation–compensation (SOC) model depicts the life mastery processes for adults and leaders. However, these processes do not necessarily represent a natural trajectory that adults or leaders take up. Rather, these individuals need to go through a continuous and conscientious learning process to acquire and master the SOC skills, as life challenges vary drastically from one individual to another and from one stage of life to another.

The continuous building-up process of adaptation and transformation helps shape two important pillars for adult and leader developments—change and growth. According to Day et al. (2004, p. 41), growth is inherent in change. As organisms grow, they evolve. Quantitative and qualitative changes occur in the process of growth. Quantitative growth may involve taller height and stronger muscles, but qualitative growth is more difficult to conceptualise and measure. For example, the ability to adapt and transform as a means of personal mastery is a kind of qualitative growth that is complex—both cognitively and emotionally—in terms of the underlying processes. Leaders in the process of their leadership development will inevitably find their trajectories being challenged by difficulties or problems. Very often, adaptation and transformation are repeated frequently as means of tackling challenges. The strengthening of that complexity cannot be broken down and taught separately. In fact, growth is achieved only through the repeated application of that complexity in situations that involve problem-solving; setting, pursuing, and completing goals; and evaluating outcomes for enhancement. Effectively, learning is a complexity-building process that works through experience.

Moreover, leaders do not thrive when they act as loners. Individuals usually operate in teams before they become leaders. After emerging as leaders, they steer and motivate teams. Working in teams has also proved a more effective approach to delivering the desired level of performance—for example, in meeting goals and completing tasks for organisations. Leadership training is best operated in teams so that leadership can emerge from teams. As Salas, Burke, Wilson-Donnelly, and Fowlkes (2004) point out, leadership training via teams can develop team competence and process skills including adaptability and flexibility; shared situational awareness; and performance monitoring, backup behaviour, feedback, team leadership, interpersonal relations, coordination, communication, and decision-making.

Proposition 3 Leadership development introduced to individuals in early adulthood will facilitate learning and practising coping strategies, preparing those individuals to mature and develop the same skills for tackling challenges in later life.

Proposition 4 Team-based learning will enhance students' leadership development and team competence.

Service Leadership Embedded in Self- and Relational Leadership Theories

The GE course "Leadership in Sustainability" was inspired and supported by the concept of "service leadership", a concept created and driven by two well-known Hong Kong entrepreneurs. The underlying rationale of *The Service Leader's Pledge* is very much shaped by an entrepreneurial spirit that requires individual drive and personal mastery:

> I am the entrepreneur of my life. My success will be heavily influenced by my task competencies, character strengths, and caring dispositions towards others.
>
> Whatever I do to promote my success, above all else, I am in the business of providing the highest-quality ethical service I can afford to everyone I come in contact with or whose life is affected by my actions or by my leadership. (HKI-SLAM 2014)

Another focus of the "service leadership" concept is relational capital, which may be described as a kind of "service" done for another person. This notion is where the name "service leadership" originated.

The essence of the "service leadership" concept can be found embedded in two well-discussed leadership theories: self-leadership and relational leadership. The former theory emphasises self-influence, while the latter asserts that leadership is a socially constructed entity or process that thrives within relationships.

Self-leadership theory (Manz 1986; Pearce and Manz 2005) was inspired by the social learning theory advanced by Bandura (1977) and his related works on self-control. In addition to his theory of learning by observation, Bandura's (1977) assertion of the strong human cognitive capacity and its control over self-regulation processes provided the foundation for the understanding of the human potential of self-influence. In social learning theory, human functioning relies on three regulatory processes: stimulus, cognitive, and reinforcement control. That is, both external and internal stimuli can stimulate cognitive activities that bring about control and behavioural self-regulation. For example, certain external stimuli, such as a bus timetable, may regulate the individual's daily routine. If a specific bus at a specific time can take the person to work or to school punctually and without delay, it will dictate the individual's adherence to the bus's timetable when he or she leaves home in the morning. Subsequently, if the individual's punctuality brings praise from his or her superior, the pattern of catching the same bus becomes a good control of time and punctuality. At the same time, the sense of being appreciated, owing to the praise of the superior, may become an internal stimulus. The worker/student might even consider setting punctuality as a daily target or might perceive it as a discipline, standard, or even responsibility he or she has to adhere to. This kind of target or standard, once it becomes a pattern, acts as a kind of control mechanism and source of self-influence.

Based on this ability to exercise self-influence, Manz (1986) developed the self-leadership theory. Self-leadership, according to Manz (1986), is "conceptualised as a process that encompasses behaviourally focused self-management strategies and further addresses self-regulation of higher-level control standards to more fully recognise the role of intrinsic motivation" (p. 595). In turn, Manz (1986) suggested three self-influence perspectives might shape this process: self-regulation, self-management, and self-leadership.

Self-regulation is a control process that reduces the deviation from the standard so as to meet certain targets. For example, work plans are used to regulate and control work processes at workplaces to make sure that deadlines can be met. Self-management involves strategies designed to meet standards. For example, establishing feedback loops and developing prototypes before the launch of a project are strategies that help certain standards of performance to be achieved. The self-leadership perspective proposed by Manz (1986) represents a broader view of self-influence and is closely linked to intrinsic motivation. Self-leadership goes beyond self-management and self-regulation and recognises a call beyond duty to exercise self-initiative to fulfil goals that are purposeful or meaningful. This kind of spirit is close to that embodied by perseverance.

In addition to the self-influence perspective, the role of relational capital within the "service leadership" concept is another important feature tied closely with another leadership theory—namely, relational leadership theory (Uhl-Bien 2006). *The Service Leader's Pledge* conveys the understanding that each individual is connected socially through a larger network of relations in which individuals are connected to each other by serving one another. Uhl-Bien (2006) defined relational leadership as "a social influence process through which emergent coordination (i.e., evolving social order) and change (i.e., new values, attitudes, approaches, behaviours, ideologies, etc.) are constructed and produced" (p. 668).

The dynamic and positive thrust of relational construction is embedded in the three assumptions of the relational leadership theory (Uhl-Bien 2006). First, leadership relationships are liberated from the traditional top-down perspective. The concept of relational leadership can be applied to working groups with or without a leader in a power or leading role. The relational dynamics amongst members will allow natural leaders to emerge without confining leadership to a specific set of power or role structures. Second, leadership relationships are defined by interactive dynamics rather than prescribed by the hierarchical structure. This flexibility creates the opportunity for a new social order to emerge beyond the existing role or status structure. In an organisation characterised by this approach, for example, a departmental director may become a follower in certain situations and let a subordinate or subordinates take the leading role in certain projects. Relationship leadership allows team members to be "partners, collaborators or participants" (Uhl-Bien 2006, p. 664) without focusing on their hierarchical importance. Third, the need to better understand and appreciate the context in which leadership is embedded is appreciated by all parties. Positive self-concepts are constructed within a positive context where members are connected by their work and social relations both closely and uniquely. The influence borne from the positive relations can be a crucial influence that facilitates completion of tasks and fulfilment of goals.

Based on Uhl-Bien's (2006) three assumptions vis-à-vis relational leadership, positive and mutually supportive and serving relations are the premise for leadership emergence. This reinforces the importance of team dynamics in leadership learning and development. In fact, Denis, Langley, and Sergi (2012) assert that "leadership is fundamentally more about participation and collectively creating a sense of direction than it is about control and exercising authority" (p. 44).

Proposition 5 Exercising self and relational influences are important skills that, if built into individual and group activities, will develop students' sense of leadership and responsibility for self and for others.

Sustainability Education as Part of the Higher Education Curriculum

Over the last ten years, studies have looked into the value of integrating sustainability as a topic in higher education, including studies focused on business and management education. The topic of sustainability can range from a single but complex concern for environmental issues, including air, water, land, or waste, to a systematic perspective on social, economic, and environmental challenges. Some of the recent discussions on introducing sustainability into higher education have been driven by Rusinko (2010), Benn and Martin (2010), McMillin and Dyball (2009), and Roome (2005). Out of these discussions have emerged a few common views. First, universities play an important role in nurturing a future generation of leaders who can tackle sustainability and environmental issues in communities. Second, sustainability education requires both curricular and co-curricular learning to allow students to learn about sustainability as a more holistic issue—that is, a topic that cannot be grasped completely only through classroom learning. Third, sustainability is best addressed as a broader or community issue. Students can co-learn with the communities to which they belong—for example, their campus communities. Moreover, students are encouraged to appreciate the connections between individuals, institutions, and the larger society over the issue of sustainability. Carpenter and Dyball (2006), for example, advocate a reflexive learning practice to facilitate students' reflections on how their own behaviours interact with the bigger system in which they live. Fourth, integrating sustainability education into an institution-wide curriculum requires careful consideration of resources, time, and human factors.

Rusinko (2010) has suggested that sustainability concerns are best integrated into management and business education because this area is viewed as posing an increasing threat to business decision-makers. To an ever greater extent, organisational effectiveness today hinges on the ability to resolve environmental sustainability issues. To inspire students to be change agents in their future careers, sustainability may be best taught from the perspective of how business operations tackle sustainability issues and develop solutions that can be traced back to their own operations. To achieve this goal, many different learning methods may be used, including case studies, site visits, and direct research on specific issues or companies.

Proposition 6 Using an integrated approach to help students learn about sustainability will facilitate them in understanding, discovering, and appreciating the importance of preserving the environment as a holistic issue.

The Multidimensional Learning Spirit of Whole-Person Education

Whole-person education is about multidimensional learning opportunities, including cognitive, affective, and behavioural development of learners who can then bring meaningful outcomes such as application of their learning into their lives or benefits for others.

Both Yorks and Kasl (2002) and Hoover, Giambatista, Sorenson, and Bommer (2010) asserted the importance of combined cognitive and affective experience for whole-person development. However, pure action learning experience does not provide whole-person development. Learners need to go through different stages of "knowing" (Yorks and Kasl 2002, p. 182), moving from "experiential", to "presentational", to "propositional", to "practical" knowing. Experiential knowing, according to Yorks and Kasl (2002), is apparent when learners meet and feel the presence of "energy, entity, person, place, process, or thing". When learners can grasp the imaginal patterns—whether they involve verbal, musical, or graphical expression—presentational knowing is evident. When learners can express the knowing using intellectual statements, whether verbally, numerically, or in other forms, then they have demonstrated propositional knowing. Finally, if a skill developed can be applied, learners have reached the practical knowing stage.

Skill learning without application does not lead to whole-person development because the learning will not take firm root. Understanding students' lack of appreciation for skill learning alone, Hoover et al. (2010) adopted an intensive whole-person approach in their MBA programmes, combining the behavioural and emotional dimensions to provide whole-person education to MBA students so that their students could develop personal responsibility in their actions and decisions. Students were put into different skill learning and application scenarios, including those focusing on leadership, decision-making, planning and organisation, communication, and teamwork. In an assessment centre, pretests and posttests were conducted to gauge the improvements in students' skill development from this intensive learning experience. Hoover et al.'s assessment showed that all learners' skills, except for teamwork, were improved after the students completed the whole-person approach to learning. The results of this study demonstrate how pure skill learning, if it is not accompanied by efforts to ensure whole-person development, will not allow learning to take hold.

Yorks and Kasl (2002) also proposed that a "learning-within-relationship" approach will support learners in discovering more about their fellow learners. This opportunity is suggested to encourage the development of empathic knowing in a diverse environment. Moreover, while Rogers (1975, p. 3) stated empathy 'is possibly the most potent factors in bringing about change and learning', Kellet et al. (2002) asserted that empathy was linked to effective leadership. According to Yorks and Kasl (2002), learners' greater awareness of their fellow learners and their ability to establish "balance and congruence among the different ways of knowing are central to holistic learning" (p. 187).

Proposition 7 Facilitating affective and emphatic development in conjunction with skill learning will enhance students' self-perceived competence in related skill areas, thus achieving whole-person education.

A Leadership General Education Course Directed Toward Achieving Adult and Leadership Development

The propositions derived from the related literature became the guiding principles for designing the GE course "Leadership in Sustainability". It adopted mixed learning methods to maximise students' learning experience, thereby ensuring that their learning journey in relation to leadership and sustainability could become part of their adult development.

How Was the "Leadership in Sustainability" Course Delivered?

The course description (Fig. 1) and learning objectives (Fig. 2) presented in the course programme documents sought to engage prospective students and stimulate

---

Course Description

Leadership in Sustainability, the first leadership general education course launched in Hong Kong, will help you develop your leadership skills so as to decipher the importance of leadership practiced by sustainability leaders in the corporate world. The aspects of good practice include environmental protection, good governance, quality and safe product and service offerings, motivational human resources management, and proactive stakeholder engagement.

This new course will extend beyond the classroom. It includes several teaching and learning methods, including case studies, mentoring by corporate leaders, field studies, innovative problem solving, experiential learning, and even online simulation games!

The objective is to maximise your exposure to real leadership cases in driving sustainability. In the process, you will generate intrinsic motivation to delve into the understanding of related issues, develop the right values for ethical and responsible management, and be prepared to become change agents. Corporate partnership will be sought so you can conduct research in real companies on sustainability areas.

This course will facilitate self-transformation in yourself, developing the right mind-set to serve responsible management practices with the goal of achieving sustainability for our future. It is this kind of "transform-synthesis" that will equip you to understand and meet the ecological, social, and economic opportunities of our time.

Fig. 1 Course description

Learning Objectives

- Develop your leadership and followership skills required to implement changes
- Sharpen your strategic thinking and problem-solving skills when challenged to provide solutions
- Allow you to discover the success of sustainability practices through research methods to compile a case report that can unfold how specialised expertise, organisational processes, and human factors work together to bring about sustainable practices
- Encourage you to use critical thinking skills and environmental management skills and related knowledge in identifying sustainability reporting weaknesses practised by business organisations
- Awaken your service leadership awareness and deepen your strong sense of responsibility, work ethics, and care for communities

Fig. 2 Course objectives

their interest in choosing this GE course as their elective. In support of this goal, the tone and the language were direct and upbeat.

The 38 students who enrolled in the "Leadership in Sustainability" course had a mixed profile. Because this was a GE interdisciplinary elective course, students from different disciplines, including the business school, social sciences, and humanities, were in the same class. Diverse impacts on students resulted from their participation, as some of them had never pondered the issue of sustainability. Few of them had engaged in any leadership development learning prior to this course.

The course components were organised into three areas: lectures, co-curricular activities, and assignments. There were no examinations. The key approach for each component is discussed next, and the detailed content and intended learning outcomes are provided in Fig. 3.

In the lectures, the key knowledge imparted included (1) the importance of sustainability issues from the perspective of business operators, (2) the concept of common pool resources management and environmental management systems, (3) sustainability and stakeholders' communication, (4) leadership and followership, and (5) change management. A mixed mode of instruction, consisting of lectures, case studies, class discussion, scenario simulation, and online simulation games, was adopted within the classroom environment.

The co-curricular activities were mainly action learning activities. They included two experiential learning workshops (the class size was too big to accommodate all students in a single workshop session) and a full-day outdoor leadership challenge activity. Two sessions of an experiential workshop called "Dialogue in the Dark" were organised on the Saturdays in Weeks 2 and 3. This workshop prepared the students to reflect on their own limitations as they operated in darkness. They experienced first-hand, albeit briefly, the life difficulties of visually impaired persons. This exercise was designed to develop students' empathy and encourage them to reflect on the importance of social inclusion. Along with a brief session of team-building exercises, some of the students experienced their first taste of leadership and teamwork in the workshop, a way to immerse them in whole-person education at the beginning of the course.

In Week 10, the students attended a one-day outdoor leadership challenge. Forming themselves into five teams, they faced the physical challenge of navigating

Course Components	Details of Components	Intended Learning Outcomes
Lectures A mixed mode, consisting of lectures, case studies, simulation games, and class discussions, was adopted in the classroom learning.	*Topics on Environment, Management, and Leadership* 1. Management practice and externalities 2. Leadership and followership 3. Change management 4. Stakeholder management and sustainability *Topics on Sustainability* 1. Common pool resources management 2. Environmental management systems and ISO standards 3. Global reporting initiative and stakeholders' communication	1. Acquire knowledge in leadership and sustainability 2. Obtain insights and exercise critical thinking in two business cases 3. Digest and apply knowledge learned for critical group discussions 4. Identify practical challenges through participating in online simulation scenario management
Activities A variety of activities were incorporated in the course to maximise students' learning opportunities.	*Experiential Learning (co-curricular activity)* A 3-hour experience going through activities in a darkness workshop and a team-building session in Week 2 of the course	*Ice-breaker and basic skills:* 1. Ice-breaker for class members to get to know one another 2. Develop self-awareness of limitations 3. Exercise empathy 4. Recognise importance of communication for teamwork
	Online Simulation Scenario 1 (classroom activity) Leading and climbing Mount Everest	*Simulated leadership and team skills:* 1. Build, participate in, and lead teams effectively 2. Practise problem solving 3. Rehearse decision making and dealing with trade-offs
	Online Simulation Scenario 2 (classroom activity) Change management in a sustainability project launch	*Advanced influencing skills:* 1. Practise diagnostic and action-planning skills with regard to leading strategic change 2. Gain insights into why individuals and groups might resist change 3. Develop understanding of how to choose appropriate change strategies and tactics
	Outdoor Challenge in the Morning (co-curricular activity) Each team had to do a hike in a country park and engage in joint decision making regarding whether they would pick the Lion Rock (495 m high) top as their team challenge.	*Leadership and team skills in action:* Goal setting, teamwork, decision making, perseverance, resources (time, money, and team talents) management, importance of leadership and followership
	City Expedition in the Afternoon (co-curricular activity) Each team had to organise and collect materials in a city expedition to prepare for a presentation to persuade a home-bound vulnerable individual (e.g., elderly or disabled person) to join the team for an outing.	*Taking interest in the wider community:* 1. Increase awareness of the wider community 2. Relate to vulnerable others 3. Exercise relational persuasiveness
Assignments A variety of both individual and group assignments were made.	*Individual* 1. Personal reflections on either lectures or activities 2. Critique of real corporate sustainability reports	1. Exercise reflection throughout the course to deepen learning 2. Exercise critical thinking to understand corporate sustainability reporting
	Group 1. Case study research 2. Group presentation	1. Learn from corporate mentors as role models 2. Investigate good sustainability practice 3. Exercise presentation skills

Fig. 3 Detailed course content and intended learning outcomes

their way to the summit of a peak of 460 m high. The groups had to exercise their orienteering skills to find their way up. Later, in the afternoon of the same day, they were presented with another task: preparing a presentation to convince a home-bound disadvantaged person to join their own group for a "proposed outing" to appreciate both the nature and the city life in Hong Kong. This exercise encouraged the students to think about the wider community—one that included people who were less fortunate than themselves. The goal was to develop students' empathy and teamwork in thinking about the broader community beyond their own familiar circle.

Both individual and group assignments were also part of the "Leadership in Sustainability" course. In the individual assignments, students completed four reflection tasks that required them to reflect on topics of knowledge or the action learning that they had experienced. The structure of the reflection was to be organised into "Reflect", "Build", "Recommend", and "Share" sections. In the group assignment, each group of students had to develop and analyse a case study. Each group was assigned a corporate mentor and researched a sustainability case. Through this effort, students had the opportunity to learn in a real business context and understand real sustainability practice. At the end of this assignment, the students had to produce a report and a presentation on the case study.

Students' Perceptions of Their Learning Experiences

Both qualitative and quantitative evaluation methods were used to gather students' feedback on their learning experiences.

Quantitative Evaluation of Key Activities

Students were asked to rate their perceptions of their learning experience using a 5-point Likert scale (where 5 = excellent and 1 = poor) at the end of the course. All seven course components were evaluated: two action learning activities (the "Dialogue in the Dark" workshop and the one-day leadership challenge), two types of simulation games (an in-class simulation game on "common pool resources" and two online simulation games on change management and leadership), and three assignments (the group case study, an individual paper, and four individual self-reflection tasks). Out of 38 students, 34 returned their ratings (see Table 1).

All of the co-curricular action learning activities were rated higher by students than the assignments. Clearly, the students preferred the co-curricular activities to the assignments. The activity that received the highest rating was the one-day leadership challenge—the 9-h activity including a physically demanding hike and a city expedition with a purpose. This result provided good evidence that students enjoyed learning through direct and personal experience and participation.

Table 1 Students' ratings of key activities

Learning experience	Mean
One-day leadership challenge	4.38
"Dialogue in the Dark" experiential workshop	4.21
Online simulation games	4.06
Business case research project	3.94
Common pool resources simulation game	3.74
Individual self-reflection	3.59
Individual paper	3.18

The one-day leadership challenge activity had a few key features that stimulated student enthusiasm. First, there were two specific goals: (1) finishing the hike to obtain monetary rewards for funding their afternoon city expedition, including transportation, lunch, and purchase of a souvenir and (2) designing a presentation for a home-bound disadvantaged individual. With these specific goals in hand, the teams knew the tasks that they had to complete in advance, but did not truly appreciate their difficulty until they actually participated in doing them. For example, some students had never gone on a proper hike and wore canvas shoes even though they were told to wear trainers. The actual team synergy that evolved while in completing the tasks also differed depending on the team members' physical fitness and the team dynamics. The one-day action learning experience not only allowed students to learn about their own limitations and strengths, but, more importantly, provided valuable lessons about the way to work with others. In addition to setting goals and completing them, students emphasised how they learned to provide care and support for one another. A "learning-within-relationship" approach was adopted, and it showed that students appreciated action learning that challenged them in a multidimensional way—in terms of their physical fitness; the cognitive process of planning, selection, decision-making; and the relational support embedded in teamwork.

The online simulation scenario games, which were rated third highest out of the seven course components, provided students with opportunities to develop heightened awareness of more sophisticated skills and challenges in two scenarios: an extreme expedition of climbing Mount Everest and handling a corporate sustainability project. Although these were only simulations, they were deemed important to prepare students to appreciate the more sophisticated situations that they would have to tackle in their future careers. The simulation games were intended to make students aware of how sophisticated situations would require them to be better equipped with sophisticated skills.

The individual assignments were rated the lowest. Conversely, all the group activities received the highest ratings. To a great extent, these differences indicated that team learning was successfully received. Moreover, the students' high ratings of the team-oriented experiences offered a useful reference for future leadership development education to consider when using team learning activities. However, to put things into perspective, 28 of the 34 students gave ratings ranging from 3 to 5 to the individual assignments; in other words, the majority of the students still appreciated the emphasis placed on individual work.

Looking at the detailed student evaluation breakdown, out of the 34 students who responded, 21 (more than 50 %) rated at least five out of the seven course components as 4 or 5; that is, more than half of the students perceived their learning experience as "good" to "excellent". These findings indicate that the mixed approach combining pedagogy and andragogy received positive feedback from most of the students in terms of their learning experience. This important evidence reveals that "learning from experience" for this course, focusing on leadership, was effectively designed from the learners' perspective.

Qualitative Feedback Through Focus Group Interviews, Written Comments, and Reflections

In terms of gauging students' qualitative feedback, inferences have been drawn from three sources of data: focus group interviews with 12 students, students' written comments, and students' self-reflection submissions.

Students' self-awareness relative to leadership, followership, and sustainability was clearly raised through their participation in the "Leadership in Sustainability" course. In terms of their views on sustainability, all of the students' reflections showed a clear journey of deep thinking, heightened awareness of happenings around them, and recognition of their own behaviours in the past and their change of behaviour. One student reflected on how he/she did not understand why a friend became a vegetarian a few years ago. After embarking on the course, the student better understood the endangered food chain and started to appreciate why some people chose to adopt a vegetarian lifestyle. Some students provided in-depth discussion of how business operations were cutting down trees, causing soil erosion, and polluting water with discharged chemicals. As the class included students from different disciplines, some had never thought about how nature could be so drastically polluted and affected by human activities. For these individuals, the course provided a wake-up call. Moreover, because the self-reflection assignment required students to build a glossary of new terms and to find new web resources related to sustainability and leadership, most students made conscientious efforts to share their search results. All of these efforts demonstrated how students' self-awareness and interest in the importance of sustainability and leadership were heightened. In terms of leadership development, all of the written comments appeared upbeat and positive, with students asserting they could be leaders and had a better understanding of followership, especially after they participated in the one-day leadership challenge activity.

Their action learning in the one-day leadership challenge also helped unleash the authentic selves of students in regard to leadership and followership. The positive feedback of students, both in their written comments and shared in the focus group interviews, showed that action learning was a good method for learners to apply lessons received in the classroom to practice. Some of the shared comments included "We are all leaders in our specialised area" and "Everyone has his unique talent". More than 95 % of the students made remarks similar to this one: "Just because we may be a follower most of the time, it does not mean that we cannot be a leader one day". Clearly, students perceived that they could unleash their potential for team learning when they were called to action. Moreover, students' confidence in their abilities was obvious in their assertions that they would attempt to take up a future leadership role.

Another important area of learning was students' greater awareness of the importance of relationships in the process of team learning. When students were asked to comment about whether they appreciated the importance of the relational aspect of their teamwork, all responded positively in writing. Most of them remarked that the one-day leadership challenge had the biggest impact in encouraging them to appreciate that facet of teamwork. However, some also mentioned how their self-reflections and the group research project helped them understand the relational importance in teams.

The learning in a real business context, as students met with their business executive mentors, was received positively. Students, divided into nine groups, were assigned to study real companies and their corporate sustainability practices. As the groups enjoyed having real business executives explain their organisations' sustainability practices, students remarked that these encounters enhanced their belief that sustainability issues could be tackled. It was through this immersion in actual business practices that students were stimulated to know more about the practical side of solving sustainability problems. "I realise that it is possible to achieve sustainability in real life", remarked one student.

Conclusion

The "Leadership in Sustainability" GE course achieved the intended goal of activating students' minds and making them think about their roles as future change leaders. The course provided initial leadership development to students by raising their awareness of three issues: (1) everyone can be a leader; (2) relationships are a core part of leadership; and (3) caring for others and the environment is achievable.

The seven propositions presented in this chapter, which were drawn from the literature, acted as good guidelines and paved the way for designing the content of this leadership GE course. Matching these propositions with students' feedback revealed that whole-person development can be achieved through multidimensional learning. Experiential and team learning approaches that allow students to apply their learning in practical situations will encourage their learning to take firm root and serve as a solid foundation for adult development. This was evidenced by students' evaluations, which reinforced how rewarding they found it to embark on the learning process inherent in this course.

The "Leadership in Sustainability" course was able to fulfil the intended goal of nurturing students to aspire to be change agents by heightening their leadership and sustainability awareness. Most importantly, two action learning experiences facilitated whole-person development in students. Both the "Dialogue in the Dark" workshop and the one-day leadership challenge, which built in empathy experiences (direct interface with visually impaired trainers and design and delivery of a presentation to an imaginary disadvantaged person, respectively), received students' highest ratings in terms of their learning experience. In their qualitative feedback, most students also expressed great appreciation of the relational experience—including its support, care, and teamwork components—that they went through.

Nevertheless, three learning points are worth considering when providing future leadership education. First, this course was privileged to have obtained a teaching grant to support the co-curricular learning activities. Without the grant, it might not have been possible to include the highly rated activities in the course. Amongst the co-curricular activities, the one-day leadership challenge was the most highly rated activity. Such an integrated and well-thought-out co-curricular activity that involves action learning is likely to benefit students most in sharpening their leadership and followership skills.

Second, the incorporation of sustainability and leadership as two knowledge domains in the same course was an ambitious attempt. No ready-made textbook could be adopted to support the lecture portion of this course. It was a time-consuming effort to create the teaching and learning resources that students needed to absorb the necessary knowledge within a short span of time. Any attempt to teach sustainability education will require a long period of preparation time, and a very specific scope should be crafted before the course is launched. Moreover, designing sustainability education for undergraduates and postgraduates will require very different breadth and depth in terms of the teaching resources, learning resources, and co-curricular activities. It might be wise to adopt a "gradual enhancement" approach and perform continuous reviews to bring about a successful course. Students' diverse academic and personal backgrounds can be an important variable with this kind of venture and can provide many surprises in terms of the learning and teaching in such a course.

Third, pretest and posttest assessments for any leadership courses that adopt a mixed learning approach should be built into the course to more accurately evaluate the effectiveness of action learning from experience to facilitate course enhancement. Moreover, participatory action research that seeks to explore and examine students' motivation in relation to self-regulated learning, leaders' role identification, and trust within teamwork will help all parties better understand the effectiveness of leadership development through action learning.

In summary, leadership and sustainability education should be promoted and further enhanced in higher education. "Learning by experience" is an impactful approach that can be fruitfully adopted to nurture adult and leadership development amongst learners of different ages.

Acknowledgement Mr. Antony Lock, CEO, Tsui Wah Holdings Ltd
Mr. Chris Cheung, Director of Power Generation, CLP Power
Mr. Randy Yu, General Manager, Sino Land Company Ltd
Mr. Terence Ng, Director, Best Result Environmental Services Ltd & Associate Director of Sino Property Services.

References

Baltes, P. B., Staudinger, U. M., & Lindenberger, U. (1999). Lifespan psychology: Theory and application to intellectual functioning. *Annual Review of Psychology, 50*, 471–507.
Bandura, A. (1977). Self-efficacy: Toward a unifying theory of behavioural change. *Psychological Review, 84*(2), 191–215.

Benn, S., & Martin, A. (2010). Learning and change for sustainability reconsidered: A role for boundary objects. *Academy of Management Learning & Education, 9*(3), 397–412.

Bischof, L. (1969). *Adult psychology*. New York: Harper and Row.

Brown, E. M. (2004). Leadership for social justice and equity: Weaving a transformative framework and pedagogy. *Educational Administration Quarterly, 40*(1), 77–108.

Carpenter, D., & Dyball, R. (2006). "Outside in": Experiential education for sustainability. In W. Leal Filho (Ed.), *Innovation, education and communication for sustainable development* (pp. 379–394). Frankfurt: Peter Lang.

Day, D. V., Harrison, M. M., & Halpin, S. M. (2009*). An integrative approach to leader development*. New York: Taylor and Francis.

Day, D. V., Zaccaro, S. J., & Halpin, S. M. (Eds.). (2004). *Leader development for transforming organisations: Growing leaders for tomorrow*. Mahwah: Lawrence Erlbaum Associates.

Denis, J. L., Langley, A., & Sergi, V. (2012). Leadership in the plural. *Academy of Management Annals, 6*(1), 211–283.

Elkjaer, B. (2009). Pragmatism: A learning theory for the future. In K. Illeris (Ed.), *Contemporary theories of learning* (pp. 74–89). New York: Routledge.

Etzioni, A. (1961). *A comparative analysis of complex organisations*. New York: Free Press.

Goulet, L. R., & Baltes, P. B. (Eds.). (1970). *Life span developmental psychology: Research and theory*. New York: Academic Press.

Havighurst, R. J. (1973). History of developmental psychology: Socialisation and personality development through the life span. In P. B. Baltes & K. W. Schaie (Eds.), *Life span developmental psychology* (pp. 3–24). New York: Academic Press.

HKI-SLAM. (2014, December 10). *The service leader's pledge*. Retrieved from http://hki-slam. org/index.php?r=article&catid=2&aid=20

Hoover, J. D., Giambatista, R. C., Sorenson, R. L., & Bommer, W. H. (2010). Assessing the effectiveness of whole person learning pedagogy in skill acquisition. *Academy of Management Learning & Education, 9*(2), 192–203.

Illeris, K. (2009). A comprehensive understanding of human learning. In K. Illeris (Ed.), *Contemporary theories of learning* (pp. 87–100). New York: Routledge.

Kegan, R. (2009). What "form" transforms? A constructive–developmental approach to transformative learning. In K. Illeris (Ed.), *Contemporary theories of learning* (pp. 35–52). New York: Routledge.

Kellet, J. B., Humphrey, R. H., & Sleeth, R. G. (2002). Empathy and complex task performance: Two routes to leadership. *The Leadership Quarterly, 13*, 523–544.

Knowles, M. S. (1972). Innovations in teaching styles and approaches based upon adult learning. *Journal of Education for Social Work, 8*(2), 32–39.

Knowles, M. S. (1990). *The adult learner: A neglected species*. Houston: Gulf.

Kolb, A. Y., & Kolb, D. A. (2005). Learning style and learning spaces: Enhancing experiential learning in higher education. *Academy of Management Learning & Education, 4*(2), 193–212.

Lewin, K. (1951). *Field theories in social science*. New York: Harper and Row.

Manz, C. C. (1986). Self-leadership: Toward an expanded theory of self-influence processes in organisations. *Academy of Management Review, 11*(3), 585–600.

McMillin, J., & Dyball, R. (2009). Developing a whole-of-university approach to educating for sustainability: Linking curriculum, research and sustainable campus operations. *Journal of Education for Sustainable Development, 3*(1), 55–64.

Mezirow, J. (1978). Perspective transformation. *Adult Education Quarterly, 28*(2), 100–110.

Mezirow, J. (2000). *Learning as transformation: Critical perspective*. San Francisco: Jossey-Bass.

Mischel, W., & Morf, C. C. (2003). The self as a psycho-social dynamic processing system: A meta-perspective on a century of the self in psychology. In M. R. Leary & J. P. Tangney (Eds.), *Handbook of self and identity* (pp. 15–43). New York: Guilford Press.

Pearce, C. L., & Manz, C. C. (2005). The new silver bullets of leadership: The importance of self- and shared leadership in knowledge work. *Organisational Dynamics, 34*(2), 130–140.

Overstreet, H. A. (1984). *The mature mind*. New York: W. W. Norton & Co.

Piaget, J., & Cook, M. (1952). *The origins of intelligence in children*. New York: W. W. Norton & Co.

Poggeler, F. (1957). *Einführung in die Andragogik.Grundfragen der Erwachsenenbildung*. Ratingen: Henn Verlag.

Rogers, C. R. (1975). Empathic: An unappreciated way of being. *The Counseling Psychologist, 5*(2), 2–10.

Roome, N. (2005). Teaching sustainability in a global MBA: Insights from the OneMBA. *Business Strategy and the Environment, 14*(3), 160–171.

Rusinko, C. A. (2010). Integrating sustainability in management and business education: A matrix approach. *Academy of Management Learning & Education, 9*(3), 507–519.

Ryan, R. M., & Deci, E. L. (2002). *Handbook of self-determination research*. Rochester: The University of Rochester Press.

Salas, E., Burke, C. S., Wilson-Donnelly, K. A., & Fowlkes, J. E. (2004). Promoting effective leadership within multicultural teams: An event-based approach. In D. V. Day, S. J. Zaccaro, & S. M. Halpin (Eds.), *Leader development for transforming organisations: Growing leaders for tomorrow* (pp. 293–323). Mahwah: Lawrence Erlbaum Associates.

Uhl-Bien, M. (2006). Relational leadership theory: Exploring the social processes of leadership and organizing. *Leadership Quarterly, 17*(6), 654–676.

Yorks, L., & Kasl, E. (2002). Toward a theory and practice for whole-person learning: Reconceptualising experience and the role of affect. *Adult Education Quarterly, 52*(3), 176–192.

Developing Video-Enhanced Pedagogical Cases in Service Leadership

Hugh Thomas

Abstract The paper describes how CUHK is developing video-assisted case sets (Cases) as part of the Service Leadership Initiative (SLI). Cases can be effective in supplementing traditional lecture-based methods to train leaders, introducing interactive and applied pedagogy, and assessing students. As a part of the flipped classroom, videos are increasingly and effectively used in education and can promote the goals of SLI. Production of a Case involves a writer, a producer, a camera person, and an editor. Six Cases have been completed; another six are in various stages of production, and 13 have been indefinitely postponed. We conclude that finding compelling Case subjects is challenging; leadership issues are more understandable for students in the words of the leader expressed through videos; obtaining academic faculty commitment for Case development with real-world leaders is difficult; the risks of non-completion of Case writing are high because of leader risk aversion; video production and editing services may be more effective if accomplished by in-house expertise; instructor risk aversion militates against Case adoption, and placement of a Case with platforms cross listed with Harvard Business Publishing is a necessary but not sufficient condition to effective distribution.

Introduction

The Service Leadership Initiative (SLI) has given the Center for Entrepreneurship (CfE) at The Chinese University of Hong Kong (CUHK) a unique opportunity to conduct applied, pedagogically oriented case research around an important aspect of business – service leadership – while not being constrained by the requirements for publishing in more conventional, peer reviewed journals. The Victor and William Fung Foundation (the Foundation) identified as principal investigators (PIs) respected researchers sympathetic to the goals of SLI and amenable to

H. Thomas, Ph.D. (✉)
Department of Finance, Center for Entrepreneurship, The Chinese University of Hong Kong, Room 1201, Cheung Yu Tung Building, 12 Chak Cheung Street, Shatin, N.T., Hong Kong, Hong Kong
e-mail: hugh-thomas@cuhk.edu.hk

© Springer Science+Business Media Singapore 2015
D.T.L. Shek, P. Chung (eds.), *Promoting Service Leadership Qualities in University Students*, Quality of Life in Asia 6, DOI 10.1007/978-981-287-515-0_11

interuniversity cooperation in each of the eight University Grants Commission-financed universities in Hong Kong and gave each considerable freedom to make his or her contribution to SLI as he or she saw fit. As Victor Fung, one of the two benefactors of the Foundation, said to the SLI Action Research Team (ART), he wished to "... let 100 flowers bloom ...."[1]

Professor Chan, Kin-man, a sociologist in the Faculty of Social Science and the CUHK SLI PI, considered that SLI's objectives would best be achieved through cooperation with the CUHK Faculty of Business Administration. He based his assessment of the importance of business to SLI on views expressed by Victor Fung:

> Hong Kong derives more than 90 % of its GDP from the services sector. For Hong Kong to maintain its competitiveness in the prevailing trend of globalization, we must maintain leadership in the Services Sector. In this regard, I believe our young people will benefit greatly from an education which will provide them with a good framework and hands on experience to make a long-term commitment to Service Leadership. (Fung Foundation 2012)

Professor Chan's role as an Associate Director and Executive Board Member of the CfE, a research center within CUHK's Faculty of Business Administration with predisposition to promote student practice and a track record of supporting social enterprises,[2] led him to plan with the CfE how best to use SLI funding to promote such service leadership. The plan submitted to and accepted by the Foundation involved initiating and teaching a general education (GE), three-credit course on service leadership, implementing SLI modules consistent with the SLI and Service Leadership and Management (SLAM) Curriculum Framework,[3] and producing locally sourced, globally applicable, current, video-enhanced cases to facilitate instructor-led student discussion on service leadership within the GE courses, SLI modules, and other courses in CUHK and other academic institutions around the world. We describe the structure of our main SLI GE course, UGED 1251 *Service Leadership in an Uncertain Era*, in a separate paper in this volume. In this paper, I discuss the Cases.

---

[1] SLI PIs and their teams met with the Foundation director and SLI advisors on an approximately quarterly basis from March 20, 2012, until the date of this publication to discuss progress, share practices and research, and suggest future development. Victor Fung's comments were made at the January 15, 2013, meeting of ART held in the Li and Fung Tower.

[2] The CfE promotes student practice, instruction, and research in entrepreneurship and for over a decade has emphasized social entrepreneurship, particularly through competitions, including, for the last 8 years, the Hong Kong Social Enterprise Challenge. See http://hksec.hk/

[3] SLAM, a nonprofit company founded by Po Chung, provided inspiration for, guidance to, and staff support of SLI, a framework for curricula of SLI GE courses and advice to ART.

Case Teaching in Business

Cases can be effective in supplementing traditional, lecture-based methods to train leaders when applied interactively in a discussion session. In such a situation, students can develop discipline-specific knowledge (e.g., in accounting, decision science, economics finance, management, marketing, information systems, etc.) and hone analytical skills. Where student contributions to class analysis is assessed, teaching effectiveness can be enhanced (Sparks and Langford 2012).

Currently, over ten million teaching cases are sold each year, with sales of about US$40 million but over 80 % of those cases are produced by and distributed on Harvard Business Publishing's website[4] (Korn 2012). Harvard cases, however, have drawbacks. Notwithstanding Harvard's global perspective, most cases from Harvard have a recognizably American bias. When an instructor wishes to teach Hong Kong, Chinese, or other Asian-based students about service leadership, we believe it is useful to have local pedagogical materials.

The Internet poses a serious problem for the instructor using cases. Given levels of connectivity, if an instructor assigns questions prescribed in a published Harvard-distributed case or its teaching note, to which students are to give written answers, students with Internet access can locate within seconds blogs posted by other students that give "correct" formula answers, regardless of whether or not they read the case. Such student activity can severely reduce the effectiveness of case teaching (Sparks and Langford 2012).

Implementing a flipped classroom offers a good way to increase the effectiveness of cases, mitigating the adverse effects and using the benefits of Internet connectivity (Gerstein 2012). Videos can enhance education and student preparation for a flipped class (Anderson 2010) and can be used in the classroom to enliven case teaching. Three years before SLI was launched, the CUHK CfE together with the Hong Kong Design Center developed a set of video-assisted cases that we found effective in teaching design entrepreneurship.[5]

---

[4] See http://hbsp.harvard.edu/. The HBSP website also cross lists cases from 33 other sources including ABCC at Nanyang Tech University, Babson College, Berrett-Koehler Publishers, Business Enterprise Trust, California Management Review (CMR), The Crimson Group, Darden School of Business, Design Management Institute, ESMT, Global Health Delivery / Harvard Medical School, Harvard Kennedy School of Government, HEC Montréal, IESE, IMD, Indian Institute of Management – Bangalore, Indian School of Business, INSEAD, Ivey Publishing, Journal of Information Technology, Kellogg School of Management, McGraw Hill, MIT Sloan Management Review, NACRA Case Research Journal, Perseus Books, Princeton University Press, Public Education Leadership Project, Rotman Magazine, Social Enterprise Knowledge Network, Stanford Graduate School of Business, Thunderbird School of Global Management, Tsinghua University, UC Berkeley – Haas School of Business, and the University of Hong Kong's Asian Case Research Centre.

[5] See Center for Entrepreneurship *Design Entrepreneurship in Hong Kong: Roadmaps and Cases* http://research.hkdesign.org/content.php?nid=16. Accessed 12/12/2014.

Production of Cases

Based on the above, CUHK made the production and use of Cases a key part of SLI, with the Cases to be produced under the leadership of the writer of this article. Cases were planned to have dual uses (1) in our credit-bearing, GE service leadership course and (2) in discipline-specific courses. In producing the Cases, we held to the principle that discipline-related pedagogy takes precedence over leadership training. This approach was based on our belief that leadership requires context and that academic rigor is best achieved through the interaction of leadership concepts with discipline-specific theories and practices. Moreover, this approach accords with a view expressed at ART meetings that leadership principles should be integrated into courses beyond GE (SLI MOU 2012, Annex B, p. 21). By satisfying the discipline-specific pedagogical needs of professors and other instructors, teaching a specific discipline-specific course first, a Case, and its leadership ideas can be projected into non-GE courses in other modules of other programs throughout the teaching community.

Production of each Case was organized as follows. Each Case was directed academically by a professor who said that he or she would use the Case in his or her discipline-specific course(s). The professor committed to provide guidance to a production team that included a case writer, a producer, camera people, and an editor. Overall process oversight was handled by me. The iterative production process involved leader/institution identification, pedagogical goal setting, framework development, issue identification, consent clearance, interviewing, filming, teaching note and video script writing, post-production, classroom testing, reediting, case network application, copyright clearance, and video posting. See Fig. 1.

As of the date of writing (December 2014), six Cases (including a 15–20-page write-up for distribution to students, a 10–30-page instructors' note, and a 15–30-min video) were completed (with four accepted into case clearing systems cross listed with Harvard Business Publishing (hbsp.harvard.edu/) and two in the peer review process); another six were in various stages of production, and 13 had been indefinitely postponed. See Tables 1, 2, and 3.

The completed Cases have been classroom tested in the discipline-specific courses for which they were created and have been found to be very effective. Students commented that the videos increased their personal identification with the leaders and the decision he or she was making. Within the GE course, we found the videos to be highly effective in illustrating various concepts of leadership. For example, Ms. Aglaia Kong in *Cisco and Cloud Education in China* presents an effective way of showing the difference between leadership with authority and leadership without authority. Ma Weihua in *China Merchants Bank: Business Model Transformation* provides a framework for discussing transformative versus transactional leadership. Whereas in discipline-specific courses the 15–20-page write-ups were critical to instruction, in the GE leadership course, the write-ups were far less effective than the videos and were often not useful.

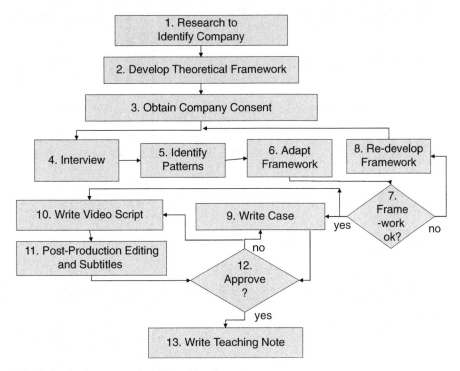

Fig. 1 Production process for video-assisted case

Problems

When we started Case production, we planned to produce 15 cases in 3 years. The fact that, 2 years into SLI, we have completed only six Cases and have indefinitely postpone 13 other Cases illustrates that we have faced more problems than we anticipated initially. These problems include difficulties in motivating professors to supervise cases, insufficient incentives for leaders to submit to case research, technical difficulties, and failure to promote cases effectively to SLI colleagues.

Motivating Professors

As discussed above, each Case team includes a professor who has discipline expertise. The primary purpose of each Case is to use a real business or other organizational situation to achieve a discipline-specific teaching objective. The second purpose of the dual-purpose case – illustrating a leadership issue – takes a subordinate role because we believe that most interactions in business or other organizations can yield insights into service leadership but, in general, most

Table 1 Completed cases

No	Professor	Department	Title	Leader	Question to decide	Leadership issues	Writer	Video	Status	Full video
1	Julie Yu	Marketing	WebOrganic: Creating a Blue Ocean for a Social Cause	Erwin Huang, CEO	Marketing and partnering strategy for social enterprise creating an uncontested market space within an e-learning market	Strategic relationship management and the rationale behind running a social enterprise	Penny Lau	Pauline Ng/HKU Journalism Acacia/Joshua	Placed at Harvard/ ACRC HK1001-PDF-ENG	https://www.youtube.com/watch?v=VRLn3Sk-aoM
2	Kevin Au	Management	Diamond Cab: Investment of a Venture Philanthropy Fund	Doris Leung, CEO	Determining a sustainable strategy of a social enterprise	Profit from providing a social service	Anna Tsui	Acacia/ Joshua	Placed at Harevard/ Ivey W13587-PDF-ENG	https://www.youtube.com/watch?v=4iiuhNxDz5k
3	Liu Minkang and Hugh Thomas	Finance	China Merchants Bank: Business Model Transformation	Ma Weihua, CEO	Banking Strategy in the face of capital constraints; stakeholder theory	Publically traded SOE bank leadership responsibilities to bank regulator, shareholders, and customers	Du Gang	Acacia/ Joshua	Placed at Harvard/ Ivey W14297-PDF-ENG	https://www.youtube.com/watch?v=KwMdKTew4nE&feature=em-share_video_user
4	Hugh Thomas and	Management	Cisco and Cloud Education in China	Aglaia Kong, CTO	Shifting from a horizontal to a vertical approach;	Reorientation of product-based company into service	Hugh Thomas	Acacia/Joshua	Accepted at Ivey; in final editing	https://www.youtube.com/watch?v=Fa9uTc1JKDI

#									
	Robert Lee				market entry strategies	approach; cultural and institutional differences of US and Chinese companies			
5	Hugh Thomas	Finance	Constellation: The Distribution of Minibonds	Front line service staff; YK Choi, Deputy CE, Banking HKMA	Pricing and risk of complex securities; Banker-customer relationship on sales of complex wealth management products	Fiduciary responsibility, remuneration, service culture; regulatory role in service	Hugh Thomas	Acacia/Joshua	Completed: submitted to HKU ACRC	https://www.youtube.com/watch?v=o6BzUnbfddk
6	Shige Makino and Hugh Thomas	Management of Nonprofits	Serving The Chinese University of Hong Kong: Leadership Challenges for Professor Joseph Sung	Joseph Song	Dealing with student, alumni and political issues concerning Goddess of Democracy, language policy and Shenzhen campus	University social responsibility	Anna Tsui	Acacia/Joshua	Completed: submitted to Ivey; rejected because insufficient market anticipated	https://www.youtube.com/watch?v=O9VugMr7dEM

Table 2 Cases in process

No	Professor	Department	Title	Leader	Question to decide	Leadership issues	Writer	Video	Status
1	Shige Makino and Hugh Thomas	Environmental Responsibility, PR and Management	Asia Pulp and Paper	Aida Greenbury, MD for sustainability	Meeting environmental performance standards in supply chain management	Corporate social responsibility	Boby Shiu	In-house	Draft in process; shooting and interviews in Indonesia, Nov 17–20
2	Hugh Thomas	Finance	Young Financial Professionals	15 graduates on business programs with from 4 to 8 years of experience	The applicability of taught theory	Leadership from the middle of an organization	David Tam	In-house	Two of 15 click-throughs produced
3	Andrew Chan, Howard Lam, and Hugh Thomas	Marketing	Hung Fook Tong	Ricky Szeto	Applying a Hong Kong marketing model to China	To be determined	Elise Sairojpand	In-house	First draft completed; scheduling interview
4	Joyce Wang Linghua and Hugh Thomas	Finance	Dividend Policy at Fuyao	Cao Dewang	What is the appropriate dividend policy for the company	Aligning differing interests of stakeholders	Joyce Wang Linghua	To be determined	In early draft writing; interview to be scheduled
5	Hugh Thomas	Finance	Financial Management /flipped classroom	Students embarking on their careers	Various applied theories in finance	Financial service leadership	Hugh Thomas	In-house	Software and equipment installed; first scripts written

Table 3 Cases indefinitely postponed

No	Professor	Department	Title	Leader	Question to decide	Leadership issues	Writer	Video	Status
1	Howard Lam and Hugh Thomas	Marketing	MTR Service Quality and Public Relations	Jay Herbert Walder/ May Wong GM – Corporate Relations	A marketing case assessing and addressing the gaps between internal and external perceptions of quality in a difficult PR period	Team building	Boby Shiu	Public segments; in-house editing	Case completed; click-through video completed; clearance denied
2	Zhao Xiande	Decision Sciences	Ritz Carleton	Front line QC manager	How to implement a QC system	Improving quality control in an acquisition	Jack Lee	–	Prof left CUHK; management left RC
3	Zhang Meng, Robert Lee and Hugh Thomas	Marketing / China Strategy	JD.com	Richard Liu Qiangdong	Marketing strategy of Internet B2C distributor	–	–	–	Liu Qiangdong not available
4	Howard Lam and Hugh Thomas	Marketing	Disneyland Hong Kong	Top management – to be identified	Strategies to address threat of Shanghai Disneyland	–	–	–	Disney not keen
5	Franko Wong	Strategy: Hotel Project Development	Starwood Meridien	Top management – to be identified	Whether or not to proceed with a new hotel project	–	–	–	Project not current
6	Waisun Chan and Hugh Thomas	Insurance and Actuarial Science	CPD cases	Front line actuaries	A series of ethical issues arising from business situations faced by actuaries	Service leadership of front line staff	–	–	Institute not keen

(continued)

Table 3 (continued)

No	Professor	Department	Title	Leader	Question to decide	Leadership issues	Writer	Video	Status
7	Bernard Suen and Hugh Thomas	Political Science	Political Leadership in Hong Kong	15 leaders from Hong Kong politics including the CE, the chief secretary, KM Chan and Robert Chow Yung	Strategies to approach political organization, policy, and democracy in Hong Kong	Leadership with and without authority	–	In-house editing and shooting	Unable to identify academic professor with political science expertise keen to proceed
8	Hugh Thomas	Finance	m.paani	Hazari	How can Akanksha Hazari, Founder, use $1 m Hult Clinton Global prize to start her social enterprise	–	–	–	Leader too busy to proceed
9	Fu Pingping	Management	Yangguang Nina Beauty, Spa and Club	Nina Yang	How to reset company strategy to develop whole person (body, mind, soul) and set appropriate personnel policies	As a company grows, can it keep its value system	–	–	Materials insufficiently strong
10	Wilton Chau	Finance	Pheim Capital	–	Relocation strategy of fund manager	The "fit and proper person" and the regulator	–	–	Leader unwilling
11	Hugh Thomas	Finance	Alpha	–	Exit of a private equity investment in kiln brick production	–	Virendra Nath	–	Leader unwilling

12	Robert Lee and Hugh Thomas	China Business Strategy	NewsCorp in China	Jack GAO, Senior Vice President	How can a global mass media giant approach best work in the China market	To be determined	–	–	Leader unwilling
13	Terence Yuen	Management of Social Enterprise	Fullness Salon	Ted Kwan	Assessing the SROI and a social venture	Leadership styles training former offenders to serve customers	–	–	SROI study results not as anticipated

interactions do not illustrate a theory or concept th*at a professor instructing in a classroom will find useful*. This need to obtain a professor's discipline-specific buy-in if a Case is to be useful creates a problem in sourcing Cases. We have talked with many leaders who wish to be the subject of a Case writing. But if no professor finds the situation illuminated by the leader pedagogically interesting, then no Case can be produced.

Virtually, all professors we talked to in the CUHK Faculty of Business Administration said that they used cases, and most said that they designed their own and would continue to do so. However, the cases they designed tended to be examples, using current publically available materials and personal experiences, that were never formally organized into written pedagogical materials for sharing with colleagues. Although many initially generated suitable ideas, most demonstrated insufficient motivation to participate in our Case production. Their time tends to be spent pursuing research to write top tier-refereed publications necessary for tenure and promotion. Although the Cases we write *do* go through a peer review process before acceptance in a Harvard-cross listed platform, the process is not sufficiently rigorous to rank the Case with top or even second tier-refereed journal article publications.

We have not so far offered the professors wishing to participate in Case writing any monetary incentive. We do offer the services of a case writer and video team and the overall coordination of the CUHK SLI team, primarily myself. But the supervision of the pedagogical direction of the case and the teaching note still requires a substantial commitment. We have found that more professors who have had careers in business as well as academic careers tend to value case production.

One of our hopes at the outset of SLI was that other ART members and their colleagues might join Case teams. So far, that hope has proved vain.

The difficulty in finding professors who are keen to produce Cases has led to an undesirable outcome. A disproportionate number of our Cases are finance related, because I am a finance professor. While finance is a very important service industry in Hong Kong, we would rather have more cases in tourism, business services, logistics, etc., as well as service functions in goods companies.

Incentives for Leaders

Leaders of companies, especially of listed companies, tend to be loath to disclose information. They shy away from case research in the same way that many shy away from reporters. Most leaders tend to avoid revealing negative aspects of their organizations, a tendency that may constrain case contents. Leaders may perceive little benefit beyond fulfilling corporate social responsibility in hosting case research while seeing significant potential risks should research uncover inconvenient truths. In our experience, the cautious leader avoids case research.

In SLI, every Case uses information beyond that which is already in the public domain, and therefore every Case needs to receive prior written authorization for publication from the leader in the Case. This constrains Case writing to situations where a high degree of trust between the Case team and the leader exists. In our Case research, most Case ideas and leaders were sourced by the sponsoring professor. This allowed trust to be engendered from the moment of contact. The Case team, the professor, and the leader all understood from the outset that we were working toward a case release at the end of the process.

However, circumstances often evolve, as Table 3 shows. For example, our research at MTR on the gap between customers' and corporate officers' perceptions of customer satisfaction was a potentially sensitive topic – although one critical to service leadership – before the protagonist, Jay Herbert Walter, was fired. His dismissal rendered our case writing, which had already gone to draft and video scripting, infeasible.

Production Difficulties

Through most of the production process to date, we have used case writers hired one at a time on a part-time basis. In each Case, the role of the case writer has differed. Some have actually written the entire case. Others have assembled exhibits. Others have administered the process. The ability of case writers to grasp the pedagogical points of the professor has varied considerably causing complete forgoing of their use in some Cases.

For most of the Cases, we subcontracted video production while maintaining script writing and editing authority. Video production companies tended to bid low for the contract and then be upset when our requirements for quality exceeded their expectations. This proved somewhat problematic when the video-producing company itself subcontracted production to individual editors, recording studies, etc. The attenuation of the chain, sometimes as long as from professor to producer to assistant to contractor to subcontractor proved unwieldy, so in later videos, we have chosen to hire in-house full-time production expertise. What we lose in professionalism we believe we gain in immediacy of conveying purpose. We also think that we can build in-house, increasingly professional capacity in video that will be useful in future pedagogical projects.

We attempted click-through techniques[6] using public domain videos located on YouTube and YouKu but encountered technical difficulties which we are still addressing. While our experience on YouTube, where we currently place all of our completed videos, has been generally good, we have had experiences of being frozen out of the site. These technical difficulties lead us to prefer, in the future, to use our own streaming server, costs permitting.

---

[6] On a click-through video, a single web page contains embedded videos that may be hosted on other sites, where only a portion of each embedded video is used for the pedagogical tool.

Failure to Promote

A substantial disappointment, shared by most case writers, is to find that, after they have invested considerable work in producing a case, no other instructor (i.e., nobody but the case writer himself or herself) uses the case. Yet this condition is the rule, not the exception in case writing. As Read, Goldsmith, and Egeli (2009) show in their study of more than 3.89 million sales of some 21,000 cases registered in the European Case Clearing House from 1993 to 2008, just over half of listed cases sold *no* copies. The largest single determinants in sales are the presence of a teaching note (selling 135 copies more than the average) and the presence of a video (selling 414 more than the average).[7] By including videos and teaching notes in our Cases, we hoped to increase our sales. Although given the life span of most cases from 5 to 10 years, this is still in the early days; we are not encouraged by enthusiasm for our cases to date. The substantial amount of time necessary for an instructor to learn a new case militates against new case adoption. Placement with a case clearing house with cross listing to Harvard Business Publishing is a necessary but not sufficient condition to effective distribution. And presence of a teaching note and a video is helpful in promoting the case but do not guarantee success.

Somewhat optimistically, we considered we had a captive audience in SLI as all ART members teach GE courses on service leadership. Our ART colleagues teaching GE courses could largely avoid pay Harvard's high prices: listing with a clearing house is a lengthy process that takes up to a year. During that time, draft Case use is free of charge through direct contact with us. Following a clearing-house listing, use of the video will always be free of charge. Instructors can access free of charge the case and teaching note for their own benefit and can distribute the video to their GE students. As we noted above, for GE classes, the video is by far the most useful part of the Cases. Only in discipline-related classes, where instructors and their students typically are used to pay for cases, would the prices of Harvard-cleared Cases be required. Unfortunately, to our knowledge, no member of SLI has used any of our Cases (or used any video from any of our Cases) in his or her classes. This may be the downside of that very positive aspect of SLI to let a hundred flowers bloom.

Conclusion

With one year to the completion of SLI, we are committed to pursue Case production. We are hopeful that the Cases can contribute to service leadership pedagogy and promotion in Hong Kong. We welcome both ART members and

---

[7] ECCH, renamed The Case Centre in 2013, cross lists its cases with Harvard. Harvard, however, does not release figures on sales of any of their own cases.

wider members of the service leadership pedagogical community to review our Cases and contribute to our Case production process.

References

Anderson, C. (2010, July). *How web video powers global innovation: TED Ideas Worth Spreading [Video]*. Retrieved from http://www.ted.com/talks/lang/en/chris_anderson_how_web_video_powers_global_innovation.html

Fung Foundation. (2012). *Victor and William Fung Foundation commemorates 105th anniversary of Li & Fung Group with grant to strengthen service leadership education* [Press release]. Retrieved from http://www.funggroup.com/eng/sustainability/foundations_vwf.ph

Gerstein, J. (2012). *User generated education – flipped classroom: The full picture for higher education [Video]*. Retrieved from http://usergeneratededucation.wordpress.com/2012/05/15/flipped-classroom-the-full-picture-for-higher-education/

Korn, M. (2012). Business education: The business of case studies. *Wall Street Journal*. Eastern Edition, NY, B.8.

Read, S., Goldsmith, H., & Egeli, P. (2009). *What drives case sales?* ECCHO issue 42, IMD International. Retrieved from www.thecasecentre.org/files/downloads/research/whatdrivescasesales.pdf

Service Leadership Initiative Memorandum of Understanding Annex B SLAM Curriculum Framework. (2012). *Signed by each PI within the SLI*.

Sparks, R. J., & Langford, J. (2012). An examination of traditional business case studies – Are they outdated in today's technology connected environment? *Journal of Business Case Studies, 8* (2), 217–222.

University Students' Socially Responsible Values and Capacities for Service Leadership

Joan Y.H. Leung, Raysen W.L. Cheung, and Hang Chow

Abstract This chapter uses the questionnaire survey method to examine the socially responsible values of university students in Hong Kong. It aims specifically to test the reliability and validity of the Socially Responsible Leadership Scale (SRLS) – a framework widely used in American higher education – as an appropriate tool to measure the leadership capacity of Hong Kong university students. The survey instrument used in the study captures the data related to Hong Kong students' scores on the seven values (including Consciousness of Self, Congruence, Commitment, Collaboration, Common Purpose, Controversy with Civility, Citizenship) of Socially Responsible Leadership Scale (SRLS) and the students' attitude toward change and Leadership Efficacy. Apart from demographic factors, it analyses the relationships between students' university experience and their capacity for socially responsible leadership. The discussion of SRLS also makes reference to the Hong Kong Institute of Service Leadership and Management (HKI-SLAM) approach of Service Leadership, both of which define leadership as a valued-based process for the purpose of self-enhancement (individual), service to others (group), collaborative actions (community) and positive social change.

The data discussed in this paper was collected from a questionnaire survey of undergraduate students in one of the eight public universities in Hong Kong. The permission to use the Socially Responsible Leadership Scale Revised Version 2 (SRLS-R2) instrument has been granted by the patent holder, the *National Clearinghouse for Leadership Programs (NCLP)*.

J.Y.H. Leung (✉)
Department of Public Policy, City University of Hong Kong, AC1-B7408, Tat Chee Avenue, Kowloon, Hong Kong, Hong Kong
e-mail: sajoan@cityu.edu.hk

R.W.L. Cheung
Department of Applied Social Sciences, City University of Hong Kong, Y7311 AC1, Tat Chee Avenue, Kowloon, Hong Kong, Hong Kong

H. Chow
Project Flame, City University of Hong Kong, 3A, To Yuen Street, Kowloon, Hong Kong, Hong Kong

© Springer Science+Business Media Singapore 2015
D.T.L. Shek, P. Chung (eds.), *Promoting Service Leadership Qualities in University Students*, Quality of Life in Asia 6, DOI 10.1007/978-981-287-515-0_12

Introduction

Historically, leadership theories tend to identify leadership as innate traits or the behaviour of an individual holding a position or a title. The post-industrial approaches to leadership, however, are nonhierarchical, relating to flatted and decentralised structure of authority. They conceive leadership as a process of development that can be learned and accessible to all people and a vehicle for social change. The Hong Kong Institute of Service Leadership and Management (HKI-SLAM), hereafter referred as the SLAM model, for example, defines leadership as a "service aimed at ethically satisfying the needs of self, others, groups, communities, systems and environments" (Chung 2011, quoted in SLAM 2014). Along similar lines, the Social Change Model (SCM) defines leadership as "a purposeful, collaborative, value-based process that results in positive social change" (Komives et al. 2009, p. xii). Indeed, there are many commonalities between the SLAM and the SCM models. Both view leadership as an inclusive, relational, empowering and purposeful process. Most crucially, both approaches associate leadership with ethically oriented values and transformational change for the common good. The cornerstone of these two approaches is a value-based developmental process. With the ethical values as the foundation, both frameworks embrace common civic values, such as self-awareness, social justice, empathy, care, commitment and collaboration as their guiding principles. Moreover, both view leadership as a service or socially responsible behaviour to effect positive change for self, others and the community (HERI 1996; HKI-SLAM 2014).

Socially Responsible Leadership (SRL) Values and Service Leadership

Given that "leadership" can be learned and all people are potential leaders, education plays a crucial role in shaping the socially responsible values and developing the leadership capacity of today's youth. Universities, in particular, are in a unique position to promote the knowledge, skills and behaviour associated with the socially responsible values in students that are so needed by society. Ethical organisations are important in all work sectors. One of the central purposes for higher education is to develop students' ethical values and sense of social responsibility before their promotion into decision-making roles in society upon graduation and employment. It is, therefore, important to have an understanding of the socially responsible values and leadership capacity of university students nowadays. According to Dugan (2011, p. 60), leadership capacity refers to an individual's "enacted leadership beliefs, style, and approach", and a research measuring leadership capacity should be "grounded in a particular theoretical context".

Among the various post-industrial leadership theories, this paper uses the SCM as the theoretical framework to examine the leadership capacity of university students in Hong Kong. The SCM instrument is chosen because it is specifically designed to examine the leadership capacity development of university students and has been widely used in the American higher education sector. Above all, as mentioned above, the central principles of the SCM are in congruence with the core beliefs of the SLAM approach of Service Leadership.[1] Fundamentally, both models are rooted in a commitment to the core civic values, predicated on individuals' self-knowledge, and associate leadership with collaboration, social responsibility, service to others and positive change (HIRI; HKI-SLAM, op. cit.). The next section explains further the SCM of leadership conception whose theoretical foundation is predicated on a set of socially responsible values. The main section of the paper then discusses the survey methods, findings and implications.

Social Change Model (SCM) of Leadership Conception

Conceptually, the SCM is built on seven critical values of leadership which is known as the 7Cs: Consciousness of Self, Congruence, Commitment, Collaboration, Common Purpose, Controversy with Civility and Citizenship. Table 1 and Fig. 1, which give a brief description of each of these seven values (the 7Cs) and a visual presentation of the SCM, are extracts from Wendy Wagner's paper available online (Wagner 2006). Adapting her materials from the original research produced by Higher Education Research Institute (1996), Wagner's paper gives a very good summary of the SCM of leadership development. The 7Cs fall into three clusters: individual, group and community values which are interrelated. The dynamic interaction among the seven critical values, which operates at both the individual and group levels, in turn, gives force to the eighth value of change. Change, a key assumption of the SCM, is at the centre. These eight values embody the principles of social responsibility and positive change, in which leadership is conceived as a process of continual learning and self-evaluation for individuals (Dugan and Komives 2011). Nevertheless, individuals might face values conflict during their interactions with others and groups. The uneasy tensions are part of the developmental process of socially responsible leadership (SRL). The SCM not only has a strong theoretical underpinning, it is also supported by extensive research in the United States. Yet, as far as the authors are aware, the SCM has not been applied to analyse the socially responsible leadership of Hong Kong students.

---

[1] The SLAM framework of leadership has two main dimensions: service competency and domain competency. In this paper, the analysis focuses mainly on the *values* underpinning the SLAM framework *of Service Leadership*.

Table 1 The values of the socially responsible leadership values of the social change model

Individual values	
Consciousness of self	Being self-aware of the beliefs, values, attitudes and emotions that motivate you to take action. Being mindful, or aware of your current emotional state, behaviour and perceptual lenses
Congruence	Acting in ways that are consistent with your values and beliefs. Thinking, feeling and behaving with consistency, genuineness, authenticity and honesty toward others
Commitment	Having significant investment in an idea or person, both in terms of intensity and duration. Having the energy to serve the group and its goals. Commitment originates from within, but others can create an environment that supports an individual's passions
Group values	
Collaboration	Working with others in a common effort, sharing responsibility, authority and accountability. Multiplying group effectiveness by capitalising on various perspectives and talents and on the power of diversity to generate creative solutions and actions
Common purpose	Having shared aims and values. Involving others in building a group's vision and purpose
Controversy with civility	Recognising two fundamental realities of any creative effort: (1) that differences in viewpoint are inevitable and (2) that such differences must be aired openly but with civility
Community values	
Citizenship	Believing in a process whereby an individual and/or a group become responsibly connected to the community and to society through some activity. Recognising that members of communities are not independent, but interdependent. Recognising individuals and groups have responsibility for the welfare of others
Change	Believing in the importance of making a better world and a better society for oneself and others. Believing that individuals, groups and communities have the ability to work together to make that change

Source: Wagner, W. (2006)

Research Questions

The purpose of this exploratory study is to test initially the SCM of SRL as the theoretical framework to examine the leadership capacity of university students in Hong Kong. The study specifically aims to address the following questions:

1. How do Hong Kong students score on the eight values of Socially Responsible Leadership Scale (SRLS)?
2. How far the Socially Responsible Leadership Scale (SRLS) is a reliable and valid measure to apply in Hong Kong?

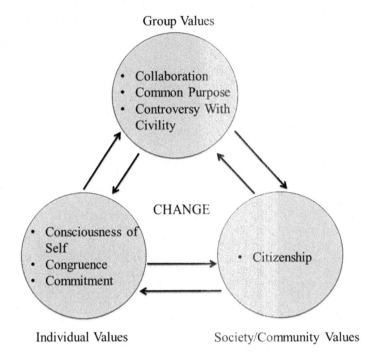

Fig. 1 The social change model of leadership (Source: Wagner, W. (2006))

3. What are the relationships between the independent variables (demographic factors and university experience) and the dependent variables (students' capacity for SRL)?

Methods

The instrument used in this study was the revised Socially Responsible Leadership Scale (SRLS-R2) which consisted of 68 items. The survey employed a convenience sampling method, and the data were collected between September and December of 2013 in forms of paper questionnaires and Qualtrics, a web-based survey system, in a public university in Hong Kong. In order to draw a meaningful sample, undergraduate students from three major disciplines of science and engineering, business studies, as well as liberal arts and social sciences were included as respondents. Moreover, residents in the student halls and members of the university sport teams were specifically invited to complete the questionnaires. There were a total of 1,344 responses, and the final dataset contained 918 valid cases. The profile of the 918 respondents is given in Table 2.

To compute and analyse the students' scores on the SRLS with SPSS, all the data on a Likert scale of 1 to 5 ranging from "strongly disagree" to "strongly agree" was

Table 2 Profiles of
918 respondents

Items		N	Valid percent
Disciplines			
Business		259	28.2
Liberal arts and social sciences		286	31.2
Science and engineering		320	34.9
Creative media		32	3.5
Law		13	1.4
Energy and environment		8	.9
Total		*918*	*100*
Gender			
Male		343	37.4
Female		575	62.6
Total		*918*	*100*
Religion			
No religion		511	59.7
With religion	Protestant	197	23.0
	Catholics	47	5.5
	Muslim	12	1.4
	Buddhist	76	8.9
	Taoist	13	1.5
	SUBTOTAL	345	40.3
TOTAL		*856*[a]	*100*

[a]62 missing cases were excluded

first input and "cleaned". The validity and reliability of the original SRLS and the SRLS-R2 have been extensively tested by Tyree and Dugan respectively (NCLP 2013). Since the SRLS measures were a self-report tool and it is the first time that this instrument was used to survey Hong Kong students, this study therefore included the scales of Self-Leadership (Houghton et al. 2012) and Leadership Efficacy (Dugan and Komives 2010) to examine the validity of the SRLS. Pearson correlations analyses were applied to examine the Pearson correlations of SRLS scales with measures of Self-Leadership and Leadership Efficacy respectively. The SRL subscales and the measures of Self-Leadership and Leadership Efficacy were all inter-correlated. The solidarity of the results was supported with a significant level all below 0.01, and the $r =$ range from .784 to .402 as indicated in Appendix 1. In addition, the Cronbach's alpha levels of the eight SRLS, Self-Leadership and Leadership Efficacy were calculated to estimate the reliability of the instrument. The alpha coefficient ranged from .71 for the Controversy with Civility to .83 for the Citizenship subscales, and the reliability estimate of the omnibus SRLS measure is .93. The alpha coefficients of the eight SRLS are found in Table 3.

The variables of this study, including the eight SRLS, as well as the measures of Leadership Efficacy are found in Appendix 2. First, the measures of each SRLS, Self-Leadership and Leadership Efficacy were calculated by adding the composite variables and dividing by the total number of items. Next, statistically tests were

Table 3 Leadership outcomes: measures of the SRLS, self-leadership and leadership efficacy

	Mean			SD			Cronbach's alpha	
	American students (nationwide)[a]	Asian American students[b]	Hong Kong students	American students (nationwide)[a]	Asian American students[b]	Hong Kong students	SRLS-R2, Dugan (2010)[a]	This particular study
Consciousness of Self	3.95	3.77	3.58	.51	.54	.49	.78	.78
Congruence	4.18	4.04	3.77	.46	.51	.48	.79	.78
Commitment	4.24	4.10	3.92	.47	.52	.49	.83	.77
Collaboration	3.98	3.93	3.8	.45	.49	.46	.80	.80
Common Purpose	4.04	3.97	3.87	.42	.46	.44	.81	.83
Controversy with Civility	3.84	3.73	3.63	.42	.43	.40	.72	.71
Citizenship	3.84	3.74	3.75	.46	.48	.48	.89	.83
Change	3.75	3.68	3.62	.47	.47	.46	.82	.81
Omnibus SRLS[c]	3.96	–	3.74	.38	–	.46	.96	.93
Self-Leadership	–	–	3.71	–	–	.51	–	.83
Leadership Efficacy	–	–	3.69	–	–	.65	–	.81

[a]Dugan and Komives (2007) [b]Dugan et al. (2009) [c]Overall of the Socially Responsible Leadership Scale

Table 4 Results of multiple analyses of variance (MANOVA) for the 8 measures of SRL

Effect (Wilks' Lambda)	Gender	Religion	Academic discipline
Value	.958	.977	.944
F	4.787	2.456	3.018
Sig.	.000	.012	.000
Partial Eta squared	.042	.023	.029

Table 5 Results of univariate analysis of variance (ANOVA) for each of the SRLS

	Gender			Academic discipline		
	F	p	n_p^2	F	p	n_p^2
Consciousness of Self	3.813			11.680	**	.027
Congruence	1.803			3.477	*	.008
Commitment	12.791	**	.014	4.538	*	.010
Collaboration	17.339	**	.019	9.945	**	.023
Common Purpose	8.740	**	.010	8.864	**	.020
Controversy with Civility	.182			1.526		
Citizenship	7.766	**	.008	8.630	***	.020
Change	.010			2.393		

$*p < 0.05 **p < 0.01$

conducted to examine the relationship between demographic factors and university experience and students' SRLS mean scores. Given there were eight measures of the SRL outcomes, multivariate analyses of variance (MANOVA) were conducted to test the mean differences between the independent variables and the dependent variables, as found in Table 4. The Pearson correlation analyses also indicated strong inter-correlations between each of the eight measures of the SRL outcomes (r ranges from .402 to .784). Finally, for SRLS measures with significant mean differences as indicated by MANOVA, follow-up tests using univariate analysis of variance (ANOVA) were conducted to compute their mean differences in each SRL outcomes. Results of the ANOVA analyses were given in Table 5.

Findings and Discussion

General Leadership Outcomes

In this study, we have obtained initial reliability data of all subscales of this leadership measure in Hong Kong, including Consciousness of Self (Cronbach's alpha = .78), Congruence (Cronbach's alpha = .78), Commitment, (Cronbach's alpha = .77), Collaboration, (Cronbach's alpha = .80), Common Purpose

(Cronbach's alpha = .83), Controversy with Civility (Cronbach's alpha = .71), Citizenship (Cronbach's alpha = .83) and Change (Cronbach's alpha = .81).

In addition to the mutual correlations among the eight subscales (Appendix 1), we also find all subscales are correlated to the measures of Self-Leadership and Leadership Efficacy. Self-Leadership has significant correlations with Consciousness of Self ($r = .558$, $p < .01$), Congruence ($r = .601$, $p < .01$), Commitment ($r = .566$, $p < .01$), Collaboration ($r = .536$, $p < .01$), Common Purpose ($r = .567$, $p < .01$), Controversy with Civility ($r = .402$, $p < .01$), Citizenship ($r = .587$, $p < .01$) and Change ($r = .488$, $p < .01$). Similarly, Leadership Efficacy is also significantly correlated with Consciousness of Self ($r = .581$, $p < .01$), Congruence ($r = .456$, $p < .01$), Commitment ($r = .418$, $p < .01$), Collaboration ($r = .523$, $p < .01$), Common Purpose ($r = .473$, $p < .01$), Controversy with Civility ($r = .490$, $p < .01$), Citizenship ($r = .500$, $p < .01$) and Change ($r = .539$, $p < .01$). On the whole, good initial reliability and validity support are found for further development and application in the Hong Kong context.

Hong Kong (HK) students exhibited a medium level of leadership capacity as indicated by the SRLS of the SCM. Table 3 shows that their omnibus (overall) SRLS score was 3.74; the highest score was found on the Commitment value ($M = 3.92$); the second highest score was found on the Common Purpose value ($M = 3.87$); and the lowest score was found on the Consciousness of Self value ($M = 3.58$). It is of interest to compare these with the American student findings conducted by Dugan and Komives (2007). Generally, HK students had lower scores on all the eight measures of the SRLS than American students. This was in agreement with the findings of Dugan, Komives and Sega (2009) that Asian American scored significantly lower than the Whites and Africa Americans. It is also noteworthy that HK students' omnibus SRLS score ($M = 3.74$) reported a high level of agreement with their scores on Self-Leadership ($M = 3.71$) and Leadership Efficacy ($M = 3.69$).

In terms of the score ranking of the SRLS, both HK and American students scored high on the Commitment and Common Purpose values, which were among the top two or three on their lists. Similarly, both HK and American students scored low on the Change value, which ranked second last or the last on their lists respectively. Yet, it is of interest to note that HK students were weak on individual values, such as the values of Consciousness of Self and Congruence which ranked last and fourth respectively on the list. Yet, the Congruence value ranked second and the Consciousness of Self value ranked fifth on the American students' score list. However, HK students were relatively strong on the group and societal values as compared to the American students. The values of Collaboration and Citizenship, for example, ranked third and fifth on HK students' list and fourth and seventh on the American students' list, though both were low on the Controversy with Civility value.

MANOVA analyses with independent variables found significant mean differences across the SRL outcomes in the following categories: gender (Wilks'

Lambda $= .958$, $F = 4.787$, $p < .000$, $n_p^2 = .042$), religion (Wilks' Lambda $= .977$, $F = 2.456$, $p < .012$, $n_p^2 = .023$) and academic discipline (Wilks' Lambda $= .944$, $F = 3.018$, $p < .000$, $n_p^2 = .029$), as indicated in Table 4. No significant mean difference was found on age, students' experience in residential halls or participation in sport teams. Follow-up ANOVA analyses with gender and academic disciplines found significant mean differences in some SRL values. The results were given in Table 5. Yet, the ANOVA analysis with religion found no significant mean difference in any SRL values, though there was significant mean difference with the MANOVA analysis. Moreover, Pearson correlation analyses between students' CGPA and the SRLS also demonstrated significant mean difference in most of the SRL outcomes. A breakdown of student groups under different categories (gender, religion and academic discipline) and their mean scores across the SRLS are given in Table 6. The correlation coefficients between students' CGPA and their scores of the SRLS, Self-Leadership and Leadership Efficacy are found in Table 7.

Gender

Same as previous findings from the research conducted in the States (Dugan and Komives 2007), HK female students exhibited stronger SRL outcomes than males. Table 6 showed that though difference existed, both men and women scored lowest on the same values: Consciousness of Self, Controversy with Civility and Change. Further analysis with ANOVA also found that there were significant mean differences between females and males in the following SRL values: Commitment ($F = 12.791$, $p < .01$, $n_p^2 = .014$), Collaboration ($F = 17.339$, $p < .01$, $n_p^2 = .019$), Common Purpose ($F = 8.740$, $p < .01$, $n_p^2 = .010$) and Citizenship ($F = 7.766$, $p < .01$, $n_p^2 = .008$). Apart from the Citizenship value in which the effect size was trivial, the effect sizes for the values of Commitment, Collaboration and Common Purpose were notable for consideration. The findings in this study affirmed that HK women, like those in the States, were more committed, participative and relational than man (Dugan and Komives 2007).

Academic Discipline

The findings suggested that the academic discipline that students studied in university also had implications for their SRL capacity. Table 6 shows that students studying Liberal Arts and Social Sciences, relatively, had the highest mean scores across all SRL values, followed by the business students, and then the science and engineering students. ANOVA analysis also found that these three groups of students exhibited significant mean differences on most of the SRL values except

Table 6 Means and standard deviations for gender, religion and academic disciplines across the SRLS

		Consciousness of Self			Congruence			Commitment			Collaboration			Common Purpose			Controversy with Civility			Citizenship			Change		
		Mean	SD	Valid N	Mean	SD	Valid N	Mean	SD	Valid N	Mean	SD	Valid N	Mean	SD	Valid N	Mean	SD	Valid N	Mean	SD	Valid N	Mean	SD	Valid N
Gender	Male	3.54	.54	339	3.74	.52	341	3.85	.56	341	3.71	.51	340	3.81	.50	338	3.62	.44	336	3.69	.53	341	3.62	.51	336
	Female	3.61	.45	568	3.79	.46	574	3.97	.44	571	3.84	.41	572	3.90	.40	573	3.63	.38	574	3.78	.45	574	3.62	.44	574
Religion	With religion	3.60	.48	343	3.79	.49	345	3.91	.52	344	3.79	.46	342	3.85	.45	341	3.63	.41	342	3.79	.48	344	3.62	.46	341
	No religion	3.59	.49	506	3.78	.48	509	3.95	.48	510	3.82	.45	509	3.90	.43	509	3.65	.40	506	3.75	.47	509	3.63	.48	508
Academic discipline	Business	3.60	.49	257	3.78	.47	259	3.93	.50	256	3.82	.47	257	3.88	.43	257	3.64	.44	255	3.74	.50	259	3.65	.48	257
	Liberal arts and social sciences	3.67	.48	281	3.81	.46	285	3.98	.42	286	3.86	.39	284	3.94	.39	285	3.65	.37	285	3.83	.45	285	3.63	.44	285
	Science and engineering	3.48	.49	317	3.71	.50	318	3.86	.54	317	3.70	.49	318	3.79	.48	316	3.60	.39	317	3.67	.48	318	3.57	.47	315

Table 7 Pearson correlations coefficients between the CGPA and SRLS

		CGPA	Consciousness of self	Congruence	Commitment	Collaboration	Common purpose	Controversy with civility	Citizenship	Change
CGPA	Pearson correlation	1	.160**	.096	.180**	.162**	.173**	.099	.139**	.074
	Sig. (2-tailed)		.001	.055	.000	.001	.001	.050	.006	.140
	N	400	399	399	397	397	398	396	399	397
	Mean	3.18	3.58	3.77	3.92	3.80	3.87	3.63	3.75	3.62
	Stdn deviation	.44	.49	.48	.49	.46	.44	.40	.48	.47

**Correlation is significant at the 0.01 level (2-tailed)

Controversy with Civility and Change. It is of interest to note particularly the magnitude of the effect sizes in the following values: Consciousness of Self ($F = 11.680$, $p < .01$, $n_p^2 = .027$), Collaboration ($F = 9.945$, $p < .01$, $n_p^2 = .023$), Common Purpose ($F = 8.864$, $p < .01$, $n_p^2 = .020$) and Citizenship ($F = 8.630$, $p < .01$, $n_p^2 = .020$). These effect sizes were much higher than those found in gender. These findings were not unexpected as both social science and business curricula focused more on humanity, moral reasoning, ethical implications, political, economic and social developments in society. Such studies tend to be more conducive to fostering the development of self-awareness and better understanding of group and societal values than the science and engineering disciplines. The findings therefore suggest that science and engineering students should be more exposed to liberal arts and general education and get more involved in community work and civic engagement.

Students' GPA (Academic Achievement)

Last but not least, students' GPA (academic achievement) was a major factor which affected their SRL capacity and development. Table 7 shows that there were significant correlations between CGPA (cumulative grade point average) and five out of the eight SRL values, namely, Consciousness of Self ($r = .160$, $p < 0.01$), Commitment ($r = .180$, $p < 0.01$), Collaboration ($r = .162$, $p < 0.01$), Common Purpose ($r = .173$, $p < 0.01$) and Citizenship ($r = .139$, $p < 0.01$). The findings showed that students with good academic results are more self-conscious, steadfast and committed in their work and studies. With good results, they would be more self-confident and relational to the community.

Conclusions and Discussion

In this chapter, we have taken an established framework of student leadership and tested it initially in the Hong Kong context. We have applied it in a public university in Hong Kong. Good reliability and validity support are initially established. We have also tested relationship between its subscales and the variables of gender, discipline of study and academic attainment. This is an ongoing project.

On the other hand, we are aware of the limitations of this initial study. This model of the leadership is developed in the United States and should be further tested in Hong Kong and other Chinese cultural context to further establish the cultural appropriateness of SRL. We are currently working on further to establish the factor structure and construct validity of this leadership framework.

Longitudinal studies to examine causal relationship as well as pre- and post-assessments for leadership related interventions are being planned.

In conclusion, this study is our first endeavour to introduce an approach of post-industrial leadership for college students to Hong Kong, which is relevant for preparing students to become future leaders of the society in the twenty-first century. With our introduction of the leadership framework and publication of initial validation results, we hope to stimulate the interests of both researchers and practitioners to further test and apply the framework or its individual scales.

Appendixes

Appendix 1: The Correlation Matrix of the Socially Responsible Leadership Scales (SRLS) Subscales, Self-Leadership and Leadership Efficacy

		1	2	3	4	5	6	7	8	9	10
1. Consciousness of Self	Pearson correlation	1	.610**	.588**	.617**	.594**	.582**	.592**	.650**	.558**	.581**
	Sig. (2-tailed)		.000	.000	.000	.000	.000	.000	.000	.000	.000
	N	907	904	903	902	902	899	904	901	901	904
2. Congruence	Pearson correlation	.610**	1	.681**	.636**	.670**	.526**	.642**	.543**	.601**	.456**
	Sig. (2-tailed)	.000		.000	.000	.000	.000	.000	.000	.000	.000
	N	904	915	909	909	909	908	913	907	909	912
3. Commitment	Pearson correlation	.588**	.681**	1	.692**	.727**	.573**	.674**	.568**	.566**	.418**
	Sig. (2-tailed)	.000	.000		.000	.000	.000	.000	.000	.000	.000
	N	903	909	912	908	906	904	909	905	907	909
4. Collaboration	Pearson correlation	.617**	.636**	.692**	1	.784**	.634**	.721**	.646**	.536**	.523**
	Sig. (2-tailed)	.000	.000	.000		.000	.000	.000	.000	.000	.000
	N	902	909	908	912	906	904	910	905	907	909
5. Common Purpose	Pearson correlation	.594**	.670**	.727**	.784**	1	.594**	.735**	.600**	.567**	.473**
	Sig. (2-tailed)	.000	.000	.000	.000		.000	.000	.000	.000	.000
	N	902	909	906	906	911	904	909	906	905	908
6. Controversy with Civility	Pearson correlation	.582**	.526**	.573**	.634**	.594**	1	.570**	.700**	.402**	.490**
	Sig. (2-tailed)	.000	.000	.000	.000	.000		.000	.000	.000	.000
	N	899	908	904	904	904	910	909	904	904	907
7. Citizenship	Pearson correlation	.592**	.642**	.674**	.721**	.735**	.570**	1	.617**	.587**	.500**
	Sig. (2-tailed)	.000	.000	.000	.000	.000	.000		.000	.000	.000
	N	904	913	909	910	909	909	915	908	909	912

(continued)

		1	2	3	4	5	6	7	8	9	10
8. Change	Pearson correlation	.650**	.543**	.568**	.646**	.600**	.700**	.617**	1	.488**	.539**
	Sig. (2-tailed)	.000	.000	.000	.000	.000	.000	.000		.000	.000
	N	901	907	905	905	906	904	908	910	904	907
9. Self-Leadership	Pearson correlation	.558**	.601**	.566**	.536**	.567**	.402**	.587**	.488**	1	.409**
	Sig. (2-tailed)	.000	.000	.000	.000	.000	.000	.000	.000		.000
	N	901	909	907	907	905	904	909	904	912	909
10. Leadership Efficacy	Pearson correlation	.581**	.456**	.418**	.523**	.473**	.490**	.500**	.539**	.409**	1
	Sig. (2-tailed)	.000	.000	.000	.000	.000	.000	.000	.000	.000	
	N	904	912	909	909	908	907	912	907	909	915

$**p < .000$ (2-tailed)

Appendix 2: Composite Measures of the SRLS, and Leadership Efficacy

Consciousness of Self
I am able to articulate my priorities
I have low self-esteem
I am usually self-confident
The things about which I feel passionate have priority in my life
I know myself pretty well
I could describe my personality
I can describe how I am similar to other people
Self-reflection is difficult for me
I am comfortable expressing myself
Congruence
My behaviours are congruent with my beliefs
It is important to me to act on my beliefs
My actions are consistent with my values
Being seen as a person of integrity is important to me
My behaviours reflect my beliefs
I am genuine
It is easy for me to be truthful
Commitment
I am willing to devote the time and energy to things that are important to me
I stick with others through difficult times
I am focused on my responsibilities
I can be counted on to do my part
I follow through on my promises
I hold myself accountable for responsibilities I agree to
Collaboration
I am seen as someone who works well with others
I can make a difference when I work with others on a task
I actively listen to what others have to say
I enjoy working with others toward common goals
Others would describe me as a cooperative group member
Collaboration produces better results
My contributions are recognised by others in the groups I belong to
I am able to trust the people with whom I work
Common Purpose
I am committed to a collective purpose in those groups to which I belong
It is important to develop a common direction in a group in order to get anything done
I contribute to the goals of the group
I think it is important to know other people's priorities
I have helped to shape the mission of the group

(continued)

Common values drive an organisation
I know the purpose of the groups to which I belong
I work well when I know the collective values of a group
I support what the group is trying to accomplish
Controversy with Civility
I am open to others' ideas
Creativity can come from conflict
I value differences in others
Hearing differences in opinions enriches my thinking
I struggle when group members have ideas that are different from mine
Greater harmony can come out of disagreement
I respect opinions other than my own
I am uncomfortable when someone disagrees with me
When there is a conflict between two people, one will win and the other will lose
I am comfortable with conflict
I share my ideas with others
Citizenship
I believe I have responsibilities to my community
I give my time to making a difference for someone
I work with others to make my communities better places
I have the power to make a difference in my community
I am willing to act for the rights of others
I participate in activities that contribute to the common good
I believe I have a civic responsibility to the greater public
I value opportunities that allow me to contribute to my community
Change
Transition makes me uncomfortable
I am comfortable initiating new ways of looking at things
Change brings new life to an organisation
There is energy in doing something a new way
Change makes me uncomfortable
New ways of doing things frustrate me
I work well in changing environments
I am open to new ideas
I look for new ways to do something
I can identify the differences between positive and negative change
Leadership Efficacy
Leading others
Organise group tasks to accomplish goal
Taking initiative to improve something
Working with team on group project

Source: NCLP (2013), Dugan and Komives (2010)

References

Chung, P. (2011). HKI-SLAM definition of leadership. *Hong Kong Institute of Service Leadership & Management*. Retrieved from http://hki-slam.org/index.php?r=article&catid=1&aid=11

Dugan, J. P. (2011). Research on college student leadership development. In S. R. Komives, J. P. Dugan, J. E. Owen, C. Slack, W. Wagner & Associates (Eds.), *The handbook for student leadership development* (2nd ed.) (pp. 59–83). San Francisco: Wiley.

Dugan, J. P., & Komives, S. R. (2007). *Developing leader capacity in college students: Findings from a national study*. A Report from the Multi-Institutional Study of Leadership. College Park: National Clearinghouse for Leadership Programs.

Dugan, J. P., & Komives, S. R. (2010). Influence on college students' capacities for socially responsible leadership. *Journal of College Student Development, 51*(5), 525–549.

Dugan, J. P., & Komives, S. R. (2011). Leadership theories. In S. R. Komives, J. P. Dugan, J. E. Owen, C. Slack, W. Wagner & Associates (Eds.), *The handbook for student leadership development* (2nd ed.) (pp. 35–57). San Francisco: Wiley.

Dugan, J. P., Komives, S. R., & Segar, T. C. (2009). College student capacity for socially responsible leadership: Understanding norms and influences of race, gender, and sexual orientation. *Journal of Student Affairs Research and Practice, 45*(4), 927–952.

Higher Education Research Institute (HERI). (1996). *A social change model of leadership development: Guidebook version III*. College Park: National Clearinghouse for Leader Programs.

HKI-SLAM. (2014). HKI-SLAM introduction. *Hong Kong Institute of Service Leadership & Management*. Retrieved from http://hki-slam.org/index.php?r=article&catid=1&aid=1

Houghton, J. D., Dawley, D., & DiLiello, T. C. (2012). The abbreviated self-leadership questionnaire (ASLQ): A more concise measure of self-leadership. *International Journal of Leadership Studies, 7*(2), 216–232.

Komives, S. R., Wagner, W., & Associates. (2009). *Leadership for a better world: Understanding the social change model of leadership development*. San Francisco: Wiley.

National Clearinghouse for Leadership Programs (NCLP). (2013). *Socially responsible leadership scale revised version 2: Using the SRLS-R2 for research and assessment*. A manuscript in PDF format was sent to the authors for use in this research.

Wagner, W. (2006). The social change model of leadership: A brief overview. *Conceptions & Connections: A Publication for Leadership Educators, 15*(1), 8–10. Available at http://web.trinity.edu/Documents/student_affairs_docs/Assessments/Social%20Change%20Model%20of%20Leadership%20-%20A%20Brief%20Overview%20(Wagner).pdf

Evaluating Service Leadership Programs with Multiple Strategies

Daniel T.L. Shek and Li Lin

Abstract Despite the growing numbers of leadership programs, little is known about the effectiveness of such programs. In view of this, evaluation research is integrated into the implementation of service leadership programs at The Hong Kong Polytechnic University (PolyU). In this chapter, evaluation methods based on objective outcome evaluation, subjective outcome evaluation, process evaluation, and qualitative evaluation are outlined. The findings of evaluation research adopting these methods are reported to show the effectiveness of service leadership programs at PolyU. Overall, results indicate that service leadership programs at PolyU have a beneficial impact for students.

Introduction

Youth leadership education and training is prosperous in the past decades (Brungardt et al. 2006; Ngai et al. 2012). Different parties are involved in cultivating tomorrow's leaders, while colleges and universities offer many opportunities for student leadership development (Astin and Astin 2000; Komives 2011). Leadership educators are eager to nurture students to be great leaders, while evidence is insufficient to inform whether these efforts are rewarding (Owen 2011; Posner 2009). As noted by Rohs (2002), "Although it is widely accepted that these programs possess considerable potential for increasing knowledge and producing change, documenting these changes have haunted many educators" (p. 50). In the

This preparation for this paper and the Service Leadership project are financially supported by the Victor and William Fung Foundation. The authorship is equally shared by the first author and second author.

D.T.L. Shek, Ph.D., S.B.S., J.P. (✉)
Department of Applied Social Sciences, The Hong Kong Polytechnic University, HJ407, Hunghom, Hong Kong, China
e-mail: daniel.shek@polyu.edu.hk

L. Lin, Ph.D
Department of Applied Social Sciences, The Hong Kong Polytechnic University, V1214, Hunghom, Kowloon, Hong Kong

© Springer Science+Business Media Singapore 2015
D.T.L. Shek, P. Chung (eds.), *Promoting Service Leadership Qualities in University Students*, Quality of Life in Asia 6, DOI 10.1007/978-981-287-515-0_13

"National Leadership Education Research Agenda 2013–2018," Andenoro et al. (2013) underscored the value yet deficiency of evaluation evidence for leadership program – "Programmatic monitoring and evaluation are critical for leadership educators to consider as they attempt to determine if their practice is achieving the desired outcomes. However, there is a deficiency in the research and resources aimed at addressing this need" (p. 13). Clearly, it is imperative to carry out evaluation research for leadership program.

Evaluation research refers to "systematic investigation to determine the success of a specific program" (Barker 2003, p. 149). Usually, findings of evaluation research serve two purposes: to acquire information that helps to improve the program (i.e., formative evaluation) and to demonstrate the accountability, outcomes, and impacts of the program (i.e., summative evaluation; Mertens and Wilson 2012). Systematic evaluation is important for leadership programs. As underscored by Chambers (1994), there are at least four reasons to integrate rigorous assessment into leadership programs: (a) to document the outcomes of student learning and development, (b) to ensure the accountability of leadership development activities, (c) to gain for more support from publics through justification of resources, and (d) to provide guidance for future programs. Many other researchers also emphasize the significance of evaluation and assessment for leadership program (e.g., Komives 2011; Owen 2011; Posner 2009; Riggio 2008).

Despite the heightened awareness of the importance, rigorous and systematic evidence of program effectiveness is still scarce in leadership programs, no matter in organizational training or university education. As noted by Riggio (2008), "Those of us involved in efforts to develop leadership need to be very concerned about evaluation of our programs. We need to demonstrate the effectiveness of what we are doing and, in short, justify our existence. Organizations should be assured that their investment in leadership development does indeed pay off. Because of this, it is somewhat disheartening that there is not more attention to evaluation, both in the research literature and in practice" (p. 388).

Posner (2009) also argued that, "despite the plethora of leadership programs scattered across college campuses, scant empirical investigation has been conducted into the benefits of such education efforts" (p. 551).

Evaluation Methods

Given the importance yet paucity of evaluation research in leadership program, leader educators and researchers should take action to measure the effectiveness of leadership programs. According to the previous literature on program evaluation (Mertens and Wilson 2012; Royse et al. 2006; Shek 2013; Weinbach 2005), multiple evaluation methods can be applied. These methods include but not limited to objective outcome evaluation, subjective outcome evaluation, process evaluation, and qualitative evaluation.

Objective Outcome Evaluation

Objective outcome evaluation is frequently used in evaluating the effectiveness of programs and service. The optimal design normally includes an experimental group (participants receiving intervention) and a control group (participants not receiving intervention) based on random assignment of participants. Participants in both groups would be assessed before and after the program, in which their changes could be compared. In this way, many alternative explanations such as personal history, natural maturity, and test effect can be ruled out when explaining the changes of participants. Thus, if a greater positive change is observed in the experimental group (vs. control group), we could infer that the intervention has a positive impact on the participants. When random assignment of group is not applicable, quasi-experiment would be used. For example, in order to test whether outdoor management training was more effective to the development of leadership in MBA students, Kass and Grandzol (2011) conducted a quasi-experiment. The enrollment of students into different classes was not based on randomization. Similar to experimental design, the pretest-posttest changes of the students receiving outdoor experiential training (i.e., experimental group) and the students receiving traditional in-class training were compared (i.e., control group).

However, it is often difficult and costly to recruit a control group in program evaluation. As noted by McCall et al. (1998), "methodologically, it is now acknowledged that conducting robust true experiments in the field ...... is extremely difficult and often impossible" (p. 982). Hence, a one-group pretest-posttest design is often adopted to show the changes of participants in the program, though it cannot lead to any causal conclusion of the program impact. Keating et al.'s (2014) study can exemplify this design, in which a single group of students who joined an introductory leadership course reported their leadership self-efficacy, motivation to lead, and leadership behavior before and after the class learning.

Objective outcome evaluation can provide potent evidence of program effectiveness. Nevertheless, it is not free of limitations, especially for the less rigorous design (i.e., one-group pretest-posttest; Royse et al. 2006). For example, in self-report measures, response shift bias may occur when participants' self-evaluation standard changes during the intervention (Howard 1980). It will pollute the changes caused by the program impact. In addition, objective outcome evaluation ignores the participants' perception on the program, leaving participants' voices unheard.

Subjective Outcome Evaluation

Subjective outcome evaluation tries to hear participants' voices by soliciting participants' feedback toward the program. It roots in customer satisfaction approach, which concerns about the extent to which the clients feel content with the program process and outcome and perceive that their needs, wishes, or desires for intervention are gratified (Brestan et al. 1999; Lebow 1983). This approach usually taps into participants' perception of program content and format, program implementers, and program effectiveness via standardized self-report instruments, though the use of open-ended question is on the rise. It has been widely applied in education (Marsh 2007), health service (Brestan et al. 1999), and other settings. For instance, plentiful teaching evaluation scales were developed to measure teaching quality, such as Students' Evaluations of Educational Quality Instrument (SEEQ; Marsh 2007; Marsh et al. 1997), Instructional Development and Effectiveness Assessment (IDEA; Cashin 1990), and Student Instructional Report (SIR; Centra 1998). Researchers inquire into students' perception on the content and organiza-tion of lecture, teacher performance, students' own learning progress toward the course objectives, as well as other feelings about the course (Cashin 1990; Centra 1998; Ma and Shek 2010; Marsh 2007). In the health service field, diverse inven-tories like Client Satisfaction Questionnaire (CSQ-8; Attkisson and Zwick 1982), Youth Client Satisfaction Questionnaire (YCSQ; Shapiro et al. 1997), the Therapy Attitude Inventory (TAI), and the Workshop Attitude Inventory (WAI; Eyberg 1993) were made to understand how the clients feel about the treatment process and outcome.

The advantages of subjective outcome evaluation are clear, such as inexpensive, simple to administrate, and easy to interpret. However, its fundamental assumption that clients' satisfaction is an excellent judge of the impact and effectiveness of the service (Royse et al. 2006) is controversial. Some researchers criticized that participants' satisfaction is not equal to effective intervention (Weinbach 2005). Also, positive response may be influenced by other confounding factors such as completion bias or bias due to "I appreciate your asking" phenomenon, which makes its internal validity questionable (Shek 2013; Weinbach 2005). On the other hand, some studies have evidenced that subjective outcome evaluation is meaningfully related to objective outcome evaluation. For example, Brestan et al.'s (1999) study found that parent satisfaction with the treatment was associated with greater improvement in child compliance and greater reduction of child behavior problems. Shek's (2009) study on the evaluation of a positive youth development program also showed that students' satisfaction about program process, program content, and program effectiveness was positively associated with their enhance-ment in positive youth development from the pretest to the posttest. These findings support the external validity of subjective outcome evaluation. Despite its inherited validity problem, client perspective is still widely used in different fields, because "professionals do not experience the agency in the same way as the clients" (Royse 2007, p. 303).

Process Evaluation

The aforementioned evaluation approaches primarily provide information about the outcomes of the program, leaving the implementation process unexamined. It is important to know what happens during the implementation, which can help researchers understand the program effects. Process evaluation can help to understand the process involved.

A variety of components are often included in process evaluation (Durlak and DuPre 2008; Dusenbury et al. 2003; Hall et al. 2012; Kalafat et al. 2007; Law and Shek 2011). These include fidelity (i.e., the extent to which the program was implemented according to the plan), adaptation (i.e., the modification of the original content during implementation), dosage (i.e., the amount of original content implemented in reality), participant responsiveness (i.e., the degree to which the program has aroused participants' attention and interest), quality of program delivery (i.e., the degree to which the program has been well conducted), program differentiation (i.e., the extent to which the current program can be differentiated from other programs), and the association of program implementation and program outcomes. Multiple approaches can be used for evaluating the program implementation, such as independent observation, interview, and survey (e.g., Delp et al. 2005; Hall et al. 2012; Helitzer et al. 2000).

Compared to other evaluation methods, less effort has been made in the process evaluation (Durlak and DuPre 2008; Shek 2013). Although there is a consensus that process evaluation focuses on implementation, there has been no agreement on what should be included in the process evaluation (see descriptions about process evaluation in Durlak and DuPre 2008; Royse et al. 2006). Nevertheless, emerging arguments highly advocate the need to understand the implementation in addition to outcomes of the program. With carefully overseeing the implementation, program implementers could timely identify the program problems and adjust the program according to the information gathered. This is very important because poor implementation can result in lower levels of effectiveness. In addition, information in the "black box" can also provide clues about what the influential factors of program efficacy are (Durlak and DuPre 2008; Harachi et al. 1999; Royse et al. 2006).

Qualitative Evaluation

Despite the dominance of quantitative methods in program evaluation, qualitative evaluation has gained wider acceptance and application. Qualitative research focuses on naturalistic inquiry, relies on researchers as the instrument of data collection, and emphasizes narrative over numbers (Royse et al. 2006). Documents, interview, and observation are often used in qualitative evaluation (Patton 1990).

While quantitative approach has an advantage in its generalizability because of its usual reliance on large samples, qualitative approach is able to generate abundant detailed information with a small amount of people, which increases the depth of the information, though at the cost of generalizability (Patton 1990). For example, to understand the effect of a mentoring program, Priest and Donley (2014) conducted individual interviews on mentors and mentees. In this way, both mentors and mentees could make meaning of their experiences and provide detailed information for researchers to evaluate the program. Additionally, while quantitative approach is based on standardized questions, which is facilitative to the comparison of research across samples and settings, qualitative approach is more flexible in question design. For example, the interviewer could ask follow-up questions upon participants' responses, which thus deepens the experiences and insights we could obtain from participants. Furthermore, qualitative approach can capture the sentimental and abstract ideas of individuals, which standardized close-ended question can hardly get. For example, making a metaphor could be an effective approach to help people make meanings from their personal experiences and articulate their self-reflection which is novel, abstract, and complex (Thomas and Beauchamp 2011). Finally, qualitative approach is especially useful to further understand unexpected findings.

On the other hand, qualitative evaluation is time-consuming and labor-intensive in the implementation, and the validity of findings depends very much on the research skills of the researchers. As noted by Patton (1990), "the researcher is the instrument…Validity in qualitative methods, therefore, hinges to a great extent on the skill, competence, and rigor of the person doing fieldwork" (p. 14). However, qualitative evaluation can be rigorous if self-disciplined data collection, data analysis, and documentation are carried out.

Mixed-Methods Design

As every evaluation method has inherent strengths and limitations, comprehensive program evaluation requires the use of multiple data based on different methodologies (i.e., mixed-methods design). According to Shek (2013), there are two philosophical strands supporting mixed-methods design. From the perspective of critical realism, truth can only be partially and probabilistically understood (Denzin and Lincoln 2011). Through triangulation of using different methods, data, and stakeholders, biases and errors associated with each method or data type can be neutralized, and strengths can be complemented. As a result, convergent and triangulated findings can render the "truth" uncovered. On the other hand, from the perspective of pragmatism, a combination of multiple methodologies is needed when different approaches are applied to solve one evaluation question or different evaluation questions require different approaches (Datta 1997). Different data and methodologies offer distinct information, which is very useful for evaluating a program. The application of mixed methods broadens and deepens the information we gather and thus enhances the confidence in the results (Boatman 2000). One example of using multiple methods to evaluate leadership program is Brungardt and Crawford's (1996) comprehensive approach which includes pretest and posttest objective outcome evaluation, post-course subjective outcome evaluation (including close-ended questions and open-ended questions), and instructor interview. In their study, the combination of different evaluation approaches enabled researchers to acquire broad while deep information about students' reaction, changes in knowledge and behavior, and results of learning.

Evaluation Research on Service Leadership Programs

The service leadership program at The Hong Kong Polytechnic University began in 2012. Besides several one-shot training programs and a subject on service learning, we have offered three classes of 2-credit "Service Leadership" subject and one intensive non-credit-bearing subject in Global Youth Leadership Program (4.5 days of class learning). There were 60, 88, and 42 students participating in the first, second, and third class, respectively. In addition, there were 48 students joining "Global Youth Leadership Program" in which class learning of service leadership was offered at the inception of the program.

In order to understand the effectiveness of the service leadership subject and program, we implemented different evaluation studies. As shown in Table 1, objective outcome evaluation, subjective outcome evaluation, and qualitative evaluation (descriptors and metaphors) were administrated in the credit-bearing subjects as well as the non-credit-bearing subject in Global Youth Leadership Program. In addition, process evaluation was conducted in the first two classes of credit-bearing subjects, while focus group interview was conducted for all the classes of credit-bearing subjects. In this book chapter, we briefly presented the results from the first two classes of credit-bearing subjects and non-credit-bearing subject in Global Youth Leadership Program.

Objective Outcome Evaluation Results

Objective outcome evaluation was administrated at the beginning and the end of the course with identical questionnaire (Shek et al. 2014e). Students were invited to report their positive youth development (i.e., cognitive-behavioral competencies, positive identity, and global positive youth development), life satisfaction and service leadership qualities (i.e., self-leadership, caring disposition, and character strength), and beliefs in this questionnaire.

Merged data based on the two classes of credit-bearing subjects (Shek et al. 2014b) showed that there was enhancement in the cognitive-behavioral competences, positive identity, life satisfaction, and character strength among the participating students. In Global Youth Leadership Program, a follow-up test was added 12 days after the completion of the class learning in order to see if the improvement could be maintained. As predicted, significant improvements were observed in all of the indicators of positive youth development, life satisfaction, and service leadership qualities and beliefs from the pretest to the posttest, and furthermore, these improvements maintained till the follow-up test. These results indicate

Table 1 Evaluation studies for the 2-credit subject "Service Leadership" and the intensive program in the Global Youth Leadership Program

Program	Methodology	Publication
First class (i.e., credit-bearing subject "Service Leadership" 2012–2013 academic year 2nd semester)	Objective outcome evaluation[a]	Shek et al. (2014e)
	Subjective outcome evaluation[a]	Shek et al. (2014a)
	Process evaluation[a]	Shek et al. (2014c)
	Qualitative evaluation (descriptors and metaphors)[a]	Shek et al. (2014d)
	Focus group[a]	Shek et al. (in press-a)
Second class (i.e., credit-bearing subject "Service Leadership" 2013–2014 academic year 1st semester)	Objective outcome evaluation[b]	
	Subjective outcome evaluation[a]	Shek and Liang (in press)
	Process evaluation[b]	
	Qualitative evaluation (descriptors and metaphors)[b]	
	Focus group[a]	Shek et al. (in press-b)
Third class (i.e., credit-bearing subject "Service Leadership" 2013–2014 academic year 2nd semester)	Objective outcome evaluation[c]	
	Subjective outcome evaluation[b]	
	Qualitative evaluation (descriptors and metaphors)[c]	
	Focus group[c]	
Global Youth Leadership Program	Objective outcome evaluation[d]	
	Subjective outcome evaluation[a]	Shek and Li (in press)
	Qualitative evaluation[b] (descriptors and metaphors)	

Notes:
[a]Published
[b]Data analyses completed
[c]Data collected
[d]Manuscripts completed

that service leadership education is able to promote youth thriving, enhance service leadership qualities, and even make students endorse service leadership beliefs to a greater degree.

Subjective Outcome Evaluation Results

Subjective outcome evaluation was administrated at the end of the service leadership course. Students were required to fill out a questionnaire, in which quality of program content (i.e., program objective, design, classroom atmosphere, interaction among the students, and the student participation during class), performance of program implementers (i.e., preparation, professional attitude, involvement, and interaction with the students), perceived program effectiveness (i.e., promotion of different psychosocial competencies and overall personal development and achievement of the intended learning outcomes), and overall satisfaction (i.e., recommend this program, join similar program in the future, and general satisfaction) were assessed.

According to the results of the first class and second class (Shek et al. 2014a; Shek and Liang in press), most of the students rated positively on the program content (64–84 % and 62–83 % for the first course and second course, respectively), program implementers (78–98 % and 79–95 % for the first course and second course, respectively), perceived program effectiveness (62–88 % and 72–90 % for the first course and second course, respectively), and overall satisfaction (50–76 % and 62–83 % for the first and second class, respectively). Students in the Global Youth Leadership Program were even more satisfied with the program (Shek and Li in press), with higher proportion of students reporting positive evaluation on the program content (83–96 %), the program implementers (89–100 %), perceived program effectiveness (68–96 %), and overall satisfaction (68–87 %). Generally speaking, students had a high degree of satisfaction with the service leadership program.

Process Evaluation Results

In the first class and second class of the subject "Service Leadership", ten out of 14 lectures were observed by two independent raters. Based on Law and Shek's (2011) framework, there are different aspects of process evaluation, including student interest, active involvement of students, classroom management, interactive delivery method, strategies to enhance the student motivation, the use of positive feedback, familiarity of implementers with the students, reflective learning, program goal attainment, time management, the quality of preparation, overall implementation quality, and success of implementation. These aspects were carefully observed and evaluated. In addition, program fidelity was rated in terms of the degree of adherence to the original curriculum in the first class.

Results showed that program fidelity was very high across two raters (mean $= 97.8$ %), which indicated that lecturers basically adhered to the curriculum. In addition, the mean ratings of other aspects were all positive (4.95–5.95 and 5.55–6.00 for the first class and second class, respectively). In particular, the quality of preparation, time management, program goal attainment, overall implementation quality, and success of implementation were perceived to be very positive across different classes. In brief, independent raters perceived the class to be successfully delivered (Shek et al. 2014c; Shek 2014).

Qualitative Evaluation: Descriptor and Metaphor Results

Students were invited to use three descriptive words and one metaphor to portray their perceptions or feelings about the subject by the end of the course. Among the descriptors collected in all the analyzed data (Shek 2014; Shek et al. 2014d), over 90 % of them were positive in nature, with a few negative (e.g., not very meaningful, idealistic, or boring). Common descriptors included "interesting," "helpful," "inspiring," and "meaningful." Similarly, among the metaphors collected in all the analyzed data, a roughly 90 % were positive in nature, with a few negative (e.g., kindergarten class, chores, and normal student). Students across different class settings preferred to use metaphors representing guidance, self-reflection, and journey. For example, "mirror" that represents more self-understanding, "compass" that stands for a tool of guidance, and "journey/tour" that indicates a learning process emerged across different datasets. A few extracts were presented here:

- *Mirror*: "I can see my true self under this course. This course helps me to reflect on my character clearly. At the same time, it may also reflect some of my classmates' characters which I may learn from." (from first class of subject "Service Leadership")
- *Compass in life*: "The course is just like pointing out correct directions in my future life, including the attitudes in working, learning, treating others, etc." (from second class of subject "Service Leadership")
- *An enjoyable tour:* "In the first place, the tour is enjoyable, because we played many games in the course, which made us feel very happy. What's more, I made many friends here. Last but not least, I learned a lot from the course. I know what the meaning of service leadership is, how to be a service leader, and so on. I gained many things from the course. In a word, the course is just like an enjoyable tour, making me learn new things happily." (from Global Youth Leadership Program)

From students' personal reflection via descriptor and metaphor, we know that students generally had a positive perception toward the subject in terms of joyfulness and usefulness. Furthermore, they appreciated self-reflection practice in this subject and regarded this subject as a guidance or reference that would help with their personal growth and leadership development.

Qualitative Evaluation: Focus Group Results

At the end of the credit-bearing subject, students were invited to join a focus group interview, so that we could gain deep understanding about the subject through students' narratives and lived experiences. In each round of the evaluation, two focus groups were conducted with 3–6 students in each group. Each focus group was moderated by a registered social worker equipped with qualitative research skills. Their discussion mainly covered six topics: (1) how students perceived the subject, (2) how students perceived their learning process in the subject, (3) how students perceived the performance of lecturer(s), (4) what benefits students obtained from the subject, (5) what students' overall impression of the subject is, and (6) what recommendations students would provide for the improvement of the program.

According to the findings of two rounds of focus groups (Shek et al. in press-a, in press-b), students generally appreciated the course and the effort of the lecturers. In particular, they appreciated the interaction in class, as students shared below:

- "The major uniqueness of this subject in comparison to others resides in the intensive interactions. If there were no such activities like role-play or drawing, it would be quite boring. Moreover, for those abstract concepts, only through discussions and activities could we comprehend more and better." (from first class of subject "Service Leadership")
- "When the instructor divided us into small groups, I interacted a lot with other group members. When working on one project together, I knew more students and interacted with them." (from second class of subject "Service Leadership")

Lecturers performance was appreciated by the students as well, which can be exemplified by the following narratives:

- "The three instructors are highly enthusiastic. We feel that they teach with their heart and try different ways to communicate with us." (from first class of subject "Service Leadership")
- "I felt that she well prepared the whole course. She used different methods to enrich the course." (from second class of subject "Service Leadership")

Finally, students reported they obtained benefits from the course, such as:

- "After that course, I learned that when I experience adversities or negative emotions, I must remind myself not to be too negative but to apply the strategies recommended in the lectures to cope with the difficulties. It was really helpful!" (from first class of subject "Service Leadership")
- "Service leadership is applicable in many aspects in our life, especially when we are in the workplace in the future. For example, what we learned in this course can be applied to the interactions with others." (from second class of subject "Service Leadership")

In the focus group interview, students also offered their suggestions for further improvement of the course such as suggestion for improving teaching skills, increasing practical opportunity, and strengthening the link between theory and reality. The following extracts illustrated students' comments for further improvement:

- "The practical experience is very different from that of sitting in a classroom and listening to the teachers. Even if one writes a good term paper, can he/she perform well in the real-world settings?" (from first class of subject "Service Leadership")
- "I felt that some theories introduced in this course were very complicated and hard to understand. When mentioning the theories, it would be better to provide some daily examples which could be applied in our usual life. When the learning contents are too intricate, it is not easy to be remembered." (from second class of subject "Service Leadership")

Conclusion and Future Direction

In response to the call for more systematic evaluation on the effectiveness of leadership education and training (Posner 2009; Riggio 2008), the research team of service leadership program at The Hong Kong Polytechnic University has conducted a series of evaluation studies with multiple methodologies. Across different methodologies and different datasets, results are convergent to suggest that service leadership education was successfully delivered at The Hong Kong Polytechnic University. The utilization of different evaluation methods enlarges the range of data collected and enhances data and methodological triangulation, which further strengthens the validity of conclusions (Helitzer et al. 2000). From the research aspect, future studies could examine the associations among different methodologies and data, which may help to answer a further question about why the program is effective. In addition, additional evaluation methods that increase the breadth and depth of the evaluative information such as case study, reflective journal analysis, and longitudinal outcome evaluation should be used in the future. Practically speaking, these findings serve to demonstrate the value of the subject and also serve to guide our further work in maintaining the effectiveness of the program and improving the practice.

References

Andenoro, A. C., Allen, S. J., Haber-Curran, P., Jenkins, D. M., Sowcik, M., Dugan, J. P., & Osteen, L. (2013). *National leadership education research agenda 2013–2018: Providing strategic direction for the field of leadership education*. Retrieved from Association of Leadership Educators website: http://leadershipeducators.org/ResearchAgenda

Astin, A. W., & Astin, H. S. (2000). *Leadership reconsidered: Engaging higher education in social change* [Online]. Retrieved from: http://www.wkkf.org/Pubs/CCT/Leadership/Pub3368.PDF

Attkisson, C. C., & Zwick, R. (1982). The client satisfaction questionnaire: Psychometric properties and correlations with service utilization and psychotherapy outcome. *Evaluation and Program Planning, 5*(3), 233–237.

Barker, R. L. (Ed.). (2003). *The social work dictionary* (5th ed.). Washington, DC: NASW.

Boatman, S. A. (2000). Assessment of leadership programs: Enhancing student leadership development. *Concepts & Connections, 9*(1), 5–8.

Brestan, E. V., Jacobs, J. R., Rayfield, A. D., & Eyberg, S. M. (1999). A consumer satisfaction measure for parent-child treatments and its relation to measures of child behavior change. *Behavior Therapy, 30*(1), 17–30.

Brungardt, C., & Crawford, C. B. (1996). A comprehensive approach to assessing leadership students and programs: Preliminary findings. *Journal of Leadership & Organizational Studies, 3*(1), 37–48.

Brungardt, C., Greenleaf, J., Brungardt, C., & Arensdorf, J. (2006). Majoring in leadership: A review of undergraduate leadership degree programs. *Journal of Leadership Education, 5*(1), 4–25.

Cashin, W. E. (1990). *Student ratings of teaching: Recommendations for use.* Manhattan: Center for Faculty Evaluation and Development (IDEA No. 22).

Centra, J. A. (1998). *Development of the student instructional report II.* Princeton: Educational Testing Service.

Chambers, T. (1994). Criteria to evaluate student leadership programs: What leadership educators consider important. *NASPA Journal, 31*(3), 225–234.

Datta, L. E. (1997). A pragmatic basis for mixed-method designs. *New Directions for Evaluation, 1997*(74), 33–46.

Delp, L., Brown, M., & Domenzain, A. (2005). Fostering youth leadership to address workplace and community environmental health issues: A university-school-community partnership. *Health Promotion Practice, 6*(3), 270–285.

Denzin, N. K., & Lincoln, Y. S. (Eds.). (2011). *The Sage handbook of qualitative research.* Thousand Oaks: Sage.

Durlak, J. A., & DuPre, E. P. (2008). Implementation matters: A review of research on the influence of implementation on program outcomes and the factors affecting implementation. *American Journal of Community Psychology, 41*(3–4), 327–350.

Dusenbury, L., Brannigan, R., Falco, M., & Hansen, W. B. (2003). A review of research on fidelity of implementation: Implications for drug abuse prevention in school settings. *Health Education Research, 18*(2), 237–256.

Eyberg, S. M. (1993). Consumer satisfaction measures for assessing parent training programs. In L. VandeCreek, S. Knapp & T. L. Jackson (Eds.), *Innovations in clinical practice: A source book* (Vol. 12). Sarasota: Professional Resource Press.

Hall, W. J., Zeveloff, A., Steckler, A., Schneider, M., Thompson, D., Pham, T., . . . & McMurray, R. G. (2012). Process evaluation results from the HEALTHY physical education intervention. *Health Education Research, 27*(2), 307–318.

Harachi, T. W., Abbott, R. D., Catalano, R. F., Haggerty, K. P., & Fleming, C. B. (1999). Opening the black box: Using process evaluation measures to assess implementation and theory building. *American Journal of Community Psychology, 27*(5), 711–731.

Helitzer, D., Yoon, S. J., & Wallerstein, N. (2000). The role of process evaluation in the training of facilitators for an adolescent health education program. *Journal of School Health, 70*(4), 141–147.

Howard, G. S. (1980). Response-shift bias a problem in evaluating interventions with pre/post self-reports. *Evaluation Review, 4*(1), 93–106.

Kalafat, J., Illback, R. J., & Sanders, D. (2007). The relationship between implementation fidelity and educational outcomes in a school-based family support program: Development of a model for evaluating multidimensional full-service programs. *Evaluation and Program Planning, 30* (2), 136–148.

Kass, D., & Grandzol, C. (2011). Learning to lead at 5,267 feet. *Journal of Leadership Education, 10*(1), 41–62.

Keating, K., Rosch, D., & Burgoon, L. (2014). Developmental readiness for leadership: The differential effects of leadership courses on creating "ready, willing, and able" leaders. *Journal of Leadership Education, 13*(3), 1–16.

Komives, S. R. (2011). Advancing leadership education. In S. R. Komives, J. P. Dugan, J. E. Owen, W. Wagner, C. Slack & Associates (Eds.), *Handbook for student leadership development* (pp. 1–34). San Francisco: Wiley.

Law, B. M. F., & Shek, D. T. L. (2011). Process evaluation of a positive youth development program: Project P.A.T.H.S. *Research on Social Work Practice, 21*, 539–548.

Lebow, J. L. (1983). Research assessing consumer satisfaction with mental health treatment: A review of findings. *Evaluation and Program Planning, 6*(3), 211–236.

Ma, H. K., & Shek, D. T. L. (2010). Subjective outcome evaluation of a positive youth development program in Hong Kong: Profiles and correlates. *The Scientific World Journal, 10*, 192–200.

Marsh, H. W. (2007). Students' evaluations of university teaching: Dimensionality, reliability, validity, potential biases and usefulness. In R. P. Perry & J. C. Smart (Eds.), *The scholarship of teaching and learning in higher education: An evidence-based perspective* (pp. 319–383). Dordrecht: Springer.

Marsh, H. W., Hau, K. T., Chung, C. M., & Siu, T. L. (1997). Students' evaluations of university teaching: Chinese version of the students' evaluations of educational quality instrument. *Journal of Educational Psychology, 89*(3), 568–572.

McCall, R. B., Green, B. L., Strauss, M. S., & Groark, C. J. (1998). Issues in community-based research and program evaluation. In W. Damon, I. E. Sigel & K. A. Renninger (Eds.), *Handbook of child psychology* (5th ed., Vol. 4): *Child psychology in practice* (pp. 955–997). New York: Wiley.

Mertens, D. M., & Wilson, A. T. (2012). *Program evaluation theory and practice: A comprehensive guide.* New York: Guilford Press.

Ngai, N. P., Cheung, C. K., Ngai, S. S. Y., & To, S. M. (2012). Youth leadership training in Hong Kong: Current developments and the way ahead. *International Journal of Adolescence and Youth, 17*(2–3), 165–179.

Owen, J. E. (2011). Assessment and evaluation. In S. R. Komives, J. P. Dugan, J. E. Owen, W. Wagner, C. Slack & Associates (Eds.), *The handbook for student leadership development* (pp. 177–202). San Francisco: Wiley.

Patton, M. Q. (1990). *Qualitative evaluation and research methods.* Newbury Park: Sage.

Posner, B. Z. (2009). A longitudinal study examining changes in students' leadership behavior. *Journal of College Student Development, 50*(5), 551–563.

Priest, K. L., & Donley, S. (2014). Developing leadership for life: Outcomes from a collegiate student-alumni mentoring program. *Journal of Leadership Education, 13*(3), 107–117.

Riggio, R. E. (2008). Leadership development: The current state and future expectations. *Consulting Psychology Journal: Practice and Research, 60*(4), 383–392.

Rohs, F. R. (2002). Improving the evaluation of leadership programs. *Journal of Leadership Education, 1*(2), 50–61.

Royse, D. (2007). *Research methods in social work.* Belmont: Thomson Brooks/Cole.

Royse, D., Thyer, B., & Padgett, D. (2006). *Program evaluation: An introduction* (4th ed.). Belmont: Wadsworth.

Shapiro, J. P., Welker, C. J., & Jacobson, B. J. (1997). The youth client satisfaction questionnaire: Development, construct validation, and factor structure. *Journal of Clinical Child Psychology, 26*(1), 87–98.

Shek, D. T. L. (2009). Subjective outcome and objective outcome evaluation findings: Insights from a Chinese context. *Research on Social Work Practice, 20*(3), 293–301.

Shek, D. T. L. (2013). Evaluation of the Project P.A.T.H.S. using multiple evaluation strategies. In D. T. L. Shek & R. C. F. Sun (Eds.), *Development and evaluation of positive adolescent training through holistic social programs (P.A.T.H.S.)* (pp. 53–67). Singapore: Springer.

Shek, D. T. L. (2014). *Evaluation data of subject "Service Leadership".* Unpublished data.

Shek, D. T. L., & Li, X. (in press). Evaluation of an innovative leadership training program for Chinese students: Subjective outcome evaluation. *International Journal on Disability and Human Development.*

Shek, D. T. L., & Liang, J. Q. (in press). Subjective outcome evaluation of a university subject on service leadership. *International Journal on Disability and Human Development.*

Shek, D. T. L., Lin, L., & Liu, T. T. (2014a). Service leadership education for university students in Hong Kong: Subjective outcome evaluation. *International Journal on Disability and Human Development.* Advance online publication. doi: 10.1515/ijdhd-2014-0349.

Shek, D. T. L., Lin, L., Leung, H., Law, M. Y. M., & Li, X. (2014b, May 14–15). *Evaluation of service leadership programs using multiple evaluation methods.* Paper presented at the International Conference on Service Leadership Education for University Students: Experience in Hong Kong, Hong Kong.

Shek, D. T. L., Lin, L., Liu, T. T., & Law, M. Y. M. (2014c). Process evaluation of a pilot subject on service leadership for university students in Hong Kong. *International Journal on Disability and Human Development.* Advance online publication. doi: 10.1515/ijdhd-2014-0351.

Shek, D. T. L., Lin, L., Liu, T. T., & Law, M. Y. M. (2014d). Service leadership education for university students in Hong Kong: Qualitative evaluation. *International Journal on Disability and Human Development.* Advance online publication. doi: 10.1515/ijdhd-2014-0350.

Shek, D. T. L., Yu, L., & Ma, C. M. S. (2014e). The students were happy but did they change positively? Yes, they did. *International Journal on Disability and Human Development.* Advance online publication. doi: 10.1515/ijdhd-2014-0348

Shek, D. T. L., Liu, T. T., & Law, M. Y. M. (in press-a). Focus group evaluation of a service leadership subject in Hong Kong. *International Journal on Disability and Human Development.*

Shek, D. T. L., Xie, Q. Z., Lin, L., & Law, M. Y. M. (in press-b). Evaluation of a service leadership subject in Chinese university students in Hong Kong using focus groups. *International Journal on Disability and Human Development.*

Thomas, L., & Beauchamp, C. (2011). Understanding new teachers' professional identities through metaphor. *Teaching and Teacher Education, 27*(4), 762–769.

Weinbach, R. W. (2005). *Evaluating social work services and programs.* Boston: Allyn and Bacon.

Service Leadership Community: A Seedbed of Nurturing Service Leadership Mindset in Student Learning

Leo K.W. Hui, Neil C. Mickleborough, and Ben Y.B. Chan

Abstract The service leadership mindset, unlike academic subjects, has proven difficult to "teach". To seed this mindset of service leadership in students, The Hong Kong University of Science and Technology (HKUST) strategizes the creation of a cultural environment where students understand the need to serve, and more importantly, service occurs naturally – a Service Leadership Community (SLC). The Community provides various approaches for students to achieve three different levels of service leadership learning (i.e., Service Leaders, Service Leadership Practitioners, and Service Leadership Apprentices). To help students become service leaders, two types of courses are designed for them so that they can later take an active role as learning experience designers in service leadership. For the practitioner level of learning, a peer mentoring program and a service learning course are available to engage students with an interest in services and practicing service leadership. To serve as a scaffold for average students to have an apprentice level of learning about service leadership in their university life, a well-designed leadership corner located at the Engineering Commons has been set up to raise their awareness on service leadership. This three-level design of learning is intended to sustainably nurture the service leadership mindset in students. Several components of the SLC are evaluated and some recommendations are given to enhance the influence of SLC on student learning.

Introduction

Although people are surrounded by hundreds of different forms of service, they tend to ignore its importance (Chung 2012). Service actually plays a crucial role in the global economy. Based on the World Factbook from the Central Intelligence Agency (CIA), 93 % of the Hong Kong GDP in 2013 was from the service sector and the corresponding percentage for the whole world was over 60 %. The Asian

L.K.W. Hui • N.C. Mickleborough (✉) • B.Y.B. Chan
Center for Engineering Education Innovation, The Hong Kong University of Science and Technology, Lifts 27/28, Academic Building, Clear Water Bay, Kowloon, Hong Kong
e-mail: ceneilm@ust.hk

© Springer Science+Business Media Singapore 2015
D.T.L. Shek, P. Chung (eds.), *Promoting Service Leadership Qualities in University Students*, Quality of Life in Asia 6, DOI 10.1007/978-981-287-515-0_14

Development Bank (ADB) also reported that the service sector had been a major source of growth in Asia and the share of service sector output for export rose over time in most Asian countries (Park and Shin 2012). It is clearly necessary for people to pay more attention to the service sector.

Unlike manufacturing, service has uncontrollable characteristics like people interaction and variability in delivery (Gronfeldt and Strother 2006). It is a process of dealing with human beings who are often unpredictable, and its delivery depends on each individual situation, relationship, and circumstance. These unique characteristics make service management a challenge. Merely having the specific knowledge and technical skills is not enough for university graduates to compete in the service-oriented marketplace. They should know how to interact and work in teams of people with diverse backgrounds and have soft skills in leadership, effective communication, and interpersonal relationships. Their services to others (e.g., customers/clients) should be customized (i.e., not one size fits all) in a way that they can build a trust-based rapport with their service receivers, generating more contentment and business. To obtain the competitive advantage in such an economy, university students should have the mindset of service leadership. Service leadership is about satisfying needs by providing quality personal service to everyone, including individuals, groups, communities, systems, and environments (HKI-SLAM 2014). Its core beliefs are:

- Every day, every human occupies a position of leadership and possesses the potential to improve his or her leadership quality and effectiveness.
- Leadership effectiveness and service satisfaction are dependent on a leader or service provider whether that person:
  - Possesses relevant situational task competencies and character
  - Accepts judgments from superiors, peers, and subordinates
  - Exhibits care

    These points imply that the server is the service.

- Service includes self-serving efforts aimed at ethically improving one's competencies, abilities, and willingness to help satisfy the needs of others.

The purpose of this chapter is to describe how HKUST sets up a Service Leadership Community (SLC) to seed the mindset of service leadership in students. Some community components are evaluated, and a number of recommendations are given to enhance the influence of the SLC on student learning.

Service Leadership Community (SLC)

Unlike traditional academic subjects, leadership mindset cannot be easily taught by conventional pedagogies (Doh 2003; Gunn 2000; Hay and Hodgkinson 2006; Kerfoot 1998; Roomi and Harrison 2009). Kerfoot (1998) mentioned that classroom learning was not enough to teach leadership, and the best approach would be through actual real-life experience of successes and failures to learn leadership. Some management educators also agreed that besides book knowledge, leadership should be learned in a personal, applicable, and more intuitive way that can be found in coaching, mentoring, client-consulting, internships, role-plays, and other experiential exercises (Doh 2003). Leadership is a performance sport, and it requires both thinking and doing.

One way to help students integrate the theories and practices of leadership is to create meaningful learning communities (Komives et al. 2011). In the designed community, much learning can take place informally and incidentally, beyond explicit teaching or the classroom. Learning is also grounded in particular contexts and individual experiences, requiring effort to transfer specific knowledge and skills to other circumstances and to be prepared to change their personal views and approaches when confronted by new information.

To facilitate the leadership development of students, HKUST has established a Service Leadership Community (SLC) to help students understand the need to serve as leaders, and that service leadership is an important facet of their daily life. Developing leaders relates to the "whole person," and when people are leading from their inside, actions and decisions flow naturally and without great effort (Gunn 2000). To help students achieve this, the SLC has created an environment which provides multifaceted approaches for them to develop four personal dimensions which are attributed to a service-oriented personal brand:

- *Social*: the ability to organize and interact with people
- *Mental*: the ability to help transform others (after self-transformation has occurred)
- *Spiritual*: the ability to be able to connect with the meaningful things in life – the environment, religion beliefs, and the common good
- *Emotional*: the ability to create positive feelings in other people and raise the level of positive emotions and contentment

In the SLC, there are four main components to facilitate student development and learning (Fig. 1), and students can achieve three different levels of service leadership learning through these components based on their interest and passion (Fig. 2). For a higher level of learning, a community service project course and two knowledge-based courses are designed to foster potential students who are highly interested in service leadership to become service leaders. For the second level, the School of Engineering has developed a Peer Mentoring Program (PMP) in which senior students receive training and then practice service leadership through mentoring first-year students. In addition to this program, students with an interest in serving others can also take a service learning course to learn leadership through service.

Finally, to raise the overall awareness of students about service leadership, a leadership corner (Professional Leader's Focus) was set up with different media forms to promote the concepts of service leadership, so students can learn service leadership at the apprentice level. In addition, the upper level learners can be learning experience designers for the lower level learners (e.g., service leaders for service leadership practitioners and service leaders for service leadership

Fig. 1 Service leadership
community components

Fig. 2 Levels of learning

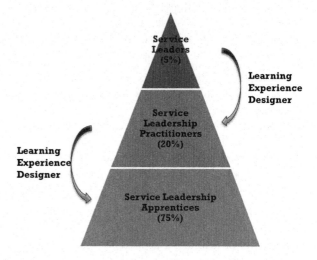

apprentices), and with this arrangement, the three-level structure forms a sustainable framework for nurturing service leadership mindset in student learning.

Service Leader Development

Becoming service leaders needs both practice opportunities and knowledge inputs. Thus, there are two types of courses which offer opportunities for students to learn and practice service leadership. Service learning courses aim at the development of the four personal dimensions of students. *ENGG 2900 (Community Service*

Program) is a service project course to help students develop in spiritual and emotional dimensions. It involves a multifaceted teaching approach including lectures, simulation exercises, self-assessment, team-building games, videos, and group discussions applied to cover the issues of personal development, leadership rules, and social skills. Students can practically learn leadership through community service projects like helping underprivileged families and ethnic minorities and saving the environment. Under the supervision of the instructor and mentors, students design their own group service projects and gain experience from plan development, service marketing, and project implementation. Although they face many difficulties and obstacles during project planning and implementation, this is a good opportunity for them to handle actual situations by themselves so that they can really learn leadership in a realistic way.

Service project have typically been diverse and original. Some students served the children of ethnic minorities by teaching them Chinese so that they can more readily assimilate into the community. The students went to the YMCA center in Cheung Sha Wan to be tutors in the Chinese class. Another group worked with the IMC Sunday School to help underprivileged primary school students to learn English through real-life practice and to explore Hong Kong at the same time by co-organizing an outdoor "City Hunt" game at the Peak, a famous tourist attraction visited by most English-speaking travelers. The young students were encouraged and supported to speak in English during the game to gather information from stores and tourists. Another group organized a campaign to show support and appreciation to janitors at HKUST. Students on campus were asked to donate bottles or cans of soft drinks which were then delivered to the janitors by the group. The janitors responded thankfully, and this encouraged the group members to care more for the people around them.

It is obvious that students in these three groups demonstrated the ability to create positive feeling in other people. The group of ethnic minority children given assistance to learn chinese, an unfamiliar language, enabled them to communicate more readily with locals within their environment, while underprivileged students achieved better results, giving both groups a more positive feeling in their school and daily lives. Janitors who are appreciated by students work more positively at HKUST, and this contagious positive feeling has served to enhance others lives.

Some other service projects were tailor-made to address the social problems faced by the general public. To raise public awareness of the food waste problem in Hong Kong, one group of students organized a seminar to spread the message to the HKUST community. They invited the founder of a social enterprise, the Hong Kong Organic Waste Recycling Center, to address the issue and share his story about starting his business of selling fertilizers and organic products converted from food waste. In organizing this seminar, the students' horizon was widened, and they valued the project more than projects tackled in other courses.

Another group collaborated with Onfire (an NGO that provides free tutoring services for underprivileged kids) to invite the kids to visit the HKUST campus. The purpose of the tour was to inspire the kids, light up their hope, and support their future goals and dreams. To lessen the financial burdens of the participating families on the trip to HKUST, the group set up a counter on campus for a week to raise funds for them. Eventually, they raised more than enough funds for the event, and the extra was donated to Onfire for charity purposes.

In these two projects, students connected their services to some meaningful things in life (spiritual development). The increase of food waste exacerbates landfill problems in Hong Kong, and students tried their best to raise public awareness on saving the environment. Bringing hope of a bright future to the underprivileged kids was the purpose of another service project, and this enhanced the growth in the spiritual dimension of connecting with the common good in life. Therefore, *ENGG 2900* can really help the spiritual and emotional development of students.

In addition to the service learning courses, there are two knowledge-based courses teaching service leadership knowledge, leadership skills, and emotional intelligence to students. *ENGG 2010* focuses on the practical skills in leadership, e.g., skills in communication, trust building, and teamwork. Since this course is for students who are peer mentors, topics related to mentoring are covered. The students are asked to make an activity plan for their mentees so that they can actively take a leadership role in their clans. Finally, they are required to submit reflection papers at the end of the course for assessment. On the other hand, *ENGG 2020* mainly talks about the principles of leadership and management. Corporate cases and recognized leaders' stories are used to demonstrate and discuss leadership skills. Topics like personal development, integrity, and emotional intelligence are also covered. Students' performance will be assessed based on a knowledge test and reflection papers.

Service Leadership Practitioner Training

Another straightforward and useful way to let students experience service leadership is to serve their peers – helping first-year students assimilate into university life. The clan-based mentoring program (PMP) was launched in 2012 and is administrated by the Center for Engineering Education Innovation (E^2I) of the School of Engineering. This program focuses on the social, mental, and emotional development of students. First-year students are required to enroll into one of the nine clans (communities), and each clan has its self-created name (e.g., Pioneers and Vulcan) and individual clan characteristics (i.e., a year plan of activities) to attract students to join. Each clan has a support team of 9–10 peer mentors who provide academic advice, campus life information, and social support to students. The mentors are senior students who are selected after a significant interview process to determine their interest and sincerity in helping first-year students.

Before being mentors, the selected senior students are trained in a series of workshops. They learn the background and purposes of the mentoring program, and previous mentors are invited to share their experience with them. Then, the roles and key competencies of peer mentors are described, and topics on communication skills, team building, and, of course, service leadership are included. In addition, to help mentors understand more about themselves so that they can support junior students more efficiently, a session on the Myers-Briggs Type Indicator (MBTI) is provided to self-assess their personality types. There is also a mental health first aid workshop for students to learn how to handle emotional issues.

To provide opportunities for mentors to practice and gain experience in service leadership, E^2I holds two major events (*Registration Day* and *Team-Building Camp*) for them to serve the first-year students. After leaving the familiar environment of their high schools, many first-year students may feel lost or unprepared for university life. Mentors can help them with course registration and then provide advice about studying in university. Some mentors may assist the students to obtain identity cards, activate university email accounts, and walk them around the campus to find the venues for classes. As clan leaders, the mentors serve the initial needs of first-year students.

Since engineers primarily work in teams, E^2I arranges training for first-year students to understand the importance of teamwork and learn teamwork skills. Each clan is led by a professional trainer who plans the activities for students. The mentors, as the camp facilitators, help the trainers set up venues and prepare games. One of the popular team building activities is to ask students to build a model through one-way communication. Students are divided into three groups (i.e., viewers, messengers, and builders), and each group can only communicate with other certain group(s) in one direction. This activity assists students to understand the importance of two-way communication and to practice teamwork. Through a series of activities and endeavors related to communication and teamwork, the mentors help the first-year students to learn and grow, while the mentors further develop their own skills.

To assess the influence of the mentoring program on students (i.e., those who were peer mentors), a simple and concise questionnaire was designed to check their understanding of service leadership. The survey was carried out by emailing a link to a questionnaire created using Google Form (a popular survey approach) to the students. About one third of the peer mentors answered the questionnaire. 88 % of them agreed that leadership is aimed at decently satisfying the needs of self and others. Over 74 % believed leadership is everywhere, and everyone can be a leader every day. However, 54 % of students were neutral in the belief that the server is the service, even though the service sector dominates Hong Kong's GDP (93 % in 2013).

Students were also asked to write a reflective statement on their learning and experience in the peer mentoring program. They showed their ability to organize and interact with people in the reflections. They also developed initiative to communicate and to help transform others. In addition, the mentors can raise the level of positive emotions and happiness among mentees using self-designed activities in the Camp, but they cannot maintain this positive relationship afterward. They also mentioned the challenges they faced in the program. The cooperation between mentors within the clans is at times not strong enough, and it is quite difficult for mentors to keep connected with mentees. Thus, the mentorship training is continuously being adjusted to enhance the bonding between mentors, and this may in turn improve their mentoring skills.

In addition to the previous activities, there is a course *ENGG 1900 (Service Learning Program)* that allows students to learn through on-/off-campus voluntary services. This course focuses on the social and mental developments of students. Lectures, talks, or training sessions are provided for students to build their communication skills, foster their personal development, and broaden their horizon. At the end of the course, students are required to submit reports or reflection papers, as appropriate.

In the reflection journals of *ENGG 1900*, students demonstrated the ability to interact with people. They learned the importance of each individual in a team and understood that without everyone's contribution, they can do nothing. They also knew people should be organized, based on their strengths and weaknesses, to do different jobs. In addition, the service learning program helped students understand more about themselves and the ways to improve their handling of problems. They identified their weaknesses and tried their best to overcome them. This confirms that they transformed themselves before serving others, but there is no evidence about their ability to transform others in their reflections.

Nurture of Service Leadership Apprentices

The purpose of the apprentice level is to raise the overall awareness of students on service leadership. A leadership corner area (Professional Leader's Focus) (Fig. 3) has been designated for promoting the concepts of service leadership in the Engineering Commons (Fig. 4) which is the physical home of SLC and the place where students meet, study, and discuss projects when they have no classes. Tailor-made slideshows and videos are shown on a 55" screen to engage students in the core beliefs of service leadership and demonstrate how these beliefs are related to their daily life and future career.

A bookcase beside the corner area houses a mini-library containing leadership/ service leadership books and selected leader biographies. Past and current leaders in recognized engineering companies are showcased with their leadership biographies and 3D-printed replicas of the products developed by those companies. There are also free copies of recommended articles on leadership and its relation to the engineering profession for students to read.

The corner area is also targeted for students to discuss their projects, as well as for other relevant leadership activities like organizing events and committee meetings. Its cozy and relaxing environment encourages students to speak out and discuss their ideas. As mentioned before, much learning can take place informally outside the classroom, grounded in particular contexts and individual experiences. Thus, an open, informal, and interactive forum (EnG Chitchat) has been organized by E^2I and GCE (Center for Global and Community Engagement) for students to

Fig. 3 Professional leader's focus

Fig. 4 Engineering commons

share their thoughts and experiences on leadership issues and engineering projects. GCE is introduced as a cocurricular program that aims to engage students in making contributions to the community as well as create and facilitate educational and leadership opportunities.

Fig. 5 EnG Chitchat promotion posters

Fig. 6 Pictures taken during EnG Chitchat sessions

The EnG Chitchat forum is scheduled weekly and focuses on how engineering is related to service leadership and can help different people, communities, and industries. Figure 5 shows the posters designed for promoting the EnG Chitchat. In each session, the speaker poses questions during the presentation, and the audience is encouraged to respond to the questions or share ideas with the speaker (Fig. 6). Through this two-way interaction, students can understand more about the role of leadership in engineering disciplines and the application of what they learn to make contributions to communities. Also, an evaluation survey was conducted for the forum. Over 76 % of attendants agreed or strongly agreed that the EnG Chitchat was fun and 74 % enjoyed learning from/with their schoolmates.

In addition to the Professional Leader's Focus area, students can learn about service leadership from the "Leadership in Engineers" (LinE) newsletter. The newsletter provides up-to-date information about leadership resources and activities held at the School of Engineering. It also contains information about various leadership topics and news related to engineering. It is available electronically from the School website or in print from the Professional Leader's Focus area.

At the curriculum level, the service leadership concepts are also introduced to the first-year students through an academic compulsory orientation course (*ENGG 1010*). The definition and core beliefs of service leadership are presented to the students so that they can start to learn service leadership as soon as they enter the university.

Recommendations

Based on the current evaluation, the outcome of SLC is satisfactory, and further assessment will be conducted to completely evaluate the SLC as a seedbed for nurturing the mindset of service leadership in students. Some tuning will be done to enhance the students' understanding of service leadership, and more components will be added into the SLC for more effective competency development of students:

- Since students do not fully comprehend the concept and significance of service in the economy, effort should be spent on explaining the service issues in the practitioner training or the EnG Chitchat forum. Promotion items like videos, posters, or articles related to these issues will also be put in the Professional Leader's Focus area to attract students' attention on service.
- Training (e.g., off-campus overnight camp) for the peer mentors should be extended and enriched in the areas of mental and emotional development so that they can build stronger and more cohesive teams to serve the first-year students and form better bonding with the mentees.
- To support the spiritual development of students, an "Engineering the Community" award will be set up to recognize students whose final year projects focus and satisfy the needs of people and communities or address the issues in society, e.g., food waste and labor shortage for dish cleaning in restaurants, poorly equipped homes for the elderly, and insufficient workforce for building sites.
- A service leadership week will be organized at the Engineering Commons to attract more students from different backgrounds for the nurture of service leadership apprentices and will include guest seminars, talks and video shows about leadership, and, of course the highlight, the presentation of "Engineering the Community" award.

- More detailed evaluations (e.g., pre- and post-assessments of students who join the peer mentoring program) of the SLC components will be applied, and adjustments for the SLC will be completed on a continuing basis.

References

Chung, P. (2012). *Service reborn: The knowledge, skills, and attitudes of service companies.* Hong Kong: Lexingford Publishing.

Doh, J. P. (2003). Can leadership be taught? Perspectives from management educators. *Academy of Management Learning and Education, 2*(1), 54–67.

Gronfeldt, S., & Strother, J. B. (2006). *Service leadership: The quest for comparative advantage.* Thousand Oaks: Sage Publications.

Gunn, B. (2000). Can leadership be taught? *Strategic Finance, 82*(6), 14–16.

Hay, A., & Hodgkinson, M. (2006). Rethinking leadership: A way forward for teaching leadership? *Leadership & Organization Development Journal, 27*(1/2), 144–158.

HKI-SLAM (2014). *Service leadership & management.* Retrieved from http://hki-slam.org/

Kerfoot, K. (1998). Management is taught, leadership is learned. *Plastic Surgical Nursing, 18*(2), 108–109.

Komives, S. R., Dungan, J. P., Owen, J. E., Slack, C., Wagner, W., & National Clearinghouse of Leadership Programs (NCLP) (2011). *The handbook for student leadership development.* San Francisco: Jossey-Bass.

Park, D., & Shin, K. (2012). *The service sector in Asia: Is it an engine of growth?* ADB Economics Working Paper Series No. 322. Asian Development Bank.

Roomi, M. A., & Harrison, P. (2009). Teaching entrepreneurial leadership: Clarifying the concept for the classroom. *ICSB World Conference Proceedings,* 1–23.

Service Leadership Education for University Students: Seven Unfinished Tasks

Daniel T.L. Shek and Po Chung

Abstract With the financial support of the Victor and William Fung Foundation, eight higher education institutions supported by the University Grants Committee were invited to develop programs and curriculum materials for the Fung Service Leadership Initiative. While the initiative counted many achievements in the first two years and the program development represents the "let a hundred flowers bloom" phenomenon, there are several unfinished tasks that service leadership educators should address. These include evaluation, identification of success factors, role of service learning, assessment, establishing the theoretical distinctiveness of the model, integration with Chinese cultural values, and the clarification of assumptions of leaders in the Service Leadership Model.

Introduction

With the support of the Victor and William Fung Foundation, eight higher institutions funded by the University Grants Committee were invited to develop curriculum materials and programs on service leadership. A midway conference was organized in May 2014. With reference to the papers presented in the conference (see Table 1), several observations are highlighted. First, some specific subjects and programs have been developed according to the Service Leadership Model (e.g., Shek et al. 2013). Second, some subjects related to parts of the Service Leadership Model, such as subjects on general education and entrepreneurship, have been

The preparation for this work and the Service Leadership Initiative are financially supported by the Victor and William Fung Foundation

D.T.L. Shek, Ph.D., S.B.S., J.P (✉)
Department of Applied Social Sciences, The Hong Kong Polytechnic University, HJ407, Hunghom, Hong Kong, China
e-mail: daniel.shek@polyu.edu.hk

P. Chung
Hong Kong Institute of Service Leadership and Management, Room 1001, Siu On Centre, 188 Lockhart Road, Wanchai, Hong Kong, China
e-mail: info@hki-slam.org

© Springer Science+Business Media Singapore 2015
D.T.L. Shek, P. Chung (eds.), *Promoting Service Leadership Qualities in University Students*, Quality of Life in Asia 6, DOI 10.1007/978-981-287-515-0_15

225

Table 1 Papers presented at the International Conference on Service Leadership Education held in May 2014

Keynote speeches
Keynote Speech 1: Dr. Victor K. Fung, Chairman of the Fung Group
Development of the Service Economy in Hong Kong: Challenges and Opportunities
Keynote Speech 2: Dr. Po Chung, Chairman of Hong Kong Institute of Service Leadership & Management Limited
Where There is No Vision, the People Will Perish
Keynote speech 3: Prof. Dayle Smith, Dean of the School of Business, Clarkson University
Relevance of the Service Leadership Model to Global Leadership and Responsibilities
Invited presentations on Service Leadership Initiatives
Service Leadership Education and Research at The Hong Kong Polytechnic University: An Overview
Daniel T.L. Shek, Rachel C.F. Sun, Lu Yu, Cecilia M.S. Ma, Andrew M.H. Siu, Li Lin, Hildie Leung and Moon Y.M. Law, The Hong Kong Polytechnic University
The Service Leadership Initiative at CityU – Service Leadership Embedded in a Social Innovation and Entrepreneurship Framework
Linda Wong and Yanto Chandra, City University of Hong Kong
Service Leadership Community – A Seedbed of Nurturing Service Leadership Mindset in Student Learning
Leo K.W. Hui, Neil Mickleborough and Ben Y.B. Chan, The Hong Kong University of Science and Technology
Development of the Service Leadership Education Curriculum at Lingnan University
Robin S. Snell, Maureen Y.L. Chan, Carol H.K. Ma and Carman C.M. Chan, Lingnan University
The Role of Service Leadership in the University's GE Curriculum: The HKBU Experience
Reza Hoshmand, Hong Kong Baptist University
Achiever – A Co-curricular Project that Integrates Service Leadership Capabilities through Experiential Learning and Actualizing Personal Development Goals
Tom W.H. Fong, Carmen W.Y. Ng, Joey Wong and Jingwen Xing, Hong Kong Institute of Education
Service Leadership in an Uncertain Era
K.M. Chan and Hugh Thomas, The Chinese University of Hong Kong
Changing Student Mindset by Community Involvement: The Impact of Service Leadership Internship
Shui-fong Lam and Jessie Chow, The University of Hong Kong
Invited presentations on service learning, general education, pedagogy, curriculum development and research
Nurturing Service Leadership through Experiential Learning: The HKU Service Leadership Internship
Jessie Chow and Shui-fong Lam, The University of Hong Kong
Experiencing Service Leadership through Collective and Interdisciplinary Efforts
Susanna Chui, Paula Hodgson and Alice Wong, Hong Kong Baptist University
The Construction of Student Leadership Development Model through Adopting the HKI-SLAM Curriculum Framework
Richard Y.F. Tsang and Loretta M.K. Leung, Hong Kong Institute of Education
Developing Video Enhanced Pedagogical Cases in Service Leadership

(continued)

Table 1 (continued)

Hugh Thomas and K.M. Chan, The Chinese University of Hong Kong
Evaluation of Service Leadership Programs Using Multiple Evaluation Methods
Daniel T.L. Shek, Li Lin, Hildie Leung, Moon Y.M. Law and Xiang Li, The Hong Kong Polytechnic University
University Students' Socially Responsible Leadership Values and Capacities for Service Leadership
Joan Y.H. Leung, Raysen W.L. Cheung and Hang Chow
Why is Service Leadership Important in University Education: A Study of the Relationship between Service Leadership and the Definitions with Close Meanings
Catherine Zhou, Ben Y.B. Chan and Neil C. Mickleborough, The Hong Kong University of Science and Technology
Service Leadership for Adaptive Selling and Effective Customer Service Teams
Alfred Wong, Ying Liu and Dean Tjosvold, Lingnan University

offered at different universities. Third, service learning has been commonly used as a vehicle to promote service leadership attributes in university students. Fourth, some attempts to develop curriculum materials have been made. Finally, some research initiatives on service leadership have been carried out. Obviously, the Fung Service Leadership Initiative had some notable achievements within a short time, and its development is consistent with the notion of "let a hundred flowers bloom." Nevertheless, there are several unfinished tasks that researchers and educators on service leadership should address.

Unfinished Tasks in Service Leadership Education Initiative

Unfinished Task 1: Evaluation of Service Leadership Education

As a starting point, it should be noted that there are different approaches of nurturing service leadership qualities in the students. However, after the initial development and consolidation process, there is a need to evaluate the developed initiatives. There are several evaluation strategies we can consider. Primarily, as subjective outcome evaluation is routinely carried out on university subjects, integration and evaluation of the findings from student feedback would be helpful. Besides quantitative ratings, qualitative comments from the student evaluation forms are also helpful. To further understand the impacts of different stakeholders, qualitative evaluation via focus groups and individual interviews can be carried out. Of course, it would be useful if objective outcome evaluation could also be carried out. Besides the simple one-group pretest-posttest design, nonequivalent control group design and true experimental designs can give more insights into the impacts of the development of the credit-bearing subjects and non-credit-bearing programs.

Some examples in the field of higher education can be used as useful references (Shek 2013; Shek and Sun 2013a, b, c).

Unfinished Task 2: Identification of Factors Governing Program Success

Based on the "5 P" model in "conductive education," there are five broad categories of factors governing program success. These include Program, People, Process, Policy, and Place. As far as "program" is concerned, the curriculum content of the program developed and the pedagogy involved are of paramount importance. In particular, the role of traditional didactic instruction methods may not meet the needs of contemporary young people. Regarding "people," teachers or program implementers are important agents who create changes in the students. Hence, two questions should be asked. First, should teachers have certain qualities before they can successfully teach service leadership subjects? Second, do potential teachers or program implementers need training before they can teach service leadership subjects? Concerning "process," we need to be conscious of the factors that would affect the program implementation quality, such as motivation of students to learn. Program adherence and fidelity are also relevant issues to be considered if the developed program is curricula based. "Policy" on service leadership and holistic development of university students is another important determinant of program success. Administratively speaking, whether the senior management endorses service leadership subjects and programs directly affects their survival. Politically speaking, whether teachers and students see the need for nurturing service leadership qualities is another factor determining the success of the related programs. Fourthly, "place" is a factor which affects program effectiveness. For example, there is a need to consider how experiential learning activities can be carried out in classroom settings. Finally, regarding "place," whether activities outside the classroom lead to successful service leadership program is another important question to be considered.

Unfinished Task 3: Nurturing Service Leaders Through Service Learning

In the Service Leadership Initiatives carried out in different universities, service learning is a common vehicle used to help students acquire the attributes of effective service leaders. Conceptually speaking, serving the people in need can help promote the moral character and caring disposition of the students. However, several questions should further be addressed if service learning is used as a vehicle to nurture service leadership qualities in university students. First, it is important to ask whether the intended learning outcomes in a service learning subject correspond to those in a typical service leadership subject. Second, as both service learning and service leadership are covered in a single subject, there are concerns regarding whether the curriculum space is large enough to accommodate both areas. Third, since some service learning projects do not require the students to provide direct service to the service recipients (e.g., needs assessment projects), whether such programs can promote caring disposition remains to be demonstrated. Finally, although it is intuitive to believe that service learning can nurture the leadership qualities, moral character, and caring disposition in university students, we need empirical evidence to substantiate such an assumption.

Unfinished Task 4: Assessment of Service Leadership

A review of the literature shows that while there are many measures of leadership, none of them are specifically developed for the assessment of service leadership. Besides, validated measures of leadership scales are very few in the Chinese contexts. Hence, in order to evaluate service leadership subjects and programs, there is a need to have validated assessment tools on service leadership. There are at least three instruments that we should develop. First, a scale on service leadership knowledge is necessary to assess how much knowledge the students have acquired after taking a service leadership subject. Second, we need a scale on attitudes and values related to service leadership such as moral character and values underpinning service leadership. Third, to understand changes in the students after joining courses on service leadership, a scale assessing skills on service leadership is also indispensable. Besides constructing these measures, there is also a need to assess their reliability and validity. With the support of the Victor and William Fung Foundation, the Research Team is currently conducting a pioneer project to develop various measures related to service leadership.

Unfinished Task 5: Theoretical Distinctiveness of Service Leadership

One question that should be addressed is how unique is the Service Leadership Model. With reference to the basic ingredients of service leadership (generic leadership competencies, moral character, and caring disposition), they are not novel in the leadership literature. As far as generic leadership competencies are concerned, they are commonly found in leadership models in the management context. For moral character, models such as authentic leadership and spiritual leadership models also highlight the importance of moral character of leaders. Regarding caring disposition, transformational leadership and servant leadership also emphasize the importance for effective leaders to develop a strong sense of care. Despite these similarities, the focus on self-leadership and the notion that "everybody can be a leader" bear some humanistic flavor. Hence, more work on integrating the Service Leadership Model with other prominent leadership models is desirable. At the same time, effort to differentiate the Service Leadership Model and other leadership models should be carried out. Some preliminary work on these issues has been carried out (Shek et al. in press).

Unfinished Task 6: Service Leadership in the Chinese Context

Besides theoretical integration, there is also a need to examine how the Service Leadership Model can be integrated with the cultural ingredients. Chung (2010) highlighted that Chinese Confucian values are important anchors for moral character in service leadership. Besides Confucianism, other Chinese thoughts have influenced the development of Chinese people for centuries. For example, it would be interesting to think of how to integrate the Buddhist values of "giving up" and "forgiveness" and Taoist concepts of "harmony" and "integration with nature" to the Service Leadership Model. Besides, it would also be interesting to explore ways to integrate Chinese values with Western leadership concepts. For example, Shek et al. (2013) examined how Confucian values can be integrated with Western concepts. If we regard Western concepts are the "Yin" of the leadership concepts, Chinese concepts are the "Yang" of the related concepts. How to integrate these two domains would be an exciting task regarding the integration of cultural concepts on leadership.

Unfinished Task 7: Assumptions of Leaders in Service Leadership

As a novel approach of addressing leadership under service economy, the Service Leadership Model has the following assumptions about leaders:

- *Freedom versus determinism*: While human behavior is governed by their habits, they are also free to make their choices, such as deciding to practice self-leadership and continuously improve themselves.
- *Holism versus reductionism:* A multilevel approach involving interrelationships among different systems, including the individual, follower, group, and environmental systems, is adopted in the Service Leadership Model. The 12 dimensions of the quality of service leadership is also a good illustration of the holistic focus of the Service Leadership Model (Chung in press-a; in press-b).
- *Self-orientation versus other orientation*: Instead of solely focusing on establishing fame and power, service leadership emphasizes the satisfaction of

one's own and others' needs, as exemplified in Core Belief 1 that "Leadership is a service aimed at ethically satisfying the needs of self, others, groups, communities, systems, and environments."

- *Elitist versus mass leadership:* In contrast to the notion of "inborn leadership" or "elite leadership," it is embedded in the Service Leadership Model that everybody is (and can be) a leader. As exemplified in Core Belief 2 – "Every day, every human occupies a position of leadership and possesses the potential to improve his leadership quality and effectiveness." The notion of leadership has a strong humanistic flavor that everybody has potentials to be a leader (Shek and Lin in press).
- *Leading others versus leading oneself:* One key belief in the Service Leadership Model is that leading oneself is very important. In fact, before one can lead others, one must lead oneself. The notion of moral character requires that a service leader must have integrity and moral conduct. The notion of requiring service leaders to make a continuous improvement also suggests that self-leadership is very important.
- *Static versus dynamic leadership development:* According to the Service Leadership Model, leadership development is a continuous rather than a static process. In other words, leadership is not defined in terms of how many leadership programs one has joined. This is shown by Core Belief 4 that "service includes self-serving efforts aimed at ethically improving one's competencies, abilities, and willingness to help satisfy the needs of others."
- *Changeable versus unchangeable leadership qualities:* With reference to the notion that "everybody is (and can be) a leader" and the expectation that service leaders will continuously improve their leadership effectiveness, the Service Leadership Model assumes that leaders can change and improve.

In the future, it is suggested that the issue regarding the assumptions of Service Leadership Model with reference to personality theories and leadership models should be further considered. By exploring these assumptions about human beings and leaders, the unique and common features of service leadership with reference to other leadership approaches can be further established.

References

Chung, P. (2010). *Distinguishing characteristics of service leadership and management education.* Hong Kong Institute of Service Leadership and Management. Available from: http://hki-slam.org/index.php?r=article&catid=2&aid=29

Chung, P. (in press-a). *The 24 principles of service leadership.*

Chung, P. (in press-b). *Your second skin.* Managing the 12 dimensions of your personal brand for the service age.

Shek, D. T. L. (2013). Promotion of holistic development in university students: A credit-bearing subject on leadership and intrapersonal development. *Best Practices in Mental Health, 9*(1), 47–61.

Shek, D. T. L., & Lin, L. (in press). Core beliefs in the service leadership model proposed by the Hong Kong Institute of Service Leadership and Management. *International Journal on Disability and Human Development.*

Shek, D. T. L., & Sun, R. C. F. (2013a). Post-course subjective outcome evaluation of a course promoting leadership and intrapersonal development in university students in Hong Kong. *International Journal on Disability and Human Development, 12*(2), 193–201.

Shek, D. T. L., & Sun, R. C. F. (2013b). Post-lecture evaluation of a university course on leadership and intrapersonal development. *International Journal on Disability and Human Development, 12*(2), 185–191.

Shek, D. T. L., & Sun, R. C. F. (2013c). Process evaluation of a leadership and intrapersonal development subject for university students. *International Journal on Disability and Human Development, 12*(2), 203–211.

Shek, D. T. L., Yu, L., & Fu, X. (2013). Confucian virtues and Chinese adolescent development: A conceptual review. *International Journal of Adolescent Medicine and Health, 25*(4), 335–344. doi: 10.1515/ijamh-2013-0031

Shek, D. T. L., Yu, L., Ma, C. M. S., Sun, R. C. F., & Liu, T. T. (2013). Development of a credit-bearing service leadership subject for university students in Hong Kong. *International Journal of Adolescent Medicine and Health, 25*(4), 353–361. doi: 10.1515/ijamh-2013-0033

Shek, D. T. L., Chung, P. P. Y., & Leung, H. (in press). How unique is the service leadership model? A comparison with contemporary leadership approaches. *International Journal on Disability and Human Development.*

Index

© Springer Science+Business Media Singapore 2015
D.T.L. Shek, P. Chung (eds.), *Promoting Service Leadership Qualities in University
Students*, Quality of Life in Asia 6, DOI 10.1007/978-981-287-515-0

CPSIA information can be obtained
at www.ICGtesting.com
Printed in the USA
LVOW01*0924170716

496656LV00009B/416/P